THE WOMAN QUESTION
IN ISLAMIC STUDIES

The Woman Question in Islamic Studies

KECIA ALI

PRINCETON UNIVERSITY PRESS

PRINCETON & OXFORD

Published by Princeton University Press
41 William Street, Princeton, New Jersey 08540
99 Banbury Road, Oxford OX2 6JX

press.princeton.edu

All Rights Reserved

ISBN 9780691183596
ISBN (pbk.) 9780691261843
ISBN (e-book) 9780691263748

British Library Cataloging-in-Publication Data is available

Editorial: Fred Appel and James Collier
Production Editorial: Nathan Carr
Jacket / Cover Design: Katie Osborne
Production: Lauren Reese
Publicity: William Pagdatoon
Copyeditor: Bhisham Bherwani

This book has been composed in Arno

10 9 8 7 6 5 4 3 2 1

For Mama Dot (1925–2022) and Tata Ellen (1923–)

CONTENTS

THE WOMAN QUESTION
IN ISLAMIC STUDIES

Introduction

IN 2007, SHORTLY after my first book was published, I spoke about gender and Qur'an interpretation at Loyola University in Chicago. During the Q&A, an audience member objected that my feminist critique imposed a Western perspective. Did I know about William Chittick's book *The Tao of Islam*, which argues for Islam's balanced treatment of the masculine and the feminine? I responded that I found the book important but unpersuasive for my purposes. I also pointed out that it was written by Sachiko Murata; Chittick is her husband. In turn, the questioner offered a compromise: they *both* wrote it. Actually, they didn't.[1]

Attributing women's scholarly achievements to men is a time-honored practice that spans fields and disciplines.[2] It is but one example of how sexism and misogyny thrive in the academy.[3]

1. Sachiko Murata, *The Tao of Islam: A Sourcebook on Gender Relationships in Islamic Thought*. Foreword by Annemarie Schimmel (Albany: SUNY Press, 1992). Murata and Chittick did, however, co-author another book that may have been the source of the questioner's confusion. For more on that book, and the reflex to attribute collaborative work solely to men, see Chapter 4.

2. For one example, see Kishonna Gray, "#CiteHerWork: Marginalizing Women in Academic and Journalistic Writing," December 28, 2015, http://www.kishonnagray.com/manifestmy-reality/citeherwork-marginalizing-women-in-academic-and-journalistic-writing.

3. Danica Savonick and Cathy Davidson, "Gender Bias in Academe: An Annotated Bibliography" summarizes the findings of dozens of studies, http://blogs.lse.ac

Discrimination occurs in its upper echelons, as men—especially straight, white, abled, cis men—are disproportionately hired into tenure-track jobs, tenured, promoted, given named chairs, and awarded prestigious lectureships. At the other end of the higher education spectrum, women are overrepresented in the gig academy, the "insecure and poorly paid" adjunct jobs that now make up close to three-fourths of instructional positions.[4] The contingency crisis itself reflects the changing demographics of the academy. As more white women and people of color of all genders have earned doctorates and pursued scholarly careers, the security and prestige attached to being a professor has declined.[5] This is not coincidental, nor, as Tressie McMillan Cottom points out, are its effects equally distributed.[6] The growth in tenure-ineligible positions in centers, programs, and areas deemed peripheral to the university

---

.uk/impactofsocialsciences/2016/03/08/gender-bias-in-academe-an-annotated -bibliography/(updated 2017); see also Kathleen E. Grogan, "How the Entire Scientific Community Can Confront Gender Bias in the Discipline," *Nature Ecology and Evolution*, 3, 2019: 3–6, https://www.nature.com/articles/s41559-018-0747-4.pdf. The short pieces collected in "The Awakening: Women and Power in the Academy" (*The Chronicle Review*, April 6, 2018, B1–B24) traverse disciplines.

4. This phrase already appears in a study written decades ago. Nadya Aisenberg and Mona Harrington, *Women of Academe: Outsiders in the Sacred Grove* (Amherst: University of Massachusetts Press, 1988), 54. On women as adjuncts, see also Sekile M. Nzinga, *Lean Semesters: How Higher Education Reproduces Inequality* (Baltimore, MD: Johns Hopkins University Press, 2020), 15, 133–37, 151.

5. Lara Deeb and Jessica Winegar discuss the way "academic minefields" in Middle East/North Africa (MENA) anthropology relate to "the broader loss of professorial legitimacy in the United States" in *Anthropology's Politics: Disciplining the Middle East* (Stanford, CA: Stanford University Press, 2016), 15 ff.

6. On the structural effects of anti-Black racism in adjunct hiring, see Tressie McMillan Cottom, "The New Old Labor Crisis," *Slate*, January 24, 2014, https://slate .com/human-interest/2014/01/adjunct-crisis-in-higher-ed-an-all-too-familiar-story -for-black-faculty.html. See also Joseph Fruscione and Kelly J. Baker, "Introduction," in Fruscione and Baker, eds., *Succeeding Outside the Academy: Career Paths beyond the Humanities, Social Sciences, and STEM* (Lawrence: University of Kansas Press, 2018), 1–7 at 3.

accounts for some disparities.[7] Humanities programs, in which men constitute a smaller proportion of faculty than in STEM fields, are shrinking or are threatened across the United States. Faculty positions are being eliminated. Professional vulnerability, like caregiving duties and service obligations, is unequally distributed.[8]

There seems to be a paradox. Academia has a reputation as a bastion of progressive values, a haven for feminists and other impractically utopian social justice advocates. But despite loud claims that conservative speech is being suppressed, those under threat from repressive policies limiting academic freedom tend to be on the left. And in its mundane practices, the academy remains thoroughly, if unevenly, (cis)sexist as well as classist, racist, ableist, and homophobic.[9] As Sekile Nzinga observes, "the structural inequities" of contemporary academic life are "encapsulated within and often hidden from our sight by the resilient enshrinement of the university as a fundamentally progressive institution."[10]

Islamic studies, an amorphous field crossing area studies, philology and textual studies, religious studies, and theology, is inescapably shaped by the contemporary academy, with its endemic

7. Such fields include women's and gender studies and ethnic studies, Black studies, and critical race studies. Cottom, "The New Old Labor Crisis," and Nzinga, *Lean Semesters*, 57, 71–75, 80–85.

8. See, e.g., Social Sciences Feminist Network Research Interest Group, University of Oregon, "The Burden of Invisible Work in Academia: Social Inequalities and Time Use in Five University Departments," *Humboldt Journal of Social Relations*, 39, 2017: 228–245. An important early study of this phenomenon is Shelley M. Park, "Research, Teaching, and Service: Why Shouldn't Women's Work Count?," *The Journal of Higher Education*, 67:1, 1996: 46–84.

9. Places to begin with this extensive literature include Lorgia García Peña, *Community as Rebellion: A Syllabus for Surviving Academia as a Woman of Color* (Chicago, IL: Haymarket Books, 2022); Deborah L. Rhode, "Women in Academia," in *Women and Leadership* (New York: Oxford University Press, 2017), 95–110; and Nicole Brown and Jennifer Leigh, eds., *Ableism in Academia: Theorising Experiences of Disabilities and Chronic Illnesses in Higher Education* (London: University College London Press, 2020).

10. Nzinga, *Lean Semesters*, 12.

precarity, hyperattention to productivity, and fetishization of metrics as well as its sexist norms. Yet even as it shares patterns with other fields and disciplines, the gender politics of Islamic studies are distinctive. The incident at my lecture illustrates the complexities of talking about women and gender in Islam. My interlocutor, a brown man from the local community, held that I, a white academic visitor, was inappropriately pushing a Western feminist agenda when Islamic gender complementarity was the answer. Although that was not my aim, he was not wrong to push back. The gender politics of Islam in the U.S. and globally are also always racial politics (and conversely, the racial politics are deeply gendered). As a white person and an American citizen, I benefit in numerous ways from the racist and colonialist status quo.[11] Deployments of liberal feminism against Muslims do real harm, helping justify military invasions overseas and expanded surveillance at home.[12] At the same time, his insistence that Muslim women's roles are sacrosanct in a way that, say, political norms are not—he agreed that electoral democracy, despite being a Western import, was compatible with Islam—is itself worth questioning and historicizing. And the fact that we were both Muslim, and I was younger and a convert, meant he felt free to encourage me to embrace what he saw as a more religiously authentic perspective on gender issues.

Conversations about women and Islam, as well as gender and sexuality in Islam, have only become more charged in subsequent

11. For an exploration of white convert privilege, especially for men, in Muslim religious organizations, see Mahdi Tourage, "Performing Belief and Reviving Islam: Prominent (White Male) Converts in Muslim Revival Conventions," *Performing Islam*, 1:2, 2013: 207–226 and Walaa Quisay, *Neo-traditionalism in Islam in the West: Orthodoxy, Spirituality and Politics* (Edinburgh: Edinburgh University Press, 2023). An account of white converts in academic Islamic studies remains to be written. I suspect that as the children and grandchildren of post-1965 immigrants to the U.S. enter the profession, and as the proportion of Black scholars increases, we make up a diminishing proportion of Muslims in the field.

12. See Rafia Zakaria, *Against White Feminism: Notes on Disruption* (New York: W. W. Norton, 2021).

years. In America, broad cultural shifts have increased awareness and acceptance of gender beyond the male-female binary and normalized same-sex marriage and, to a lesser extent, a range of queer sexualities. There is also rising backlash to these changes alongside a frightening curtailment of reproductive autonomy. Scholars who are nonbinary and/or trans are becoming a more visible presence in Islamic studies. In this book, my focus is mostly on women, with occasional reference to nonbinary scholars, as I discuss in more detail in the methodological appendix. I recognize, though, that *women* is not and never has been a natural and universal category, and gender is by no means the only useful lens through which to understand academic bias, discrimination, and privilege. I make a point of discussing, for example, the overrepresentation of white and non-Muslim women in many contexts. However, in addition to its salience as a potential site of feminist solidarity, gender is a particularly meaningful category when analyzed in conjunction with scholarship on women, gender, and sexuality.

Conjoined with the troubled cultural politics of gender and sexuality in the contemporary United States is the long-standing hypervisibility of women and gender in Islam as a topic of interest. Everyone from Islamophobic politicians to local interfaith group members to lay Muslims has perspectives and preconceptions and strong feelings. And because of the salience of such issues to contemporary life, as well as the interplay of social media and public scholarship, a lot of academic conversations on these topics cross over, sometimes for good, sometimes for ill. Even where the conversation is mostly confined to specialized publications and academic contexts, conversations on women and gender are fraught. Sometimes, the topics are avoided or treated as undeserving of serious scholarly attention. Sometimes, people take them up superficially, without engaging the substantial work that others—mostly others who aren't men—have done over the decades. Though many factors play a role, gender bias within academic Islamic studies is a crucial part of the story. Sexist bias and its detrimental effects on scholars and scholarship are the subject of this book, which aims to lay the groundwork for productive conversations about, and transformative approaches to, the gender politics of academic Islamic studies.

Islamic studies has been shaped by histories and contemporary manifestations of colonialism and imperialism as well as anti-Muslim hostility in myriad forms, in and beyond the United States, where I am based and where I focus my analysis. I began working on this book casually during the lead-up to the 2016 presidential election and in earnest after Donald Trump was inaugurated. By the time I submitted this manuscript past the halfway mark of Joe Biden's presidency, debates over putting Muslims in camps or making us register seemed a bit like a fever dream. Yet the political situation for American Muslims remains somewhat precarious, especially those from or with heritage ties to places perceived as threats to U.S. security interests. It falls outside the scope of this book to catalog these effects or predict their long-term trajectory. I can only note the fast-moving and complicated rhetorical and political dynamics that shape scholarship and teaching, including the emerging restrictions on what can be taught about gender, race, and sexuality in a variety of public and private institutions. Even as some things about the academy remain stubbornly resistant to change, colleges and universities across the country are undergoing significant and rapid transformation, both for good and for ill.

The United States academy is, of course, not hermetically sealed off from the rest of the world. Ideas, texts, and money cross borders. So do people, some more easily than others. Scholars born elsewhere train here. Scholars trained elsewhere teach here. Transnational collaborations are less common than some might wish but they are far from rare. Key European publishers have New York branches. American scholars publish in German journals, though nearly always in English. The Fulbright Program sends American scholars to Egypt and Indonesia and sponsors students and scholars from there to come to the U.S. Given that a PhD from an American institution is an advantage in some job markets, its norms matter. To the extent that English language scholarship dominates global academic Islamic studies, and its conferences and publishers have prestige, the U.S. has an outsized role. Non-anglophone scholars and scholarship are often neglected or excluded, especially in certain subfields. Discrimination here reverberates globally.

Still, higher education within the U.S. is highly stratified and internally differentiated to the point that generalizations about the American academy are suspect.[13] Elite private research universities and selective liberal arts schools operate differently from community colleges and large public institutions. And within the same school, faculty working conditions can diverge sharply. Tenured faculty teaching two courses per semester and adjuncts teaching 4/4 loads on annually renewable contracts have little common ground.

One factor distinguishing the U.S. from other Western academies is its demographics. For example, in North America, a substantially larger proportion of Islamic studies scholars is Muslim than in most of Europe—though substantially less than, say, in Iran or Indonesia.[14] Though too many events and publications

13. Raewyn Connell notes wide variation in practices among institutions within and among countries but concludes that "there is a great deal of overlap in what different universities and their workers actually do." *The Good University: What Universities Actually Do and Why It's Time for Radical Change* (London: Zed, 2019), 5.

14. I could not find firm statistics on the proportion of Muslims in Islamic studies or within religious studies, but the increase in recent decades is obvious and, for some, distressing. For one perspective, see Omid Safi, "Reflections on the State of Islamic Studies," *Jadaliyya*, July 21, 2022, https://www.jadaliyya.com/Details/30175/Reflections-on-the-State-of-Islamic-Studies. Though it tracks a different population, Deeb and Winegar's study of Middle East/North Africa-focused anthropologists in the U.S. academy estimates "an approximately 25 percent increase in region-related scholars"—which they gloss as "those with heritage ties to MENA"—"since the late 1960s" and "that at least 40 percent of those in PhD programs in the United States today are region-related" (*Anthropology's Politics*, 7). They also observe that "today, the subfield [of MENA anthropology] is 61 percent female and 39 percent male, with a notable increase in the number of women since 1990" (8). In

continue to exclude Black scholars, it is unusual to have an Islamic studies conference or volume in the U.S. that is all white or comprised entirely of non-Muslims. Consequently, the gender politics of academic Islamic studies are affected by and inflected with the gender politics of heterogeneous American and global Muslim communities. These dynamics shape the production and reception of scholarship on women, gender, and Islam.

The study of Islam and Muslims has always been political. Although one cannot reduce area studies to an "epiphenomenon of the Cold War" or Orientalism to an epiphenomenon of colonialism, early philological studies were often facilitated by European occupation of places where Muslims lived.[15] Numerous postwar anthropologists were funded by Cold War money; today,

---

comparison, Eyal Clyne estimates around 150–300 Israeli scholars of the Middle East/Arabs/Arabic/Islam, "almost all Jewish, and mostly men" (*Orientalism, Zionism and Academic Practice: Middle East and Islamic Studies in Israeli Universities* [Abingdon and New York: Routledge, 2019], 17). For the United Kingdom, see Alison Scott-Baumann, Mathew Guest, Shuruq Naguib, Sariya Cheruvallil-Contractor, and Aisha Phoenix, *Islam on Campus: Contested Identities and the Cultures of Higher Education in Britain* (Oxford: Oxford University Press, 2020), 171. On Islamic theology in the German university system, see Jan Felix Engelhardt, "On Insiderism and Muslim Epistemic Communities in the German and US Study of Islam," *The Muslim World*, 106:4, 2016: 740–758. According to Irene Schneider, in 2018 women held five of twenty-three professorships in Islamic theology at seven distinct institutions (21.7%), slightly lower than women's 25% share of such positions across disciplines. The numbers are too small for the difference to be statistically significant. Schneider, "Gender Equal Islamic Theology in Germany," in Dina El Omari, Juliane Hammer, and Mouhanad Khorchide, eds., *Muslim Women and Gender Justice: Concepts, Sources, and Histories* (New York: Routledge, 2020), 62–85 at 78.

15. Zachary Lockman, *Field Notes: The Making of Middle East Studies in the United States* (Stanford, CA: Stanford University Press, 2016), 258 (see also xii, x); Ursula Wokoeck, *German Orientalism: The Study of the Middle East and Islam from 1800 to 1945* (London: Routledge, 2009), 86, 218–9. On the intertwining of scholarly, missionary, and imperial interests, see Avril A. Powell, *Scottish Orientalists and India: The Muir Brothers, Religion, Education, and Empire* (Woodbridge, Suffolk: The Boydell Press, 2010).

it's anti-terrorism grants.[16] Dismissive talk of identity politics, which Reni Eddo-Lodge defines as "a term now used by the powerful to describe the resistance of the structurally disadvantaged," is largely absent when ROTC cadets study Arabic and Islam in preparation for possible deployment.[17] Instead, those comfortable with the status quo invoke the ideal of disinterested pure scholarship when those from marginalized and minoritized backgrounds contest it.

Issues of insiders and outsiders bedevil other fields as well. Divisions between scholars and practitioners, or academics and activists, are inseparable from debates over objectivity, feminism, and other pre-commitments.[18] Religious studies' wrangling over these issues is conditioned by its history of boundary struggles with theology. The study of Islam has become a key place where those uncomfortable with the necessarily political implications of scholarship have found their nemeses. Some criticisms of Muslim feminist work, for instance, come from committed secularists skeptical about normative projects. Yet other critics are Muslim men who locate themselves simultaneously within academia and within a scholarly tradition, usually Sunni. Muslim men aren't uniquely patriarchal, of course. Throughout this book, I show how various androcentric and misogynistic academic practices overlap with each other and sometimes align with white supremacist norms and discourses.

Four chapters illustrate the interconnected ways that sexism functions in academic Islamic studies. Chapter 1 shows how

16. Deeb and Winegar, *Anthropology's Politics.*

17. Reni Eddo-Lodge, *Why I'm No Longer Talking to White People about Race* (London: Bloomsbury, 2017), 215.

18. See, e.g., Aisha M. Beliso-De Jesús, "Confounded Identities: A Meditation on Race, Feminism, and Religious Studies in Times of White Supremacy," *Journal of the American Academy of Religion* 86:2, 2018: 307–40. After 9/11, according to Deeb and Winegar, "MENA became not just one, but *the* primary lens through which anthropology's tensions were reproduced, navigated, and debated" (*Anthropology's Politics,* 140–41).

subfields within Islamic studies are gendered, by which I mean both that they are numerically skewed in terms of who's in them and that they are treated as masculine or feminine—with work on women and gender consistently relegated to the periphery of Islamic studies. Chapter 2 looks at the citational politics of recent work, showing how despite the remarkable growth and depth of scholarship on Islam and gender, men continue to overlook scholarship by people who aren't men, even in work that purports to discuss gender issues, especially when it touches on the Muslim textual/intellectual tradition. Chapter 3 looks at public scholarship and representation in the media, considering the dynamics that both encourage scholars to talk about Islam and Muslims to broader audiences and make such engagements perilous for women, especially when the topic is gender or sexuality. Chapter 4 discusses curricula, noting widespread exclusions of women's scholarship and gender as a topic in syllabi while acknowledging that the classroom is a space where sustained, transformative learning can occur. Short interludes between the chapters provide glimpses into these broader dynamics and the feelings they engender, including irritation, frustration, disappointment, and rage. A conclusion proposes practical strategies to help those who research and write and speak and teach about Islam and Muslims avoid some of the sexist pitfalls described in this book.

The inclusion of such strategies, however, is not meant to imply that our problems will be solved if only each of us tries harder. Heroic individual exertion is not a panacea for structural problems. Second wave feminist Marilyn Frye used the image of a birdcage to describe the interconnected elements of an oppressive structure. Study any particular wire as long as you like; you'll conclude that it doesn't stop the bird from flying away. One glance at the whole, however, suffices to show how the bird is trapped.[19] The metaphor aptly captures women's disadvantage in academic

19. Marilyn Frye, "Oppression," in *The Politics of Reality: Essays in Feminist Theory* (New York: Crossing/Ten Speed, 1983), 1–17 at 4–5.

contexts.[20] As Frye observes, "the locus of sexism is primarily in the system or framework, not in the particular act."[21]

The Woman Question in Islamic Studies describes, analyzes, and suggests ways of improving existing systems. Highlighting the intertwined ethical and intellectual harms that result from others' failures to cite women and to engage work on women/gender, it provides an evidence-based discussion of how we do our scholarly work, how our current approaches hinder scholars who aren't cis men and harm the scholarship produced, and how we can all do better.[22] One of its goals is simply improved awareness. As Kate Manne points out, there is "significant value in the social support itself" of women coming together, as well as in the "enhanced pattern recognition" that comes from "being forewarned about how misogyny works."[23] Some scholars may not recognize the scope of the problem; calling their attention to harmful practices will suffice for them to adjust their own habits and to support broader transformation. Others may resist, doubling down on the spurious rhetoric of objectivity, relevance, and merit. "Misogyny is a self-masking phenomenon," Manne notes, so "trying to draw attention to the phenomenon is liable to give rise to more of it."[24] Still, if

20. For example, Chavella Pittman ("Race and Gender Oppression in the Classroom: The Experiences of Women Faculty of Color with White Male Students," *Teaching Sociology*, 38:3, 2010: 183–196) and Jennifer Thompson ("The Birdcage: Gender Inequity in Academic Jewish Studies," *Contemporary Jewry*, 39, 2019: 427–446) have used it to explain, respectively, the classroom experiences of women faculty of color and the constraints on professional advancement for women in Jewish studies.

21. Frye, *The Politics of Reality*, 19.

22. Sarah Imhoff described the pairing of an "ethical problem" and an "intellectual problem" as a way of thinking about all or mostly male collective publications. See Kecia Ali, Alison Joseph, Sharon Jacob, Sarah Imhoff, Toni Bond, Natasha Heller, and Stephanie Buckhanon Crowder, "Manthologies," *Journal of Feminist Studies in Religion*. 36:1, 2020: 145–158 at 149.

23. Kate Manne, *Down Girl: The Logic of Misogyny* (New York: Oxford University Press, 2018), 239.

24. Manne, *Down Girl*, xix.

enough come on board, the steady accrual of individual efforts and policy changes will shift our professional defaults. I pretend no objectivity here. Although I wholeheartedly favor bending wires to let birds escape, I ultimately hope to abolish birdcages.

In this book, I share some personal stories. I recount events to the best of my recollection, relying on my own files, archives, and emails for corroboration. I invent nothing but I sometimes omit or obscure details to protect others' privacy. When reporting spoken comments or unpublished correspondence, I don't name those involved. When quoting or discussing published writing, I generally do. As for social media, I draw from my own tweets freely but quote others only with permission.

There are pluses and minuses to naming names. Either way, someone will object. In a scathing assessment of Islamic legal studies, Ayesha Chaudhry refers only obliquely to the works she discusses, although specialists will find them easily identifiable.[25] Some have criticized that decision. Speaking at a conference panel after Chaudhry's essay appeared, a male full professor deemed her work "dangerous" in its vagueness. When it was my turn to talk, I noted that another male full professor had just published an article that deemed my criticisms of similar phenomena, in which I named (tenured) authors, "dangerous."[26] Chaudhry erred by

25. Ayesha S. Chaudhry. "Islamic Legal Studies: A Critical Historiography." In Anver M. Emon and Rumee Ahmed, eds., *The Oxford Handbook of Islamic Law* (Oxford: Oxford University Press, 2018), 5–44. On choosing not to cite specific figures, see also Lena Salaymeh, "Imperialist Feminism and Islamic Law," *Hawwa: Journal of Women of the Middle East and the Islamic World*, 17, 2019: 97–134 at 103–104.

26. Sherman Jackson, "The Alchemy of Domination 2.0," *American Journal of Islamic Social Sciences*, 35:4, 2018: 87–117 at 94. The lecture to which he refers is my Ismail Al Faruqi Memorial Lecture for the International Institute of Islamic Thought in November 2017 (available at IIITMedia's YouTube channel, https://www.youtube.com/watch?v=ai5XF-bP3KEis). It is forthcoming with commentary as Kecia Ali, "Muslim Scholars, Islamic Studies, and the Gendered Academy: Contingent Reflections," in Ebrahim Moosa, ed., *Contingency in Contemporary Muslim Theology: Madrasa Discourses* (Notre Dame, IN: University of Notre Dame Press, forthcoming).

omitting references, leaving her claims unsubstantiated.[27] On the other hand, by naming scholars and referencing specific works, I made people "targets" of my "invective," creating a "silencing effect" and a climate of fear for others who might be singled out.[28] We're damned if we do, damned if we don't. There's no right way to do it because the problem is that we're trying to do it at all. Any attempt to reckon with the damage done by the persistent devaluation of women's scholarship gets derailed quickly by a turn to imagined consequences for those whose reputations might be besmirched if they are called to account for their omissions.[29]

In what follows, I have tried to walk a middle path. I provide references to my evidence in my analyses of scholarly inclusion and exclusion. Singling out specific works as examples of poor citation practices can, as Chaudhry suggests, give the impression

27. Sohaira Siddiqui, who offers a nuanced and thorough engagement with Chaudhry's method and claims, criticizes her "basic failure to substantiate her argument with evidence and footnotes." "Good Scholarship/Bad Scholarship: Consequences of the Heuristic of Intersectional Islamic Studies," *Journal of the American Academy of Religion*, 88:1, 2020: 142–174 at 168. Ahmed El Shamsy also faults Chaudhry for failing to include "substantiating footnotes" in favor of "occasional anonymized examples." "How Not to Reform the Study of Islamic Law: A Response to Ayesha Chaudhry," in Intisar A. Rabb and Mariam Sheibani, eds., "Roundtable on Islamic Legal History and Historiography," *Islamic Law Blog*, December 10, 2020, https://islamiclaw.blog/2020/12/10/legalhistoryroundtable/.

28. Jackson, "The Alchemy of Domination 2.0," 87, 93, 94, 99. Although all the people I mention in the sources he cites are tenured men, Jackson writes of "the silencing effect that has already invaded the psychological space of numerous junior scholars and graduate students, male and female" (94). Won't someone please think of the children!

29. Discussing only the work of securely employed associate and full professors has been my policy from the start of this book project, expressed clearly when I've spoken about the work, and adhered to, save a couple of unintentional lapses, in talks, blogs, and tweets. Still, some have claimed hyperbolically that I'm aiming to ruin people's—by which they always mean men's—livelihoods. I'm not. On the ways that attempts to hold men accountable often result in claims that the men are now due sympathy for having been injured, see Manne's discussion of "himpathy" in *Down Girl*, 196 ff.

that the problem is individual malefactors rather than robustly self-reinforcing systems. I try to minimize this effect by showing how various forms of exclusion depend on and shore up other exclusionary practices. In analyzing book series and edited volumes, I emphasize patterns, while providing bibliographic details for reference. In other instances, as when I discuss syllabi from various data sets, I do not name faculty. Patterns matter alongside, and significantly constrain, the specific choices that individuals make. Yet some choices are at the very least questionable and deserve scrutiny. Also, not to put too fine a point on it, publications are by definition public. It says so right in the word. Still, the objective is not to apportion blame but to call our attention to existing norms and use this increased awareness to shift both individual and collective habits.

My discussions of publications and citations make no attempt at comprehensive coverage. I combine broad surveys with more focused analyses of a smaller set of texts. I rely mostly on qualitative analysis, accompanied by some quantitative reckoning with specific books, book series, and syllabi. Large-scale bibliometric analyses proved impractical for a variety of reasons, explained in the methodological appendix, but my examples are neither mere anecdote nor cherry-picked outliers. My findings here echo those in the statistically robust mixed-methods survey of gendered citation and author description in religious studies book reviews that Lolo Serrano and I conducted.[30] I encourage those who wish to contest my findings to demonstrate, with adequate evidence, that the imbalances I demonstrate aren't widespread, rather than simply claim that I've failed to meet some arbitrary standard of proof.

Islamic studies is a small field. I know many of those whose work I write about. In some cases, we are cordial acquaintances; in others,

30. Kecia Ali and Lolo Serrano, "The Person of the Author: Constructing Gendered Scholars in Religious Studies Book Reviews," *Journal of the American Academy of Religion*, 90:3, 2022: 554–578.

colleagues who have had long-standing, friendly relationships. A few have been advisors and mentors over the decades. I discussed my concerns and criticisms with several of them as I worked on this book. Reactions included chagrined acknowledgment, the abrupt severing of communication, and hostile rejoinders in person, online, or in print. As a tenured full professor, I am buffered from professional repercussions in ways that more precariously situated scholars, dependent on behind-the-scenes evaluation processes for hiring, publication, grants, and tenure, are not. It is precisely those vulnerabilities, magnified by increased reliance on algorithmic citation metrics, that make this work necessary.[31] I hope that even those who are unhappy about my analyses will understand my reasons for pursuing them.

Though I have been, in Kelly Baker's words, "scorched-earth angry" about some of the phenomena I discuss, my aim is not to ostracize anyone.[32] Although I critique specific works, mentioning several of my own failures along the way, none of these problems is reducible to individual lapses. What matters is not the purity and perfection of any single person's practice or the failings of any one book or article. We must think in terms of patterns, not merely incidents. Collectivities, not just individuals. Systems, rather than only cases. Structures as well as choices. I have tried to depict the forest by means of a few well-chosen trees. I describe some specimens in detail, down to the veining on a handful of leaves. I do not suggest that those trees are diseased and must be uprooted, much less advocate wildfire or clear-cutting. Rather, I want to focus on what kind of soil allows those trees to flourish.

31. Focusing on search engine results rather than scholarly citations, Safiya Umoja Noble shows how algorithms amplify existing biases and magnify inequalities. See *Algorithms of Oppression: How Search Engines Reinforce Racism* (New York: New York University Press, 2018).

32. Kelly J. Baker, *Sexism Ed: Essays on Gender and Labor in Academia* (Chapel Hill, NC: Raven Publishing, 2018), xvi. Baker writes about "the structural sexism of the academy" (xix), using her experiences as a lens for telling a larger story about religious studies specifically as well as the U.S. academy broadly.

What happens when their roots commandeer more than their share of nutrients? When their canopies block other saplings' access to sunlight? I want to understand the unhealthy imbalances of the current landscape in order to imagine and to begin to cultivate a healthier, sustainable scholarly ecosystem in which all inhabitants can thrive.

1

Engendering Islamic Studies

ANNEMARIE SCHIMMEL, a German scholar of Sufism with two doctorates and fluency in numerous languages, became a Harvard professor in 1967 partly because of scant prospects for advancement in Germany. Her boss there had told her: "Miss Schimmel, if you were a man, you would get a chair!"[1] She had been the first woman and first non-Muslim faculty member at Turkey's Ankara University in the 1950s. In 1980, she was the first woman and first scholar of Islam elected president of the International Association for the History of Religions.[2] In 1987, she became the first—and for nearly fifty years, only—woman to win the Giorgio Levi Della Vida Award, which honors "outstanding scholars whose work has significantly and lastingly advanced the study of Islamic civilization."[3]

1. Annemarie Schimmel, "A Life of Learning," Charles Homer Haskins Lecture, American Council of Learned Societies, ACLS Occasional Paper No. 21, 1993, https://www.acls.org/wp-content/uploads/2021/11/Haskins_1993_Annemarie Schimmel.pdf, 11.

2. Schimmel, "A Life of Learning," 13.

3. Recipients through 2019, as well as authors and chapter titles for commemorative volumes published until 2017, can be found at "Giorgio Levi Della Vida Series in Islamic Studies," https://international.ucla.edu/cnes/article/14544. As of this writing, there have been twenty-two recipients, with the prize awarded on twenty-one occasions. In 1999 two men jointly received the award and shared a commemorative volume. I discuss the prize, its recipients, and related publications in more detail below.

In the decades since Schimmel was told her gender would prevent her from getting a job, more women have earned prominence,
prizes, and professorships. The demographics of what Schimmel
called Islamology, like those of American academia more generally,
look considerably different than they did during her career. But the
field remains in key respects male-dominated, gender-segregated,
and unequal. Its forms of recognition reinscribe biased histories.
Its embedded sexism and gendered racism affect individual scholars, who lose out on myriad opportunities, and shape—indeed,
distort—scholarly subfields.[4]

These continued imbalances manifest in edited collections that
survey Islamic studies as well as in book series and edited volumes
in specific subfields. Overviews of the field minimize and marginalize women's contributions, especially those of Muslim women,
particularly Muslim women of color. They treat subfields in which
women predominate as less important and serious than those considered masculine, often ignoring them entirely or segregating
them into their own sections. Edited volumes and book series
in some areas, like the study of Islam in America, are balanced. In
others, such as the study of early Islam or Islamic law, they are
badly skewed. In choosing contributors and collaborators, men
often exclude women colleagues. Power-laden ideas about what
and who is essential (usually, masculine-coded topics and/or men
scholars) to the field and what and who is marginal (typically,
feminine-coded topics and/or scholars who aren't men, or who
are queer men) quietly shape ordinary practices of citation and

---

4. Wanda Martin Burton gives a succinct explanation of the phenomenon in
"Gendered Racism: A Call for an Intersectional Approach," *Journal of Psychosocial
Nursing and Mental Health Services*, 60:12, 2022: 3–4. As Kelly Baker points out,
"male-dominated fields seem prone to harassment" and, whether in the sciences or
the humanities, "can breed discrimination, harm, and abuse" (*Sexism Ed*, 29). That's
partly how they stay male-dominated. See Becky Mansfield et. al, "It's Time to Recognize How Men's Careers Benefit from Sexually Harassing Women in Academia,"
Human Geography, 12:1, 2019: 82–87.

inclusion in, or exclusion from, literature reviews, edited volumes, and book series, as well as honors and awards.

Mapping the field

Even as the study of women, gender, and Islam has flourished over the past decades, attempts to survey the terrain of Islamic studies consistently marginalize the study of women and gender and, not coincidentally, women's scholarly contributions. This is true for a quarter century's worth of edited volumes on Islamic studies in the U.S. and Europe, including Azim Nanji's *Mapping Islamic Studies*; Carl Ernst and Richard Martin's *Rethinking Islamic Studies*; Mumtaz Ahmad, Zahid Bukhari, and Sulayman Nyang's *Observing the Observer*; Clinton Bennett's *Bloomsbury Companion to Islamic Studies*; Léon Buskens and Annemarie van Sandwijk's *Islamic Studies in the Twenty-first Century*; Matt Sheedy's *Identity, Politics and the Study of Islam*; Majid Daneshgar and Aaron Hughes's *Deconstructing Islamic Studies*; and Leif Stenberg and Philip Wood's *What is Islamic Studies?* Excepting any chapters or sections on women and gender, these accounts of the field are overwhelmingly male-dominated.[5] This is true when we judge their own practices (most include few contributors who are not men), consider whether individual contributors account for and reference women's contributions on any topic (usually not), or assess whether they discuss scholarship on women and gender in their general accounts of the field (seldom).

The earliest of these volumes, *Mapping Islamic Studies* (1997) surveys Islamic studies in Europe and the U.S. in ten nationally or thematically focused chapters.[6] One is by a woman. Azim Nanji's

5. As its focus is pedagogy, I do not address Courtney M. Dorroll's *Teaching Islamic Studies in the Age of ISIS, Islamophobia, and the Internet* (Indianapolis: University of Indiana Press, 2019). Note, however, that fully half the chapters are by women. The book is recent, the editor is a woman, and the topic—pedagogy—is feminized.

6. Azim Nanji, ed., *Mapping Islamic Studies: Genealogy, Continuity, and Change* (Berlin and New York: Mouton de Gruyter, 1997). Seven men wrote a total of nine chapters and one woman wrote one chapter.

introduction explains that the book aims to show "how the discipline of Islamic Studies, a branch of Oriental Studies, as it has come to be understood and practiced, evolved in various historical contexts."[7] The sole woman he names in his text is contributor Sarah Roche-Mahdi. Only three of ten chapters mention women or gender at all. Several neither name nor cite any women scholars. Only seven women Islamicists are named in total, most in just one chapter. Not a single Muslim woman scholar is named in the body of the book and very few appear in its notes or bibliography. Some gender imbalance is inevitable, as contributions lean more heavily on the nineteenth century than the twentieth, but the overall vibe of this volume is not appreciably better than that found in the chapter-length "studies of the study of Islam" originally published between 1959 and 1963, which Merlin Swartz translated from the French and published in *Studies on Islam* (1981).[8]

The sidelining of scholarship on women and gender, and the relative marginalization of scholars who are not men as contributors and references, continued into the 2010s, albeit with mild improvements in contributor ratios. Carl Ernst and Richard Martin's *Rethinking Islamic Studies: From Orientalism to Cosmopolitanism* (2010) presents itself as an update to co-editor Martin's *Approaches to Islam in Religious Studies* (1985).[9] Two of its sixteen contributors are women, writing two of its thirteen chapters. Yet apart from brief summaries of their chapters and a passing mention of Marilyn Waldman in a list of otherwise male attendees at the symposium on which that earlier volume was based, Ernst and Martin's introductory overview of the field names only men

7. Azim Nanji, "Introduction," in Nanji, ed. *Mapping Islamic Studies*, xi–xxi at xi.

8. Merlin L. Swartz, *Studies on Islam*, translated and edited by Swartz (New York: Oxford University Press, 1981), vii.

9. Carl W. Ernst and Richard C. Martin, eds., *Rethinking Islamic Studies: From Orientalism to Cosmopolitanism* (Columbia: University of South Carolina Press, 2010) and Richard C. Martin, ed., *Approaches to Islam in Religious Studies* (Tucson: University of Arizona Press, 1985 and republished by Oneworld [Oxford, 2001]).

and discusses only men's work.[10] None of its twenty-eight end-notes includes publications by women. A few of the book's chapters, including some by men, address gender and cite some women's scholarship, but most have fewer than one note out of ten citing women. Only Jamillah Karim's chapter cites women's scholarship in more than one fifth of its endnotes.[11] In about half the chapters, references to women's scholarship can be counted on the fingers of one hand, not including the thumb. Two out of forty-eight citations. One of thirty-two. Zero of eighty-four. The volume was a stealth Festschrift for Bruce Lawrence, one of my doctoral instructors, whose afterword begins with an entirely male genealogy of Islamic studies even as he notes that "correcting the narrowly dyadic, male-dominant, logocentric interpretations of Islam" is a central concern of the volume.[12]

Mumtaz Ahmad, Zahid Bukhari, and Sulayman Nyang's *Observing the Observer: The State of Islamic Studies in American Universities* (2012) was organized and published by the academia-adjacent International Institute of Islamic Thought.[13] It mixes topical chapters, such as Marcia Hermansen's survey of Sufi studies, with those addressing specific cases, such as Jane Smith's

10. Carl W. Ernst and Richard C. Martin, "Introduction: Toward a Post-Orientalist Approach to Islamic Religious Studies," in Ernst and Martin, eds., *Rethinking Islamic Studies*, 1–19.

11. Jamillah Karim, "Can We Define 'True Islam'? African American Muslim Women Respond to Transnational Muslim Identities," in Ernst and Martin, eds., *Rethinking Islamic Studies*, 114–130.

12. Bruce B. Lawrence, "Afterword: Competing Genealogies of Muslim Cosmopolitanism," in Ernst and Martin, eds., *Rethinking Islamic Studies*, 302–323 at 309. Lawrence, who has been instrumental in promoting the scholarly legacy of historian Marilyn Waldman, including by posthumously editing her *Prophecy and Power* (Sheffield, UK: Equinox, 2012), does discuss and cite work by philosopher and legal scholar Martha Nussbaum.

13. Mumtaz Ahmad, Zahid Bukhari, and Sulayman Nyang, eds., *Observing the Observer: The State of Islamic Studies in American Universities* (Herndon, VA: International Institute of Islamic Thought, 2012). It is available open access at https://iiit .org/wp-content/uploads/Observing-The-Observer-1.pdf.

exploration of how Islam is taught in Christian theological schools.[14] It also contains a survey of introductory Islam courses, the findings of which I explore in Chapter 4, and a summary of a roundtable discussion among some of the contributors and other Islamic studies faculty. Three of its ten chapters are woman-authored, including one on gender by Saba Mahmood adapted from her essay for the *Encyclopedia of Women and Islamic Cultures*.[15] Other contributors discuss gender fleetingly, if at all. None of the men cites more than three items written or co-written by women. Some cite no women's scholarship at all.

Deciding not to segregate women and gender in his *Bloomsbury Companion to Islamic Studies* (2013), "intended as a companion to graduate level work on Islam," Clinton Bennett indicates that each chapter should attend to these topics.[16] However, of nine topical chapters, a third of them by women, only that on jurisprudence by Maria Curtis gives women or gender more than a passing mention.[17] Bennett's own portrait of the field is male-dominated. In his twenty-seven-page introduction, the number of women he mentions barely makes double-digits, even counting parenthetical

14. Marcia Hermansen, "The Academic Study of Sufism at American Universities," 88–111 and Jane I. Smith, "Teaching Islam in American Theological Schools," 114–136.

15. Saba Mahmood, "Islam and Gender in Muslim Societies: Reflections of an Anthropologist," 70–87. The *Encyclopedia of Women and Islamic Cultures* (2003–) is a major interdisciplinary project in several phases under the editorship of Suad Joseph. More information is available at https://sjoseph.ucdavis.edu/encyclopedia-women-and-islamic-cultures.

16. Clinton Bennett, "Introduction," in Bennett, ed., *The Bloomsbury Companion to Islamic Studies* (London: Bloomsbury, 2013) 1–27 at 1.

17. Of the topical chapters in the section "Current Research and Issues," only Maria Curtis's "*Fiqh*, The Science of Islamic Jurisprudence" (207–226) includes multiple paragraphs addressing gender, sexuality, and Islamic family law. Other chapters briefly note issues having to do with gender and dress (e.g., William Shephard's "Salafi Islam: The Study of Contemporary Religious-Political Movements," 163–184 at 164 and 175) or defer it to the book's broader apparatus: "some titles under gender in Resources are also relevant" (Mashhad al-Allaf, "Islamic Theology," 119–134 at 133). Mea culpa; it was at my suggestion that Bennett pursued this course.

citations. Most of the rest appear only in a brief in-text mention, though Annemarie Schimmel merits most of a paragraph, which ends with the observation that "the current phase sees more women contributing to Islamic studies."[18]

Islamic Studies in the Twenty-first Century: Transformations and Continuities (2016), Léon Buskens and Annemarie van Sandwijk's volume, has three chapters by women among eleven substantive chapters.[19] Two focus on gender, given a section of its own. Once again, men do very poorly at including work by women, especially Muslim women, or integrating work on gender in their essays. Buskens's account of Islamic studies within Middle Eastern studies names six men for every woman. Of the seven women he names, four appear in the paragraph that begins "Since the 1970s many scholars, especially female, have worked on gender issues."[20]

Matt Sheedy's *Identity, Politics and the Study of Islam: Current Dilemmas in the Study of Religion* (2018) and Majid Daneshgar and Aaron Hughes's *Deconstructing Islamic Studies* (2020) offer critical analyses of the way the academic study of Islam is currently practiced. Numerous contributors to these volumes view it as too often apologetic or polemical, and suggest alternatives to existing approaches.[21] Of nine chapters in *Identity, Politics and the Study of Islam,* including a substantive introduction and a lengthy afterword, two chapters are by women and one is co-authored by a

---

18. Bennett, "Introduction," 22.

19. Léon Buskens and Annemarie van Sandwijk, *Islamic Studies in the Twenty-first Century: Transformations and Continuities* (Amsterdam: Amsterdam University Press, 2016). The book is available open access at https://library.oapen.org/handle/20.500.12657/30676.

20. Léon Buskens, "Middle Eastern Studies and Islam: Oscillations and Tensions in an Old Relationship," in Buskens and van Sandwijk, eds., *Islamic Studies in the Twenty-first Century,* 241–267 at 249.

21. Matt Sheedy, ed., *Identity, Politics and the Study of Islam: Current Dilemmas in the Study of Religions* (Sheffield, UK: Equinox, 2018) and Majid Daneshgar and Aaron W. Hughes, eds., *Deconstructing Islamic Studies* (Boston, MA: Ilex Foundation, 2020).

mixed-gender team. Unusually, about half its contributors come from outside of Islamic studies, focused on theoretical approaches to religious studies or from adjacent fields such as Jewish studies or biblical studies. *Deconstructing Islamic Studies*, in which two of twelve chapters are by women, explores the way genres from classical Muslim thought such as *tafsir* (roughly, exegesis) and *tasawwuf* (sort-of-but-not-exactly mysticism) have structured modern academic work on Islam. Contributors, who apart from a few exceptions tend to ignore work on women and gender, find the uses of these genres both problematic and potentially fruitful.[22] Some modern women scholars' work appears scattered throughout the chapters, but the volume mostly discusses a male textual tradition and secondary literature by men. These volumes continue, and occasionally directly engage, the discussions of "Normativity in Islamic Studies" that Juliane Hammer and others offered in a roundtable in the *Journal of the American Academy of Religion* (2016)—unusually, for the field, with two out of every three contributions by women.[23]

Men's contributions (seven of nine chapters) in Leif Stenberg and Philip Wood's *What is Islamic Studies? European and North American Approaches to a Contested Field* (2022) attend overwhelmingly to scholarship by men.[24] For instance, the first chapter, by Aaron Hughes, includes no work by women in its bibliography. It focuses on Shahab Ahmed and Wael Hallaq, drawing on

22. The chapter by Mahdi Tourage ("Studying Sufism Beyond Orientalism, Fundamentalism, and Perennialism," 313–337) attends at some length (yes, that's a phallus joke) to masculinity, gender, and sexuality.

23. Juliane Hammer, Jonathan Brockopp, Zareena Grewal, Sarah Eltantawi, Elliott Bazzano, and Anna M. Gade, "Roundtable on Normativity in Islamic Studies," *Journal of the American Academy of Religion*, 84:1, 2016: 25–126. Two men and four women (66%) contribute one article each.

24. Leif Stenberg and Philip Wood, eds., *What Is Islamic Studies? European and North American Approaches to a Contested Field* (Edinburgh: Edinburgh University Press, 2022). Seven of nine chapters are written by men, one by a mixed-gender team, and one by a woman.

Jonathan Z. Smith and Bruce Lincoln, after kicking off with a suitable quotation from Clifford Geertz reviewing Marshall Hodgson.[25] In the second chapter, Carool Keersten briefly deploys Atalia Omer's argument in favor of "critics who also act as caretakers" to address the work of Irfan Ahmad and Hamid Dabashi, with extensive attention to writings by Dabashi's key interlocutor Gil Anidjar, and with reference to the ideas of numerous other men, including Ahmed, Smith, Lincoln, and Talal Asad.[26] In turn, Hadi Enayat's discussion of Asad's secularism in the third chapter substantively engages, apart from Asad himself, Khaled Fahmy and Colin Koopman, and, through Koopman, Michel Foucault.[27] Page after page, chapter after chapter, it's men's books all the way down.

Decades worth of reflection on Islamic studies in volumes such as these shows not only neglect of women generally but the specific marginalization of Muslim women. Muslim men continue to be cited as authorities and engaged as thinkers within these surveys, but Muslim women seldom are, except in work specifically about Muslim women's thought on gender. Otherwise, women whose ideas and publications make the cut are almost always white and non-Muslim, with the occasional white convert making an appearance. Among those named in the main text of *Mapping Islamic Studies*, for instance, all the women—except maybe Nabia Abbott, "an 'oriental' from Mardin"—are white and all the Muslims are men.[28] Ditto, Buskens's overview from two decades

25. Aaron W. Hughes, "There is No Data for Islam: Testing the Utility of a Category," in Stenberg and Wood, eds., *What is Islamic Studies?*, 32–41.

26. Carool Keersten, "Critics as Caretakers, Religion as Critique," in Stenberg and Wood, eds., *What is Islamic Studies?*, 42–59 at 43. Also see Atalia Omer, "Can a Critic Be a Caretaker Too? Religion, Conflict, and Conflict Transformation," *Journal of the American Academy of Religion*, 79:2, 2011: 459–496.

27. Hadi Enayat, "Talal Asad and the Question of Islamic Secularities," in Stenberg and Wood, eds., *What is Islamic Studies?*, 60–81.

28. My phrasing here echoes Akasha Gloria Hull, Patricia Bell-Scott, and Barbara Smith, eds., *All the Women Are White, All the Blacks Are Men, but Some of Us Are Brave: Black Women's Studies* (New York: Feminist Press, 1982). The description of Abbott,

later.[29] All but three of the women cited by other male authors in *Islamic Studies in the Twenty-first Century* are white Westerners.[30] Indeed, the women contributors to these state-of-the-field volumes are also overwhelmingly white and mostly non-Muslim.

Curating exclusion

The marginalization of gender as a topic and the sidelining of women scholars and women's scholarship can also be seen in the way subfields within Islamic studies organize their work and scholarly production. Few areas achieve gender parity, but some are substantially better than others, as a comparison of edited volumes and book series in the subfields of American Islam, Islamic law, and Qur'anic studies illustrates. Even within subfields, some areas are more or less likely to have women represented. Areas with more women in them are often treated as less prestigious and important. What Catherine Lutz observes about sociocultural anthropology holds for other areas of study as well: "It is difficult to disentangle the socially constituted value of a

who comes from a Turkish Christian background, is from Muhsin Mahdi, who explains that Mardin is located "in southern Turkey or northern Mesopotamia." Mahdi, "The Study of Islam, Orientalism and America," in Nanji, ed., *Mapping Islamic Studies*, 149–180 at 159. Who counts as white, and what counts as Europe, is complicated, especially when religious identity is considered. See Neda Maghbouleh, *The Limits of Whiteness: Iranian Americans and the Everyday Politics of Race* (Stanford, CA: Stanford University Press, 2017).

29. Buskens does, however, include parenthetical citations to several publications by Muslim women/women from Muslim backgrounds.

30. Kevin Reinhart's chapter (A. Kevin Reinhart, "What to Do with Ritual Texts: Islamic *Fiqh* Texts and the Study of Islamic Ritual," 67–86) has a half dozen items (co-)written by women in his bibliography, including two by Saba Mahmood. The only other work by women from a Muslim background I found cited in chapters by the six men contributors other than Buskens or Reinhart is a co-authored interview by Mona Anis and Amira Howeidy with Nasr Hamid Abu Zayd published in the Egyptian newspaper *Al-Ahram*.

subfield from the socially constituted value of the people who do research in it."[31]

Three factors influence the balance within edited volumes: year, subfield, and editors' genders. A collection published in 2020 is likely to be more inclusive than one published in 2000 or 2010. And, perhaps obviously, a volume in a male-dominated subfield is likely to be more skewed than one in a subfield that is more balanced. Less obviously, editors' genders also shape inclusion. Surveying two decades of classical studies handbooks, Peter Thonemann found "very striking correlations between the gender(s) of the editor(s) of 'Companion' volumes and gender representation within the volumes." Controlling for other variables, men tend to produce the most male-dominated volumes in Islamic studies, too, though I found this effect considerably blunted in subfields that are more gender-balanced overall.[32]

Editors' genders matter because collective publications are idiosyncratic. In addition to the pet concerns of proposal reviewers and the interests and aversions of publishers, edited volumes' composition depends heavily on the scholarly networks of their editors. Men's networks tend to be male-dominated. Editing what Mara Benjamin calls a "manthology" isn't a purely passive overlooking or omitting, but involves actively doing what Annette Yoshiko Reed describes as "maintaining closed networks."[33] It is integrally

31. Catherine Lutz, "The Erasure of Women's Writing in Sociocultural Anthropology," *American Ethnologist*, 17:4, 1990: 611–627 at 621.

32. Peter Thonemann, "Gender, Subject Preference, and Editorial Bias in Classical Studies, 2001–2019," *Council of University Classical Departments Bulletin*, 48, 2019: 1–24 at 1, https://cucd.blogs.sas.ac.uk/files/2019/09/THONEMANN-Gender -subject-preference-editorial-bias.pdf.

33. Mara Benjamin, "On the Uses of Academic Privilege," May 27, 2019, in the Feminist Studies in Religion @theTable blog series on "Manthologies," https://www .fsrinc.org/thetable-manthologies/. Although the term "manthology" has gained traction, edited volumes and other collective publications typically aren't anthologies in the sense that publishers use that term: books which gather previously published work or primary texts, often with a pedagogical purpose. For "maintaining

related to other patterns that include but stretch beyond editorial practice. Who holds the research professorship with the boundless budget? Who gets accepted into a conference for which there will be a publication but can't attend because they have no institutional funding?[34] Such factors, unrelated to the quality or relevance of scholarship, shape tables of contents. Some scholars are less likely to hold secure faculty positions at well-resourced institutions, less likely to be part of prestigious networks, and less likely to have their work celebrated as central to a given field.[35] My analysis here makes no attempt to probe these background occurrences or to do a deep dive into editorial practices, though someone should. One shouldn't draw grand conclusions from a handful of examples. Still, even if the sample is too small to derive statistically significant results, we can see that in male-dominated subfields, a volume with one or more women among its editors is likely to show better gender parity among contributors.

Cambridge's seven Islam-related Companions in its collection on Philosophy and Religion, published between 2006 and 2019, bear this out. Four focus on topical areas and three on significant people—which is to say, men. *Classical Islamic Theology* (male editor, 2008) is least inclusive, with just one of fifteen chapters by a woman.[36] *Muhammad* (male editor, 2010) tripled that rate, with

closed networks," see Annette Yoshiko Reed (@AnnetteYReed), Twitter, February 6, 2020, https://twitter.com/AnnetteYReed/status/1225416757369876481.

34. Sekile Nzinga recounts two instances within the same year of organizing conference panels that included Black women scholars whose work was accepted but who ultimately couldn't attend because of the cost. *Lean Semesters*, 102. I am not aware of research on this phenomenon in Islamic studies or religious studies.

35. Portions of this section are adapted from Kecia Ali, "No Manthology Is an Island," June 4, 2019, https://www.fsrinc.org/no-manthology-is-an-island/.

36. Timothy Winter, ed. There was one woman contributor and fifteen men (6.7%). I exclude from consideration *The Cambridge Companion to Arabic Philosophy* (2004), as the editors omitted "Islamic" from the title, unlike the Cambridge Companion volume on *Medieval Jewish Philosophy*.

women contributing one of every five chapters.[37] One in four contributors to *The Qur'an* (woman editor, 2006) was a woman, despite its being the earliest of the series.[38] Nearly a decade later, the *Sufism* handbook (male editor, 2015) had one woman in every three contributors.[39] Only the volume focused on *American Islam* (mixed-gender editorial team, 2013) had a majority of women contributors, nearly six out of ten.[40] But the focus on the United States does not guarantee inclusion. The Companion on Malcolm X (male editor, 2010) has the second worst ratio, with one of every seven chapters by a woman.[41] The most recent Companion, devoted to Sayyid Ahmad Khan (mixed-gender editorial team, 2019), has nearly half of its chapters by women.[42]

These texts show us three things. First, men get disproportionate scholarly attention. There is no Cambridge Companion for any woman in Muslim history. In this, Cambridge is typical. I.B. Tauris's Makers of Islamic Civilization series devotes all thirteen of its biographies to men and Oneworld's Makers of the Muslim World has two biographies of women and forty-four of men.[43]

---

37. Jonathan Brockopp, ed. There were three women and twelve men among the contributors (20%) and 3 / 14 chapters by women (21%).

38. Four of sixteen contributors were women (25%), with the same proportion of chapters by women (3.5 / 14 or 25%).

39. Lloyd Ridgeon, ed. Four of twelve contributors (33%) were women, with the same ratio of chapters by women (4 / 12 or 33%).

40. Juliane Hammer and Omid Safi, eds. Thirteen of twenty-two contributors were women (59%). Women wrote 10.5 / 18 (58%) of its chapters.

41. Robert E. Terrill, ed. Two of its fourteen chapters (14%) were by women.

42. Yasmin Saikia and M. Raisur Rahman, eds. Six of thirteen chapters (46%) were by women.

43. Information about the Oxford Center for Islamic Studies' series Makers of Islamic Civilization, published by I.B. Tauris, as of January 23, 2023, and Oneworld's Makers of the Muslim World series from 2005–2021, as of February 5, 2021. One of these biographies of men is by me. I initially agreed to write the volume on Aisha bint Abi Bakr when its original author backed out. When she decided to resume the project, I shifted to al-Shafi'i. Unfortunately, the volume on Aisha was never completed. Oxford Bibliographies Online has a section for People in its Islamic Studies section. Roughly

Second, more recent texts are typically more inclusive than older ones. The average percentage of women contributors more than doubles between Companion volumes published before 2010 and those from the following decade, from 16% to 35%. And third, editors' genders are closely tied to gender (im)balance. Volumes edited by men average 16% women contributors while for volumes with at least one woman editor, that percentage soars to 57%.

Publications in Islamic legal studies, Qur'anic studies, and American Islam demonstrate similar patterns, with the caveat that where the subfield is more balanced, editor gender seems to matter less. A cursory survey of edited volumes on Islam in the United States or the Americas from 2013 to 2020 shows that women often comprise between half and three quarters of contributors.[44] Similar

---

one entry in ten is for a woman (7 / 65 as of January 23, 2023). This is a better, although not good, ratio. https://www.oxfordbibliographies.com/obo/page/islamic-studies.

44. Aisha Khan's *Islam and the Americas* (Gainesville: University Press of Florida, 2015), has nine women authors out of twelve contributors, as does Edward Curtis's *The Practice of Islam in America* (New York: New York University Press, 2017). *Varieties of American Sufism* (Albany: SUNY Press, 2020), edited by Elliott Bazzano and Marcia Hermansen, has four of eight; while John Ghazvinian and Arthur Mitchell Fraas's *American and Muslim Worlds before 1900* (London: Bloomsbury, 2020) has six of twelve, counting the woman-authored epilogue. Mohammad Hassan Khalil's *Muslims and US Politics Today: A Defining Moment* (Cambridge, MA: Harvard University Press, 2019) has a different chronological focus but a similar breakdown: six men and six women contribute eleven chapters, one co-authored by two women. Not every volume is quite so balanced. Jessica Baldanzi and Hussein Rashid's *Ms. Marvel's America: No Normal* (Jackson: University Press of Mississippi, 2020) has nine men and four women contributors (eleven chapters, two co-authored), while in Carl Ernst's *Islamophobia in America: The Anatomy of Intolerance* (New York: Palgrave Macmillan, 2013), only the chapter on gender is by a woman; the other four are (co-)written by men. Co-edited volumes on *Africana Islamic Studies* (Lanham, MD: Lexington, 2016) and *New Perspectives on the Nation of Islam* (New York: Routledge, 2017) flip expectations about editors' genders and contributor ratios. The former, edited by James L. Conyers Jr. and Abul Pitre, has four men and nine women among its contributors, while the latter, edited by Dawn-Marie Gibson and Herbert Berg, has ten men and three women. In compiling this quick-and-dirty survey with assistance from colleagues on Twitter, I excluded edited volumes explicitly focusing on women. I also left out

ratios are found in Juliane Hammer and Omid Safi's *Cambridge Companion to American Islam* (2013) and *The Oxford Handbook of American Islam* (2014), edited by Jane Smith and Yvonne Haddad.[45] That both handbooks and many edited collections on American Islam have at least one woman editor seems to reflect gender balance in the subfield as much as explain gender balance in these books. Most of the volumes (co-)edited by men are also balanced, and of the three volumes with a surfeit of men contributors, two have women co-editors.

In contrast, in the subfields of Islamic law and Qur'an/Islamic origins, editors' genders make a substantial difference in the composition of edited volumes, reflecting the historically male-dominated subfield. Ayesha Chaudhry's critique of patriarchy and white supremacy in the Western academic study of Islamic law delineates existing approaches to the subject. Patriarchal Islamic Legal Studies and White Supremacist Islamic Studies are, as her insulting acronyms (PILS and WhiSIS) for them suggest, deeply problematic for intertwined methodological and political reasons.[46] Both center

---

Conyers's *Africana Faith: A Religious History of the African American Crusade in Islam* (Lanham, MD: Hamilton Books, 2017), since none of the contributions (from two women and twenty-six men) postdates 2020, and Edward Curtis's *Bloomsbury Reader on Islam in the West* (London, Bloomsbury: 2015), as the contributions (from seventeen men and thirteen women) vary substantially in length and style. Mehdi Aminarazvi's *Sufism and American Literary Masters* (Albany: SUNY Press, 2014), with two women out of twelve contributors, covers American poets, not American Muslims, and Micah Fries and Keith Whitfield's *Islam and North America: Loving Our Muslim Neighbors* (Nashville, TN: B&H Academic, 2018), solidly outside of Islamic studies, has one woman among a dozen contributors. As with any subfield, deciding what counts is tricky. Some might dispute my choices or find texts I have overlooked. Nonetheless, the pattern is clear and contrasts with the other areas within Islamic studies.

45. Haddad and Smith's *Oxford Handbook of American Islam* (New York: Oxford University Press, 2014) has sixteen men and seventeen women among its thirty-three contributors. I discuss Hammer and Safi's volume above.

46. She proposes, as a corrective to these "morally failed" approaches, Intersectional Islamic Studies. Chaudhry, "Islamic Legal Studies," 29. For a substantive critique of Chaudhry's approach, see Siddiqui, "Good Scholarship/Bad Scholarship."

engagement with and mastery of "precolonial" Arabic texts and, to a lesser extent, the work of scholars operating in these privileged modalities. While the former group continues to center the authority of a Muslim religio-legal textual tradition, the latter operates as though one can and should describe and analyze legal texts without any investment in their application or otherwise.

Islamic legal studies has historical imbalances to contend with that the newer field of American Islam does not. In John Makdisi's "Islamic Law Bibliography" (1986), about one in thirty of 865 secondary sources published between 1842 and 1982 has a woman as author or co-author, mostly among the more recent publications listed.[47] Just a handful of studies by women appear among the sixty-three works in "Marriage and Divorce, Women" and just one in the twenty-five entries under "Family Law." Despite the steady increase in publications in the field, R. Stephen Humphreys's *Islamic History: A Framework for Inquiry* (1991), a book I was assigned in my first semester of doctoral study, continues to impart the sense of a male-dominated field. Yet, even within this book, the chapter on Islamic law stands out as especially exclusionary. Humphreys names women scholars only in the paragraphs addressing notarial formulae.[48] (This is not inevitable. Recall that in Bennett's *Encyclopedia*, Curtis's chapter on jurisprudence does the best job of citing women's work.)

Still, beginning in the 1980s and increasing steadily to the present day, women have published more and more on Islamic law. In their *Bibliography of Islamic Law, 1980–1993* (1994), Laila al-Zwaini and Rudolph Peters use only initials instead of first names, so one cannot quickly gauge the proportion of work by women in its entries, but a preliminary survey indicates that it is

47. John Makdisi, "Islamic Law Bibliography," *Law Library Journal*, 78:1, 1986: 103–189. He also includes twenty pages of premodern legal texts by men.

48. R. Stephen Humphreys, *Islamic History: A Framework for Inquiry*, rev. ed. (Princeton, NJ: Princeton University Press, 1991), 218–19.

substantially higher than in Makdisi.[49] A good number of these publications by women are in Spanish, by Spanish scholars. Spain has a considerably higher proportion of women in Arabic and Islamic studies than most academic communities, including in the subfield of Islamic law.[50] A revised and updated version of Makdisi's bibliography, co-authored with Marianne Makdisi in 1995, limits itself to English and French publications but also attests to a significant shift between the collection of the first 865 entries in 1984 and the expanded set of 1908 items found in 1994.[51] "Marriage and Divorce, Women" has been subdivided. Seventeen works by women appear in each section. They comprise one in seven entries in "Marriage and Divorce" and two of every five in "Women."[52]

Brill's prestigious and long-standing Studies in Islamic Law and Society book series shows a male-dominated field moving toward greater parity, the way we see in these bibliographies, while preserving male dominance when men serve as gatekeepers.[53] It published fifty-one books between 1996 and 2020, forty-one

49. Laila al-Zwaini and Rudolph Peters, *A Bibliography of Islamic Law, 1980–1993* (Leiden: Brill, 1994).

50. See Maribel Fierro, "Spanish Scholarship on Islamic Law," *Islamic Law and Society*, 2:1, 1995: 43–70; Delfina Serrano Ruano, "Spanish Research on Islamic Law, 1990–1999," *Journal of Law and Religion*, 15:1–2, 2000–2001: 331–357; and Maribel Fierro et al., *Repertorio Bibliográfico de Derecho Islámico: Primera y Segunda Partes* (Murcia: Universidad de Murcia, 1999), which covers journal articles primarily in Spanish, Italian, and French.

51. John Makdisi and Marianne Makdisi, "Islamic Law Bibliography: Revised and Updated List of Secondary Sources," 87:1, 1995: 69–191.

52. "Marriage and Divorce" contains 105 items, including seventeen (16%) by women. That figure includes ten works by Lucy Carroll but not the article from 1929 by Leslie D. Gruyther, about whom I could find no further information. The section "Women" contains forty-three items, including seventeen (39%) by women.

53. One might track publications in other series and by other publishers, including Cambridge University Press, which publishes important books on law and legal thought in its Cambridge Studies in Islamic Civilization series. However, that series is broader than law, and books that deal centrally with law—e.g., Marion Katz, *Prayer in Islamic Thought and Practice* (Cambridge and New York: Cambridge University Press, 2013)—are also published in other series, making comparison trickier.

monographs and ten edited volumes. Five monographs, just under one in eight, were by women. Between its first publication of a book by a woman in 1998 and the second in 2010, the series published two dozen books by men. As with the Cambridge Companions, both single-authored and collective publications in this Brill series tend toward greater gender balance over time. The proportion of single-author books by women increased eightfold from 1996–2007 to 2010–2020.[54] Yet, although women make up an increasing proportion of those publishing monographs, men remain heavily overrepresented in collections edited by men, even as edited volumes make up a greater share of the series. Until 2007, only one in ten books in the series was an edited collection. After 2010 it was one in three.[55] Four non-Festschrift collections were published between 2017 and 2019. The three edited by women or mixed-gender teams have between 31% and 50% of their substantive chapters by women.[56] The volume edited by men has zero.[57]

54. From 1996 to 2007, just one of twenty-seven monographs ($<$ 4%) was by a woman, but nearly 30% (4 / 14) of those published from 2010 to 2020 were. No books were published in 2008–2009 or 2021–2022. As this book goes to press, all three books published in 2023 and the sole volume projected for 2024 (as of February 19, 2024) are single-author monographs by men.

55. From 1996 to 2007, 3 / 30 books in the series were edited volumes (10%). After 2010, the proportion was 7 / 21 (33%).

56. Giovanna Calasso and Giuliano Lancioni, eds., *Dar al-islam / dar al-harb: Territories, People, Identities* (Leiden: Brill, 2017) has, not counting a substantial introduction, 7.5 of 19 chapters by women (39%). Sohaira Siddiqui, ed., *Locating the Shari'a: Legal Fluidity in Theory, History and Practice* (Leiden: Brill, 2019) has four of thirteen substantive chapters authored by women (31%), while women wrote 4.5 of nine chapters (50%) in Norbert Oberauer, Yvonne Prief, and Ulrike Qubaja, eds., *Legal Pluralism in Muslim Contexts* (Leiden: Brill, 2019).

57. Ali-reza Bhojani, Laurens de Rooij, and Michael Bohlander, eds., *Visions of Shari'a: Contemporary Discussions in Shi'i Legal Theory* (Leiden: Brill, 2019) has seven substantive chapters, all by men. While there are certainly far fewer women in Shi'i legal studies than men, there are some. They include Ziba Mir-Hosseini, well known in the Western academy; Sedigheh Vasmaghi, a traditionally trained former tenured professor of law in Iran; and Jamileh Kadivar, another "learned" legal scholar. A different configuration of editors who approached the project with other networks and somewhat different framing could have gotten different results. On Vasmaghi, see

Three of the ten edited volumes in Brill's series are Festschriften. All honor men. Their contents both echo and reinforce existing exclusions. The Festschrift for Aharon Layish (2006) has ten contributors, including one woman.[58] The volume for Bernard Weiss (2014) has thirteen chapters, including one by a woman.[59] It's a suitable follow up to the volume on Islamic legal theory (2002), also in this series, that Weiss edited, which had one chapter by a (different) woman and thirteen by men.[60] The Festschrift honoring Rudolph Peters, both the most recent (2017) and only one with women among its (co-)editors, has two or three times the proportion of substantive chapters by women as its predecessors, nearly one out of four.[61] Being more recent or having a woman co-editor does not guarantee balance, of course, as we see with other collected volumes. *Dispensing Justice* (2005), co-edited by three men, also has nearly one in four of its chapters by women, while the collection of profiles of (male) jurists (2013), despite having a woman among its three editors, has a smaller proportion of its chapters by women, less than one in seven.[62]

Ziba Mir-Hosseini, *Journeys toward Gender Equality in Islam* (London: Oneworld, 2022), 16–18, 209–236. On Kadivar, see Hamid Dabashi, *Being a Muslim in the World* (New York: Palgrave, 2013), 130–31.

58. Ron Shaham, ed., *Law, Custom, and Statute in the Muslim World: Studies in Honor of Aharon Layish* (Leiden: Brill, 2006). The contributions are 10% woman-authored.

59. A. Kevin Reinhart and Robert Gleave, eds., *Islamic Law in Theory: Studies on Jurisprudence in Honor of Bernard Weiss* (Leiden: Brill, 2014). The contributions are 8% woman-authored.

60. Other women were present at the conference. Ingrid Mattson's contributions are preserved in the "Alta Discussion" transcript. A photograph in the volume shows three women, though their names are not given. Susan Spectorsky is the only woman included among the fourteen contributor biographies. The contributions are 7% woman-authored.

61. Maaike van Berkel, Léon Buskens, and Petra M. Sipesteijn, eds., *Legal Documents as Sources for the History of Muslim Societies: Studies in Honour of Rudolph Peters* (Leiden: Brill, 2017). The contributions are 23% woman-authored.

62. Muhammad Khalid Masud, Rudolph Peters, and David Powers, eds. *Dispensing Justice in Islam: Qadis and their Judgements* (Leiden: Brill 2005) has 5 / 21 chapters by women (24%). Oussama Arabi, David S. Powers, and Susan A. Spectorsky, *Islamic*

The general tendencies toward increased gender balance over time, gender segregation within certain areas of study, and more women contributors when women are editors also appears, though less distinctly, in a group of texts from 2014 to 2019. Intisar Rabb, director of Harvard Law School's Program in Islamic Law, points to a growing emphasis on "studied reflections on Islamic legal history and historiography" leading to "the publication of no fewer than *five* handbooks on Islamic law in just *five* years."[63] Along with the Weiss Festschrift and Sohaira Siddiqui's *Locating the* Shari'a (2019) in Brill's series, Rabb includes Peri Bearman and Rudolph Peters's *The Ashgate Research Companion to Islamic Law* (2014); Anver M. Emon and Rumee Ahmed's *The Oxford Handbook of Islamic Law* (2018); and Khaled Abou El Fadl, Ahmad Atif Ahmad, and Said Fares Hassan's *Routledge Handbook of Islamic Law* (2019). Three of the five are edited by male teams, one has a mixed-gender team, and one has a woman editor. The collections from 2014 have few chapters by women. The Festschrift for Weiss has more than nine in ten of its chapters by men (8% woman-authored). Bearman and Peters's Ashgate Companion has twice that proportion, with about one in seven chapters by a woman (15%).[64] The books from 2018 and 2019 are more inclusive. The Routledge *Handbook*, edited by Abou El Fadl, Ahmad, and Hassan, has more than one in four of its chapters by women (27%), Siddiqui's *Locating the Shari'a* has nearly one in three (31%), and Emon and Ahmed's Oxford *Handbook*, despite its all-male editorial team, has the highest proportion of chapters by women contributors, more than one in three

---

Legal Thought: A Compendium of Muslim Jurists (Leiden: Brill, 2013) has 3 / 23 chapters by women (13%).

63. Intisar Rabb, "Methods and Meaning in Islamic Law: Introduction," December 10, 2020, https://islamiclaw.blog/2020/12/10/legalhistoryroundtable-intro /#_ftnref12.

64. Reinhart and Gleave, *Islamic Law in Theory*, 1 / 13 (8%); Rudolph Peters and Peri Bearman, eds., *The Ashgate Research Companion to Islamic Law* (Abingdon, UK and New York: Ashgate, 2014), 3 / 20 (15%).

(37%).[65] These chapters, however, are distributed very unevenly. Women wrote roughly two-thirds of the regional or topical case studies, yet none of the five entries under legal theory which, like the study of early Islamic law, continues to be especially male-dominated. Meanwhile, the twenty-two item "Roundtable on Islamic Legal History and Historiography" (2020) that Rabb and Mariam Sheibani co-edited reflects an impressively diverse array of contributors, nearly half women (45%), at varied career stages and with numerous specializations and approaches.[66]

As in Islamic legal studies, gendered imbalances partly owed to men's editorial exclusions shape Qur'anic studies, as established series by Brill and Routledge show.[67] Brill's *Texts and Studies on the Qur'an* published eighteen books from 2003 to 2021. Sixteen are monographs and translations, only one by a woman. There are also two edited volumes. The one with a woman among its co-editors has a higher proportion of chapters by women than the one edited solely by men, even though the former was published in 2009 and the latter in 2016.[68] *Routledge Studies in the Qur'an* also

---

65. *Routledge Handbook*: 7 / 26 (27%); *Locating the Shari'a*: 4 / 13 (31%); *Oxford Handbook*: 13 / 35 (37%).

66. Intisar A. Rabb and Mariam Sheibani, eds., "Roundtable on Islamic Legal History and Historiography," *Islamic Law Blog*, December 10, 2020, https://islamiclaw .blog/2020/12/10/legalhistoryroundtable/.

67. Not all Routledge or Brill publications that could be construed as Qur'anic studies fall into these series. For instance, A. Geissinger's *Gender and Muslim Constructions of Exegetical Authority* (Leiden: Brill, 2015) appears in Brill's Islamic History and Civilization series.

68. One fifth (5.5 / 27) of the chapters in Angelika Neuwirth, Nicolai Sinai, and Michael Marx's *The Qur'an in Context* (Leiden: Brill, 2009) are by women. *Islamic Studies Today: Essays in Honor of Andrew Rippen*, (Leiden: Brill, 2016), edited by Majid Daneshgar and Walid Saleh, has three of nineteen substantive chapters by women (16%). There are four women among twenty-two contributors (18%). In final copyediting, I discovered that the series now stands at twenty-two volumes, including two more monographs, both by men, and two edited volumes, one honoring a man, both edited by men. These collections are substantially more gender-balanced than their predecessors. Majid Daneshgar and Evan Nurtawab, eds., *Malay-Indonesian*

includes both monographs and edited volumes. Between 2007 and 2020, its monographs were balanced—seven by women and eight by men. However, the six edited volumes during this period show stark gendered differences. Four are edited by one or more men, one is edited by a woman, and one by a mixed-gender editorial team. Volumes edited by men average under 10% women contributors while volumes with one or more women editors average over 40%. Balance has generally improved over time, but both co-edited volumes were published in 2016. The one with a woman editor had three times the rate of contributions from women as the one edited by men.[69]

Within Qur'anic studies, as within Islamic legal studies, the specific scholarly area often shapes gender inclusion. Books on exegesis tend to be more inclusive than those concerned with textual origins, though that is not saying much. For instance, Mustafa Shah's six-volume *Tafsir: Interpreting the Qur'an* (2012) collects eighty-one previously published articles, of which less than one in five is by a woman. Nearly half of the pieces by women are by Jane

---

Islamic Studies: A Festschrift in Honor of Peter G. Riddell (Leiden: Brill, 2023) has three chapters by women out of twelve (25%). In Nicolai Sinai, ed., *Unlocking the Medinan Qur'an* (Leiden: Brill, 2022), five of thirteen chapters (38%) are by women.

69. *Qur'anic Studies Today*, co-edited by Angelika Neuwirth and Michael Sells (New York: Routledge, 2016), has four women and seven men contributors (36% women). Marianna Klar's *Structural Dividers in the Qur'an* (New York: Routledge, 2020), four women and five men (44% women). Holger Zellentin's *The Qur'an's Reformation of Judaism and Christianity: Return to the Origins* (New York: Routledge, 2019) has three contributions by women and ten by men (23% women); Majid Daneshgar, Peter G. Riddell, and Andrew Rippin's *The Qur'an in the Malay Islamic World: Context and Interpretation* (New York: Routledge, 2016) has one of its nine substantive chapters by a woman (11%). All twelve chapters in Gabriel Said Reynolds's *The Qur'an in Historical Context* (New York: Routledge, 2007) are by men, as is the foreword (0%). Reynolds's *New Perspectives on the Qur'an, The Qur'an in its Historical Context II* (New York: Routledge, 2012) has, in addition to a foreword by Abdolkarim Soroush, twenty substantive chapters, one of which is by a woman (5%).

Dammen McAuliffe.[70] Male contributors come from a variety of backgrounds but all the women save (possibly) Abbott are white and North American or Western European. Despite the title of Mun'im Sirry's *New Trends in Qur'anic Studies: Text, Context, and Interpretation* (2019), and the refreshingly large proportion of its contributors who are from Southeast Asia, the gender ratio of contributors disappoints: fifteen of sixteen contributors are men.[71] Somewhat more balanced, perhaps because of its contemporary focus, perhaps because it attends to the U.S., perhaps because a woman is a co-editor, a third of the chapters in Emran El-Badawi and Paula Sanders's volume *Communities of the Qur'an: Dialogue, Debate and Diversity in the 21st Century* (2019) are by women.[72]

As with some of the Islamic law handbooks, volumes on the Qur'an often show gendered divisions related to topical focus. For instance, McAuliffe's *The Qur'an* in Norton's Critical Editions series (2017) offers a full translation of the scripture along with a selection of fifty texts divided into four sections, Origins; Interpretation and Analysis; Sounds, Sights, and Remedies; and The Qur'an in America. Eleven items, just over one in five, are by women, though the proportion of items by women nearly doubles if one excludes texts predating 1500.[73] There is substantial variation

70. Mustafa Shah, ed., *Tafsir: Interpreting the Qur'an* (New York: Routledge, 2012). Sixty-seven are by men and fourteen (17%) by women. In addition to six pieces by McAuliffe, Shah includes two articles by Ulrika Mårtensson and one article apiece from Nabia Abbott, Karen Bauer, Annabel Keeler (self-identified as Muslim in other writings), Leah Kinberg, Johanna Pink, and Kristin Sands. Although most of the entries are by white non-Muslim Western men academics, the collection includes contributions by several men from Muslim backgrounds, including some who write as insiders, and from non-Western countries.

71. Mun'im Sirry, ed., *New Trends in Qur'anic Studies: Text, Context, and Interpretation* (Atlanta, GA: Lockwood Press, 2019).

72. Emran El-Badawi and Paula Sanders, eds., *Communities of the Qur'an: Dialogue, Debate and Diversity in the 21st Century* (London: Oneworld, 2019). Three chapters written by, and one co-written by, women, of ten chapters total (35%).

73. Jane Dammen McAuliffe, ed., *The Qur'an: A Norton Critical Edition* (New York: W. W. Norton, 2017).

among sections. Everything in "Origins," early texts and modern scholarship, is by men.

Despite women's scholarship in the study of early Islam, Islamic law, and the Qur'an, only recently are male editors in these subfields starting to include their work. For instance, in Herbert Berg's *Method and Theory in the Study of Islamic Origins* (2003), all twelve chapters are by men.[74] Fifteen years later, nearly one in three chapters in Berg's *Routledge Handbook on Early Islam* (2018) is by a woman or nonbinary scholar.[75] Berg's choice to address modern and contemporary uses of the early Islamic past partly accounts for the shift. Two or three chapters by women and nonbinary scholars appear in the sections on "Modern and contemporary reinterpretation of early Islam," "Revisioning early Islam," and "Identities and communities in early Islam." All seven essays in the section on "The Qur'an and Muhammad" are by men.

Defining Islamic studies

The underrepresentation of women and nonbinary scholars in scholarly niches such as Islamic legal theory or the study of Qur'anic recension and early prophetic biography is not only a matter of who is included in edited volumes today but who is remembered in accounts of the field. A few women and their work appear with some regularity in histories of Near Eastern studies, including Patricia Crone (d. 2015), a historian of early Islam who spent much of her career at Princeton's Institute for Advanced Studies, and Abbott (d. 1981), the first woman appointed to a professorship in Near Eastern Languages and Civilizations at the University of Chicago.[76] In

74. Herbert Berg, ed., *Method and Theory in the Study of Islamic Origins* (Leiden: Brill, 2003). Twelve men contribute twelve chapters (100%).

75. Herbert Berg, ed., *Routledge Handbook on Early Islam* (New York: Routledge, 2018). Seven of twenty-two chapters are by women and nonbinary scholars (32%).

76. On Crone, see Michael Bonner, "The Legacy and Influence of Patricia Crone (1945–2015)," *Der Islam*, 93:2, 2016: 349–369. Her Festschrift—Asad Q. Ahmed, Behnam Sadeghi, Robert G. Hoyland, and Adam Silverstein, eds., *Islamic Cultures,*

addition to Crone and Abbott, a handful of others such as Schimmel, McAuliffe, and Wadad Kadi, an Arabist who held the Chicago
position after Abbott, are relatively well known.[77] But numerous
other twentieth-century women Islamicists have slipped into ob-
scurity. Estelle Whelan (d. 1997), who wrote about inscription
evidence for the early recension of the Qur'an, is largely unknown,
though her obituary talks about her "major contributions to the
understanding of early manuscripts of the Qur'an."[78] By chance,
Whelan's obituary appears in a 1998 issue of the Middle East Studies Association *Bulletin* directly after that for Jeanette Wakin
(d. 1998), a scholar of Islamic law whose dissertation her advisor

---

Islamic Contexts: Essays in Honor of Professor Patricia Crone (Leiden: Brill, 2014)—
has four male editors and twenty-two essays, of which seventeen are (co-)authored
by men and five (co-)authored by women. Abbott retired in 1963, having published
on a variety of topics beyond papyri, including women in the early Muslim polity.
Her book *Aishah, Beloved of Muhammad* (Chicago, IL: University of Chicago Press,
1942) was for decades the sole English-language biography of the Prophet's wife. She
was honored with a Festschrift spanning two issues of the *Journal of Near Eastern
Studies* in 1981.

77. In addition to a Middle East Studies Association graduate student travel prize
named for her, Kadi has a Festschrift in her honor: *The Heritage of Arabo-Islamic
Learning: Studies Presented to Wadad Kadi*, ed. Maurice A. Pomerantz and Aram A.
Shahin (Boston: Brill, 2016). See also Wadad al-Qaḍi, "In the Footsteps of Arabic
Biographical Literature: A Journey, Unfinished, in the Company of Knowledge,"
Journal of Near Eastern Studies, 68:4, 2009: 241–52.

78. Walter B. Denny, "Estelle Whelan," *MESA Bulletin*, 32: 1, 1998: 142–143 at 142.
As of June 2019, Google Scholar (admittedly notoriously buggy and unreliable)
counts forty-five citations for her article "Forgotten Witness: Evidence for the Early
Codification of the Qur'an" (*Journal of The American Oriental Society*, 118, 1998: 1–14).
One place her article could have been cited is in Andrew Rippin's introduction to his
all-male special issue of the *Journal of Qur'anic Studies* on "The Reception of Euro-
American Scholarship on the Qur'an and *tafsir*: An Overview" (*Journal of Qur'anic
Studies*, 14:1, 2012: 1–8). Instead, Rippin names and quotes men near-exclusively, and
despite its relevance to his topic, omits Whelan, whose article has been reproduced
in its entirety by the Muslim apologist website Islamic Awareness, with a disclaimer:
"We do not necessarily agree with everything written in this article," https://www
.islamic-awareness.org/history/islam/dome_of_the_rock/estwitness.

Joseph Schacht reportedly declared the best he ever supervised.[79] Each obituary writer laments that despite his subject's talents and skills, she suffered professional difficulties. Whelan was unable to find a secure faculty or museum position, and Wakin, a lecturer at Columbia, faced financial difficulties alongside illness as she aged. One may speculate—though neither obituary writer does—that gender bias shaped how their work was received, rewarded, and remembered. Wakin devoted significant energies to advising students but did not hold a regular faculty line. Unlike Crone, Kadi, and Schimmel, Whelan never supervised cadres of graduate students. Historiographers often gloss over both women's work— although, as the next chapter shows, even their better-known women colleagues are frequently overlooked. How we tell the story of our field is partly about which illustrious predecessors we remember, and which figures we cite or fail to cite. And although, or perhaps because, the proportion of women and attention to feminized topics in Islamic studies has risen considerably, debates over what approaches should be practiced and prized are vigorous and ongoing.

Sometimes assertions of what is in and out of the field appears in bold programmatic statements about what Islamic studies is or should be. For lay audiences, we offer simple definitions: Islam is a religion. A Muslim is a person who practices Islam. Of course, judgment calls soon arise. While religious studies scholars insist that "religion is what people do," we often use the adjective *Islamic* for what's perceived as authoritatively religious ("Islamic law") and *Muslim* to describe human behavior ("Muslim practice").[80] Or we use "Muslim law" to highlight contingent, human agency

79. Roy Mottahadeh, "Jeanette Ann Wakin," *MESA Bulletin*, 32:1, 1998: 141–142 at 141. See also Frank Vogel, "Preface," in Jeanette Wakin, *Remembering Joseph Schacht (1902–1969)*, Occasional Publication no. 4 (Cambridge, MA: Harvard Law School Islamic Legal Studies Program, 2003).

80. This resonant phrase recurs in *Keeping It 101*, the religious studies podcast by Megan Goodwin and Ilyse Morgenstein Fuerst, www.keepingit101.com. Their book *Religion Is Not Done With You* is forthcoming (Boston: Beacon, in press).

in its formulation and application—a subversive gesture doubtless lost on nonspecialist audiences. The term *Islamicate*, used by English-speaking academics and virtually nobody else, aims to distinguish cultural from specifically religious elements of the tradition.[81] It helps account for contributions by and influences on Jews and Christians in al-Andalus or non-Muslims under Mughal rule, but can falsely suggest a clear, impermeable demarcation between a purely religious domain and a larger cultural sphere.[82] Such debates over how to define *Islam* and *Islamic* are ongoing, consequential, and ultimately irresolvable.[83]

Academic Islamic studies is likewise slippery and porous: no definition captures everything essential while admitting nothing extraneous. Indeed, practitioners disagree about which is which. A kerfuffle that spread from an academic listserv to social media while I was writing this book revealed a broad divide between those who think that Islamic studies should be reserved for work on religious texts in original languages and those who advocate a more capacious understanding of the field. Those in the former camp admitted that one might study *Muslims* without knowing Arabic but defaulted to the notion that *Islamic studies* is essentially about texts, primarily premodern texts, in core languages. Now, few would disagree with one colleague's assertion that some topics require classical Arabic competence, such as "scholarship about the content of the Qur'an or Hadith or Ghazali or Ibn Arabi." This

81. Marshall G. S. Hodgson, The *Venture of Islam: Conscience and History in a World Civilization* (Chicago, IL: University of Chicago Press, 1974), 1: 58–60.

82. I made this argument as a panelist in "Hodgson at Forty," American Academy of Religion Annual Meeting. Baltimore, November 2013.

83. In his history of Middle East studies, Zachary Lockman suggests that "there has been at least de facto recognition that what gives this field coherence is, simply, the fact that those engaged in it, while doing a great many different things in intellectual terms, all relate to part or all of more or less the same geographic space and are involved with a common set of institutions and networks" (*Field Notes*, xviii; similarly, 254). Islamic studies is necessarily broader, encompassing a huge swath of the world with considerably more diversity of languages, histories, and cultures.

is a sensible observation about the requirements of responsible scholarship. Yet its author soon slips into essentialist characterizations of Muslim tradition, where some people are unreasonably "upset at the suggestion that Arabic is necessary to study Islam." Although there is an acknowledgment that other topics are possible, Islam has been collapsed to scriptural texts and the works of figures including "great Islamic polymath[s]."[84] Without specifically mentioning women or gender, Islamic studies becomes closely associated with masculinized and male-dominated subfields and practitioners: polymath is a gendered term if there ever was one. Additionally, opponents' principled arguments about disciplinary norms become reduced to emotionally charged reactions, a classic way of feminizing and disregarding some speech.

Still, Bahar Davary's description of the academic study of Islam as "an effort to understand what it is to be a Muslim" notwithstanding, there are perils to Islamic studies becoming a catch-all for "everything Muslimy."[85] Apart from a well-founded fear of reinforcing the pernicious popular habit of attributing everything about Muslims to Islam, a too-broad definition of Islamic studies could result in those who study Muslims being shunted away from other jobs for which they are qualified and toward the too-few Islamic studies posts. Yet, a vision of Islamic studies that leans into the Muslims-versus-Islam division reinforces not only the notion of a separate religious sphere but also an old-fashioned World Religions framing of traditions as centered on founders and scriptures—in the case of Islam, Middle Eastern origins and Arabic

84. Caner Dagli, "Thread(s) on Academic Islamic Studies," May 25, 2020, https://medium.com/@ckdagli/thread-s-on-academic-islamic-studies-e6bb9b501e11.

85. Bahar Davary, "Islamic Studies," in Suad Joseph, ed., *Encyclopedia of Women and Islamic Cultures*, Disciplinary Paradigms and Approaches: 2003–2013 (Brill Online, 2013), 203–226 at 208. I take the phrase "everything Muslimy" from Mohammad Fadel (@Shanfaraa), Twitter, May 22, 2020. https://twitter.com/Shanfaraa/status/1263839734733905923. In personal correspondence (January 18, 2021), he pointed out that having people doing empirical/social scientific work in other fields is a way of getting the study of Islam and Muslims into those fields. I agree.

texts.[86] Such skirmishes over where to draw the boundaries of academic Islamic studies tend to center male authorities and male-authored and male-interpreted texts as signifiers and litmus tests. What's deemed central to Islamic studies and what's considered peripheral owes both to gendered and racialized ideas of what's *really* Islamic as well as to gendered and racialized notions of what *real* scholarship looks like.[87]

It's tempting to tell this story as a grudge match between Near Eastern studies and religious studies. On one side, scholars trained in philology center an elite textual tradition, while on the other, religious studies scholars focus on people's messy lived practices. This account has some merit, especially when viewed through gendered lenses. Reserving Islamic studies for philology and its close cousins while treating everything else as "lived religion" reproduces an unhelpful Islamic/Muslim binary and affirms a gendered hierarchy. The association of texts with the core of Islam and Islamic studies diminishes Muslim women's contributions to and perspectives on Muslim histories and tradition, since women have been and still are substantially less represented in the scholarly worlds that produced those texts.[88] Explaining sexism as an artifact or correlate of text-centrism makes sense of the unenthusiastic reception of scholarship that addresses gender in Sufi narratives, legal treatises, and exegetical works. But this lets religious studies off the hook too easily. Sexism isn't just a philology problem. Gendering practices and biases channel the reception of similar religious

86. Tomoko Masuzawa, *The Invention of World Religions: Or, How European Universalism Was Preserved in the Language of Pluralism* (Chicago, IL: University of Chicago Press, 2005).

87. As Riem Spielhaus notes, "who and what is studied under the labels 'Islam' and 'Muslim' has implications for what is perceived and acknowledged as authentically Islamic by scholars." Spielhaus, "Islam and Feminism: German and European Variations on a Global Theme," in El Omari, Hammer, and Khorchide, eds., *Muslim Women and Gender Justice*, 46–61 at 51.

88. Leila Ahmed, *Women and Gender in Islam: Historical Roots of a Modern Debate*, Veritas edition (New Haven, CT: Yale University Press, 2021 (1992)), 238–240.

studies scholarship to the periphery of its various subfields or to women's and gender studies.

It's admittedly an unwieldy problem. Islamic studies emerges from and overlaps with other interdisciplinary fields ("studies" rather than "disciplines"), each bringing distinct methodological and ideological tools and baggage to the study of Islam and Muslims, as well as carrying distinctive gendered norms and histories.[89] Near Eastern studies, area studies, religious studies, and women's/gender studies are all themselves multifaceted and contentious amalgams of theories, methods, and approaches.[90] A Venn diagram would require quite a large sheet of paper.

A sampling of journals gives a sense of the range of topics that jockey for position under the Islamic studies umbrella. European titles like *Der Islam* and *Islamic Studies* (Oxford) focus, as their titles suggest, on Islam. The *Journal of the American Oriental Society* sets early Arabic epigraphy and classical Islamic texts alongside studies of Sumerian and Akkadian inscriptions and ancient Chinese scrolls. These journals are largely textual, heavily premodern, and geared to specialists. The Middle East Studies Association, founded in 1966, publishes the *International Journal of Middle East Studies*. Like the *Journal of Middle East Women's Studies*, it covers the region rather than the religion, though Islam certainly appears. *Hawwa: Journal of Women of the Middle East and the Islamic World* brings the categorizations together. Religious studies publications such as the *Journal of Africana Religions* and the *Journal of the American Academy of Religion* include Islam alongside other traditions. *JAAR* articles on Islam are generally modern or contemporary, while book reviews, typically of one to three books

89. For the distinction between studies and disciplines, see Marjorie Garber, *Academic Instincts* (Princeton, NJ: Princeton University Press, 2003), 77–78.

90. On Middle East studies, see Deeb and Winegar, "Building Disciplinary Institutions," in *Anthropology's Politics*, 115–141. On women's studies, see Alice E. Ginsberg, ed., *The Evolution of American Women's Studies: Reflection on Triumphs, Controversies, and Change* (New York: Palgrave, 2008) and Joan Wallach Scott, ed., *Women's Studies on the Edge* (Durham, NC: Duke University Press, 2008).

related to Islam per issue over the last decade, include books focused on premodern and textual topics. Various journals explicitly situate themselves within the Muslim tradition, such as the *Journal of Shi'i Studies* and the *American Journal of Islam and Society*, though non-Muslims publish in them as well.[91] Other English-language or bilingual publications from Turkey, Indonesia, and Pakistan (such as the other *Islamic Studies*) also serve as venues for U.S.-based academics, though they are less highly ranked in ways that universities increasingly value.

The study of Islam within religious studies and the study of Muslims under the aegis of area studies often conflate Islam with the Arab Middle East. Recent reflections by scholarly practitioners from both sides lament this excessive entanglement.[92] It has not always been so, especially for scholarship on gender. The 1970s and 1980s were crucial for the formation of women's studies as a field. Historians and social scientists increasingly paid attention to people other than elite men. Although ethnographers had always explored family life, women anthropologists were using gender as a lens to explore communities. In all these fields, contemporary and historical studies typically defined their subject by period, geography, and/or ethnicity, for instance: Middle Eastern, Arab, or Ottoman. Islamic or Muslim seldom appeared as a descriptive term or analytic category—and when they did, it was often negative. However, in more recent years, Middle East/North Africa anthropologists Lara Deeb and Jessica Winegar note that job applicants in their discipline have found that search committees assume or desire Islam as a research focus for those working in the

91. Formerly the American Journal of Islamic Social Sciences, published by the International Institute of Islamic Thought.

92. Charles Kurzman and Carl W. Ernst, "Islamic Studies in US Universities," in Seteney Shami and Cynthia Miller-Idriss, eds., *Middle East Studies for the New Millenium* (New York: New York University Press, 2016), 320–348 at 323; Buskens, "Middle Eastern Studies and Islam," 241, 243–245. See also Deeb and Winegar, *Anthropology's Politics*, 63–64.

region, with attention to Islam and gender when the applicant is female, especially if she is presumed Arab and/or Muslim.[93]

The increased confusion of Islam with the Middle East and with Arabic persists in part because of entrenched curricular and hiring patterns. Although many of us actively work to disrupt this easy equivalence for students and lay audiences, the reduction of Islam and Muslims to the Middle East appears so regularly in religious studies job descriptions, as Ilyse Morgenstein Fuerst has shown, that it figures in a "simple, troubling equation: Islam = Middle East + Arabic + texts."[94] Ads for faculty positions in Islam overwhelmingly single out Arabic language expertise, despite the small proportion of Muslims worldwide who speak Arabic.[95] When colleagues argue that Arabic is vital to Islamic studies, they reinforce the practice of judging Islam jobs by different criteria than, say, Christianity jobs. No one would expect a scholar of nineteenth-century African American revivalists or contemporary Brazilian Pentecostals to have impeccable Aramaic or Greek.[96]

Beyond language, geography comes into play. In religious studies job ads, geographic categories including South Asia, East Asia, the Caribbean, and Oceania appear as "drop down" searchable categories for jobs, but there is no such category for the Middle East, even though it appears in nearly eight out of ten of ads for Islam jobs. Unless otherwise specified, then—say, with a tag for South Asia— Islam is understood as "interchangeable" with the Middle East.[97] The same conflation of Islam with the Arab Middle East happens in area studies as well. *The Bulletin of the School of Oriental and African Studies* subdivides its book reviews primarily by geography, with categories such as "The Ancient Near East," "The Near and

93. Deeb and Winegar, *Anthropology's Politics*, 64.

94. Ilyse R. Morgenstein Fuerst, "Job Ads Don't Add Up: Arabic + Middle East + Text ≠ Islam," *Journal of the American Academy of Religion*, 88:4, 2020: 915–946 at 915.

95. Morgenstein Fuerst, "Job Ads Don't Add Up," 922, 930–31.

96. Ernst and Martin ("Introduction," 13–14) make a similar point.

97. Morgenstein Fuerst, "Job Ads Don't Add Up," 927, 934.

Middle East," "South Asia," "Central and Inner Asia," "East Asia," and "Africa." Some issues include a "General" category for works that cross regions or treat a theme broadly. Works on Buddhism appear under this heading, suggesting editorial reluctance to identify Buddhism with a particular region. Surveys of Islam, however, appear under "The Near and Middle East."[98]

Gendering prestige

Such emphases on Arabic and a broadly defined Middle East tend to direct attention to premodern Arabic texts and contemporary radical and political thought, especially as seen through the lens of security. These are masculinized subfields, meaning that their topics and approaches are coded masculine. They are treated as challenging, requiring expertise and mastery. Masculinized attributes, and their feminized opposites, are saturated by gendered assumptions pervasive in our culture and not always linked to the gender of any given scholar.[99] A eulogy for Schimmel provides an apt illustration. It celebrates her myriad accomplishments while casually reproducing gendered rhetoric about subfields: "Throughout her career, she combined a rigorous philological approach with the empathetic perspective of comparative religion." Philology is masculine. *Rigorous* means hard, which includes the sense of difficult. Comparative religion, in contrast, is *empathetic*, connoting feminized softness and suggesting ease, the opposite of difficulty. Beyond the recurrent association of philological and textual expertise with men, these terms masculinize women to whom they

98. For example, *BSOAS*, 76:1, 2013 and 78:2, 2015 include works on Buddhism under "General" and 74:3, 2011 and 77:1, 2014 place works on Islam (Muslim ethics, an introductory survey) under "The Near and Middle East."

99. On the gendering of Reason as masculine, see Sarah Tyson, *Where Are the Women? Why Expanding the Archive Makes Philosophy Better*, (New York: Columbia University Press, 2018), 53–60. She engages the work of Genevieve Lloyd, including *The Man of Reason: "Male" and "Female" in Western Philosophy* (Minneapolis: University of Minnesota Press, 1993).

are applied. For her linguistic skill, Schimmel is deemed "a master of Arabic."[100]

Schimmel's eulogy associates comparative religion and religious studies more broadly with feminized ideas and approaches. Some religious studies scholars, however, reject this association. The insistence that scholars of religion should be "critics not caretakers," which reflects historical anxieties about a continued association with theology, also invokes a gendered hierarchy.[101] Caretaker is a conventionally feminized role (see also: "cheerleader") while criticism is associated with masculine rationality.[102] As noted earlier, Atalia Omer has argued that religion scholars, particularly those invested in projects of social reform and transformation, can be both critics and caretakers simultaneously.[103] Russell Mc-Cutcheon vetoes this idea, holding that scholars of religion should not take on such projects.[104] The idea that caretaking involves unscholarly investments in, or inappropriate attachment to, the object of study reinforces its feminine coding while furthering the association of masculinity with detached scholarly rigor encoded in the idea of critique. Even while advocating "an approach to religion in general and specific religions in particular" that doesn't merely pit "Critics Versus Caretakers," Aaron Hughes relies on the

100. Carl Ernst, "Annemarie Schimmel (1922–2003), Honorary Fellow of MESA," *MESA Bulletin*, 37:2, 2003: 310–312 at 310.

101. Burton Mack's phrase is most closely associated with Russell McCutcheon. See Russell T. McCutcheon, *Critics Not Caretakers: Redescribing the Public Study of Religion* (Albany: SUNY Press, 2001).

102. Bruce Lincoln, "Theses on Method," *Method & Theory in the Study of Religion*, 8, 1996: 225–27 and republished at https://religion.ua.edu/external-resources/theses -on-method/.

103. Omer, "Can a Critic Be a Caretaker Too?"

104. Russell T. McCutcheon, "A Direct Question Deserves a Direct Answer: A Response to Atalia Omer's 'Can a Critic Be a Caretaker Too?'" *Journal of the American Academy of Religion*, 80:4, 2012: 1077–1082. Although her article stakes a position, Omer frames her intervention as an inquiry whereas McCutcheon offers an unequivocal declaration.

same gendered associations to argue that scholars should "combine the caretaker's sensitivity with the critic's analytic rigor."[105]

In addition to their strongly gendered connotations, *critique* and *caretaking* map roughly onto and reinforce similar binary divides between outsider/insider and expert/participant. In each, the first, masculinized, term is more highly valued. An extensive Muslim feminist literature contests this dichotomous split, refusing to associate criticism solely with outsider experts, asserting that the critical and the constructive need not be opposed, insisting that to be an insider does not preclude careful analysis, and arguing that for some forms of knowledge, insider experience grants relevant expertise.[106] And yet, the ongoing relegation of feminist work—work that explicitly asserts that there are political stakes to questions about, say, domestic violence, including the way those questions are treated in texts—to the margins is notable.[107]

Work that focuses on gender/sexuality, especially when undertaken by scholars who aren't cis straight men, tends to be devalued within prestigious subfields or categorized outside of them. As Anna Gade notes, naming subfields helps render them legitimate

105. Aaron W. Hughes, *Muslim Identities: An Introduction to Islam* (New York: Columbia University Press, 2013), 6.

106. This phrasing is drawn from the description of the Women, Ethics and Islamic Knowledge online summer school (2022) co-sponsored by the Center for Contemporary Islam at the University of Cape Town and the Center of Study for Global Mediterranean Dialogue in Barcelona, https://wi.dialogoglobal.com/. On the broader issues of experience and expertise, see Sa'diyya Shaikh, "Feminism, Epistemology and Experience: Critically (En)gendering the Study of Islam," *Journal for Islamic Studies*, 33, 2013: 14–47; Debra Majeed's discussion of Muslim womanism in *Polygyny: What It Means when African American Muslim Women Share Their Husbands* (Gainesville: University of Florida Press, 2015); and Mulki Al-Sharmani and Jana Rumminger, "Understanding *Qiwamah* and *Wilaya* through Life Stories," in Ziba Mir-Hosseini, Mulki Al-Sharmani, and Jana Rumminger, eds., *Men in Charge? Rethinking Authority in Muslim Legal Tradition* (London: Oneworld, 2015), 219–255 at 226–229.

107. Juliane Hammer, "Gender Matters: Normativity, Positionality, and the Politics of Islamic Studies," *The Muslim World*, 106:4, 2016: 655–670.

objects of academic study.[108] But their borders are subjective. So women who study gender in early Islamic legal texts, for example, may be read as treating women's experience, or, as a peer reviewer suggested about my monograph on ninth-century Sunni jurisprudential debates about marriage and divorce, writing a feminist "polemic."

When women's scholarship on exegetical, legal, or mystical writings is treated as primarily or exclusively about *gender* rather than centrally about *classical texts*, it shapes subfields and affects individual careers.[109] The placement of Marion Katz's review essay on "The Textual Study of Gender" in the section on "Gender" rather than that on "Texts" in *Islamic Studies in the Twenty-first Century* is telling.[110] Both chapters in "Gender" are written by women. All three in "Texts" are by men. Those interested in texts but not in gender will discount her essay as irrelevant, ignoring its approaches and findings and skipping over the publications, mostly by women, that she engages. When work on texts is treated as especially valuable and rigorous, and textually focused work by women or about gender, and especially work that is both by women *and* about gender, is treated as marginal to large swathes of scholarly conversation, the harms are magnified. It's not coincidental that my study of ninth-century Islamic legal conversations about marriage, which analyzes legal disagreement among early jurists, has been cited in works on women, gender, and sexuality in a wide array of historical contexts but in almost no work on Islamic law that does not also treat gender.

108. Anna M. Gade, "Roundtable on Normativity in the Study of Islam: A Response." *Journal of the American Academy of Religion*, 84:1, 2016: 113–126.

109. For example, in her review of Karen Bauer's *Gender Hierarchy in the Qur'an: Medieval Interpretations, Modern Responses* (Cambridge: Cambridge University Press, 2015), which has been widely read as a book about women/gender, Johanna Pink argues that it should be read primarily as a book about *tafsir*. https://syndicate .network/symposia/theology/gender-hierarchy-in-the-quran/.

110. Katz, "The Textual Study of Gender," in Buskens and van Sandwijk, eds., *Islamic Studies in the Twenty-first Century*, 87–107.

Since the late twentieth century, there have been overlapping bodies of work by scholars from a variety of disciplines, backgrounds, and perspectives under the rubric of Islam and gender or "Muslim women's studies," umbrella terms which encompass manifold, sometimes opposing aims, methods, and conclusions.[111] Muslim or Islamic feminism(s) are part of the story of Islam and gender as a scholarly subfield. Muslim women academics and activists in the North American context, often in collaboration with colleagues based in the global South, have worked in and on scriptural interpretation, family law reform, and toward inclusion in previously male-dominated spaces. Gender-focused scholars in religious studies have also been among those most insistent that one cannot only study religion by focusing on texts or their traditionally authoritative interpretations and clerical networks. Some have analyzed and critiqued patriarchy in extant tradition. Others have explored women's social and ritual practices and engagements with texts, as religious phenomena to be explained using the tools of religious studies and related disciplines. Scholars have explicated Muslim women's diverse lives and acknowledged women's complex realities, including their agency and flourishing within the broad framework of patriarchy. Historians and anthropologists have shown women's presence and power in venues as diverse as patronage networks, royal households, family and property courts, and popular pious movements.

Already in the 1980s, scholars had sought to replace both wholesale condemnations of Muslim women's oppression and equally baseless claims of their liberation by Islam with accounts of the specific operations of patriarchy in a variety of Muslim-majority contexts in conjunction with women's varied, and variable, sources of power and agency. Mostly, though, they didn't focus on religious elements of women's lives. Partly influenced by

---

111. The term is amina wadud's. For her account of the field's emergence and needs, see Amina Wadud, *Inside the Gender Jihad: Women's Reform in Islam* (Oxford: Oneworld, 2006), 55–86.

growing Islamist social and political movements in places like
Egypt, Iran, and Pakistan, in the 1990s scholars began attending
more directly to religious questions, including within scriptural
and interpretive texts. Ziba Mir-Hosseini has documented her own
increased engagement with Islamic feminism as necessary given
the changing political and social climates in numerous Muslim-
majority countries.[112] In the 1990s scholars sought to explore the
complexity and sophistication of Muslim history and tradition.
Although, as Chapter 3 will explore in more detail, popular media
still tend to present Muslim women as homogeneous, scholars
largely eschew such broad generalizations, recognizing the harm
they do. Careful attention to the particulars of time, place, class,
race, and more is vital to avoid depicting figures who live in what
Lila Abu-Lughod has called *IslamLand*, a timeless, unchanging
fantasy unmoored from the specifics of history.[113]

Yet, women's scholarship on and in the Muslim tradition tends to
be read as practical, grounded, or activist, even when it treats
topics and uses approaches that are philological, historical, or
theological (in the methodological sense). Here, Reviewer 2 of my
first submitted manuscript for my monograph on marriage in early
Islamic law noted my concern with contemporary Muslim gender
debates and deemed me a mere dabbler in early Islamic legal history. I "seem[ed] insufficiently familiar with this field to make a
substantial contribution at this point." Instead, I ought "to embrace [my] position as a Muslim feminist and write this book as a
polemic along the lines of similarly successful works by [Asma]
Barlas, [Amina] Wadud and [Fatima] Mernissi." While Reviewer
1 had thought I should broaden my focus from narrow readings of
jurists' texts to explore court records that affirmed women's legal

112. Mir-Hosseini, *Journeys toward Gender Equality in Islam*. Mir-Hosseini has
spoken of Islamic feminism as the legitimate, if unwanted, child of political Islam.
See Kecia Ali, "Marriage, Family, and Sexual Ethics," in Andrew Rippin, ed., *The
Islamic World* (London: Routledge, 2008), 613–27 at 618.

113. Lila Abu-Lughod, *Do Muslim Women Need Saving?* (Cambridge, MA: Harvard
University Press, 2013), 69–70.

agency (such records are nearly nonexistent for the era I was writing about), Reviewer 2 saw Muslim feminism as essentially outside of scholarly engagement with formative legal history.

The reviewers' overlapping criticisms reflected methodological and political disputes within Islamic studies, as well as the difficulties in addressing multiple audiences. I was surely at fault for inadequately explaining why a feminist was bothering with prescriptive texts by men. I was trying to intervene in contemporary conversations about Islamic law as a resource for feminist transformation while also making an argument about the internal dynamics of Islamic legal development, which emerge when the jurists navigate gendered reciprocal claims in marriage. But in that iteration my book sat uncomfortably at the intersection of three bodies of literature: studies of early Islamic jurisprudence, historical treatments of gender in the Muslim past, and feminist engagements with Muslim scripture and interpretation. Sunni legal texts were typically studied for what they could reveal about jurisprudential method in early legal history, not to ask questions about the constructions of gender and the operations of power. Such questions were typically explored in modern and contemporary contexts via court archives, ethnography, and women's testimonies, or through readings of scripture and its interpretation. So, although there were other scholars using the same or similar sources, and there were other scholars asking the same or similar questions, they were not the same scholars. Partly because of this disconnect, my dissertation's feminist interventions largely bled off into the essays that became *Sexual Ethics and Islam* (2006); the legal history, stripped of its framing within Muslim feminist debates, became *Marriage and Slavery in Early Islam* (2010)—one among a growing number of studies that looks at the Muslim intellectual and textual tradition through gendered lenses.[114]

---

114. Kecia Ali, *Sexual Ethics and Islam: Feminist Reflections on Qur'an, Hadith, and Jurisprudence* (Oxford: Oneworld, 2006) and *Marriage and Slavery in Early Islam* (Cambridge, MA: Harvard University Press, 2010). On the literature, see Katz, "The

Still, treating the study of women and gender as peripheral even as it becomes widespread remains common. Sara Parks calls this "the Brooten phenomenon," after the way insights by Bernadette Brooten have been persistently ignored to the detriment of the field of early Christianity.[115] Women comprise a significant proportion of scholars working on Second Temple Judaism and the New Testament. There is substantial scholarship on women and gender in those areas. Yet still, "there remains an impermeable conceptual wall between this and what is perceived as 'regular' scholarship," and a "largely unwritten rule, that the study of women and gender is non-mainstream or 'niche,' . . . 'ancillary' and not of general relevance."[116]

The Brooten phenomenon helps explain the shape of Islamic legal studies and Qur'anic studies. Because we do not simply slot knowledge into preexisting natural categories but create and justify the categories through which we pursue, organize, and legitimate our scholarly findings, the continued marginalization of scholarship on women and gender, disproportionately pursued by women, nonbinary, and / or queer scholars, shapes fields and subfields. When only scholars of gender take this work into account, other fields stagnate.

To say that Islamic law is male-dominated does not mean that only men write about Islamic law.[117] In fact, women probably write most of the work about Islamic family law. Yet when

---

Textual Study of Gender," and the chapters in "Part I: Foundational Texts in Historical and Contemporary Contexts" as well as Ash Geissinger, "Applying gender and queer theory to pre-modern sources," in Justine Howe, ed., *The Routledge Handbook of Islam and Gender* (London: Routledge, 2021).

115. Sara Parks, "'The Brooten Phenomenon': Moving Women from the Margins in Second-Temple and New Testament Scholarship," *The Bible & Critical Theory*, 15:1, 2019: 46–64.

116. Ibid." 46.

117. The distinctive histories, contestations, and (gendered) connotations of terms and categories including Islamic law, shariah, and *sharīʿa*, as well as Islamic family law and personal status codes, are beyond the scope of this book.

people—I mostly mean men—edit volumes or journal special issues about Islamic law, or organize conference panels on Islamic legal theory, or put together lists of top articles in the field, they routinely exclude women's publications.[118] That work is segregated into "gender and Islamic law" or even shunted into the broad category of gender and Islam. Such moves simultaneously preserve Islamic legal studies as a male-dominated domain and contribute to hasty, overly broad pronouncements about gender and Islam. When work on scripture, law, ethics, and mysticism is all lumped together because it treats gender, the rhetorical strategies, terminological nuances, and conceptual particularities of specific genres are too easily glossed over.[119]

Like Islamic legal studies, Qur'anic studies is often defined in ways that exclude the work that many women do. As Karen Bauer notes, "the academic discipline of Qur'anic Studies has been focused on historical-critical studies of the Qur'an and its milieu, and textual studies of a specific body of texts produced by the Muslim scholarly class (*'ulama'*)."[120] Much of the Qur'an-focused work women do, whether constructively engaging the scriptural text or analyzing the secondary scholarship on women's interpretation, is defined *out* of academic Qur'anic studies, at least if we go

118. Two examples suffice. Gavin R. Picken, ed., *Islamic Law*, Critical Concepts in Islamic Studies (London: Routledge, 2010) collects sixty previously published articles in four volumes totaling 1,712 pages, of which all but 28 pages are by men. The exception is an article on comparative political theory by Roxanne Euben, published in a political science journal. In late 2018, a year when five of the thirteen research articles it published were by women, the journal *Islamic Law and Society* offered free access to "15 top articles published" between 1994 and 2016, "handpicked by the ILS editors to illustrate the quality of the research and give you a flavor of the kinds of topics and coverage you will find in the journal." Fourteen of the fifteen were by men, including the three that touched on gender issues.

119. Karen Bauer, Kecia Ali, Ayesha Siddiqua Chaudhry, and Laury Silvers, "Editorial," *Comparative Islamic Studies*, 2:2, 2006 [2008]: 125–127 at 127.

120. Karen Bauer, "The Current State of Qur'anic Studies: Commentary on a Roundtable Discussion," *Journal of the International Qur'anic Studies Association*, 1.1, 2016: 29–45 at 33. I was the only panelist who wasn't a cis man.

by tables of contents, conference programs, and editorial boards. It shows up instead in events and volumes organized around gender. Meanwhile, despite increasing attention to Muslim masculinities in some contexts, the homosocial worlds of the ulama and the norms of textual masculinity that structure their interpretive lenses pass without comment or investigation. Gender remains, in practice if not in theory, largely about women.

Gatekeeping gender

Looking historically at the Giorgio Levi Della Vida Award for which Annemarie Schimmel was the first woman recipient helps illustrate both dramatic change over the decades and the distance we still have to go as a field. Since 1967, it has been awarded twenty-two times on an increasingly irregular schedule through the Center for Near Eastern Studies at the University of California, Los Angeles. CNES explains that "the recipient of the award chooses the theme of the conference" held in their honor, at which they deliver a keynote address, "and selects the other participants. The conference proceedings are published in the Giorgio Levi Della Vida Series in Islamic Studies." Since Schimmel became the first woman to win in 1987, just two others have done so. Patricia Crone won in 2014, after a quarter century during which the prize was only bestowed on men. Ottoman architectural historian Zeynep Çelik followed in 2019.[121] As the prize was not awarded in the interim, Çelik's win marks the only time in the prize's existence that one woman has followed another as honoree.

Like the winners themselves, the conference volumes skew overwhelmingly male. Of the twenty published proceedings, eighteen honor men.[122] Five of these eighteen exclude women

121. Peggy McIrney, "Acclaimed architectural historian Zeynep Çelik to organize May conference at UCLA," April 18, 2019, https://www.international.ucla.edu/cnes/article/202020.

122. As of August 9, 2023, no conference volume for Owen appears on the list ("Giorgio Levi Della Vida Series in Islamic Studies," https://www.international.ucla.edu/cnes/article/14544). According to the event description, the conference in his

entirely. Twelve have a lone woman contributor alongside five or six or ten men. In four of those twelve, that woman is Schimmel. She was the only woman included in any of the six volumes published from 1975 to 1985. One conference volume includes two chapters by women. Seventeen of these eighteen volumes celebrating men's accomplishments, then, include just one woman or none at all. "The recipient of the award," let us recall, "selects the other participants."

While it is often suggested that it is difficult to achieve inclusion of women on certain topics, the Della Vida proceedings reinforce the lesson learned from edited volumes: it matters who selects participants.[123] Neither Schimmel's nor Crone's research focused on women or gender, nor did they choose those themes for their conferences. Schimmel's theme was *Poetry and Mysticism in Islam: The Heritage of Rumi*. Crone's was *Islam and Its Past: Jahiliyya, Late Antiquity, and the Qur'an*. Neither volume contains a single contribution that refers to women, gender, or sex in its title, yet both publications model parity. After the 1985 conference honored Franz Rosenthal with a nearly all-male volume on *Society and the Sexes in Medieval Islam*, Schimmel's publication two years later had three women and four men. Crone's celebratory volume, with three women and three men, marks the only time in the award's history that women comprise fully half a volume's contributors.[124]

---

honor included his keynote plus six papers by men and three by women ("2012 Levi Della Vida Award for Excellence in Islamic Studies," http://www.international.ucla .edu/cnes/event/9389). My email query to CNES about this volume went unanswered.

123. Such questions of inclusion and gatekeeping go beyond gender. As far as I am aware, there has never been a Black recipient of the award, whether African or from the diaspora. Black scholars are at the very least underrepresented in if not entirely absent from the conference volumes.

124. Çelik's volume has not been published as of this writing. Her conference lineup included, in addition to her keynote, five papers by men and five by women. If all appear in the proceedings, it will be the only time that a majority of contributors have been women. See "Perspectives on French Colonial and Late Ottoman Cultural History," https://www.international.ucla.edu/cnes/event/13677.

The Giorgio Levi Della Vida Award guidelines state with uncommon candor how much discretion is involved in making invitations. The conference volumes demonstrate that men honorees consistently sideline their women colleagues. Parallel if sometimes less dramatic patterns in other edited volumes and book series demonstrate similar editorial impact. Men disproportionately exclude scholars who aren't men, especially in male-dominated subfields. Tables of content solidify the results of years of professional effort. Acknowledgments often reveal palimpsests of earlier invitation-only small conferences, collaborative panels among colleagues who know each other, and other collective ventures which presume on existing, and largely male, networks. Unless interrupted, these networks and patterns reproduce and reinforce themselves.

DUDE

Further Reading *DUDE*

A concise overview can be found in Wael Hallaq, *Introduction to Islamic Law* (Cambridge: Cambridge University
Press, 2009). An excellent introduction to the *hadith*, an important source for legal reasoning, is Jonathan A. C. Brown, *DUDE*
*Hadith: Muhammad's legacy in the medieval and modern
world* (Oxford: Oneworld, 2008).

Exemplary on the social and political context of the early
development of Shafi'i law is Ahmed El-Shamsy, *The Can-* *DUDE*
onization of Islamic Law (New York: Cambridge University
Press, 2013). A perceptive synthesis of the topic is Bernard
Weiss, *The Spirit of Islamic Law* (Athens: University of Geor- *DUDE*
gia Press, 1998).

A collection of excellent articles on many aspects of
Islamic law can be found in A. Kevin Reinhart and Rob- *TWO DUDES*
ert Gleave (eds.), *Islamic Law in theory: Studies on jurisprudence in honor of Bernard Weiss* (Leiden: Brill, 2014). A *HONORED DUDE?*
well-informed and engagingly written introduction to how
Islamic law evolved and continues to do so, with many contemporary examples, is Rumee Ahmed, *Sharia Compliant:* *DUDE*
A User's Guide to Hacking Islamic Law (Stanford: Stanford
University Press, 2018).

FIGURE 1. Annotated image posted to Twitter by the author.

WHEN I WAS REVISING my Islamic law syllabus a few years ago,
a colleague suggested that I assign Fred Donner's "Who's Afraid
of Shariah Law?" essay.[1] At first glance, Donner's brief synthetic
survey of key themes, pitched for undergraduates and lay readers,
seemed promising. Encouragingly, he talked about gender issues
repeatedly.

Then I got to his list of further reading.

1. Fred Donner, "Who's Afraid of Shariah Law?," in Andrew Albin, Mary C. Erler,
Thomas O'Donnell, Nicholas L. Paul, and Nina Rowe, eds., *Whose Middle Ages? Teach-
able Moments for an Ill-Used Past* (New York: Fordham University Press, 2019), 58–68.

Donner recommends six books. Five are by men. The sixth is edited by two men in honor of one of the first five men. It contains thirteen chapters of which twelve are by men.

When I tweeted my frustration with Donner's dude-centric list, a few men pushed back: what books *on those same topics* would I replace them with? Questions like this deter criticism of the status quo by dissuading anyone without perfectly formulated alternatives from expressing objections. Even if asked in good faith, it's the wrong question. It assumes one-to-one replacement, which means making a case *against* a specific book and *for* another. My point wasn't that any particular book shouldn't be on the list, but rather that the list in its totality is skewed. The way it's skewed reveals broader patterns of gendered exclusions.

Compiling a list of suggested readings is an exercise in curation. Curation involves judgments of quality, relevance, and appropriateness. As to quality, Donner praises his selections as "a concise overview" and "an excellent introduction" and "exemplary" and "perceptive" and, again, "excellent." A book which disappointingly downplays women's work on Islamic law is, in Donner's estimation, "well-informed and engagingly written."[2] Yet even if we grant that his chosen books are good, they aren't unambiguously superior to scores of other works on Islamic law. So his selection, then, must have been based on fit. But are they in fact appropriate and relevant?

Donner's essay appears in a book for students and nonspecialists. Some of his choices are beginner-friendly but others are unsuitable for those without substantial prior knowledge or professional commitment. Take the edited volume on "many aspects of Islamic law."[3] Not only are its contents quite technical, it's also expensive— as of this writing, $194 in hardback or e-book—and unlikely to be widely available in libraries outside of elite research universities.

---

2. Fred Donner, "Who's Afraid of Shariah Law?," 68. See Chapter 2 for further discussion of this book.

3. Ibid., 68.

As to relevance, one might expect "further readings" to address topics and themes mentioned in the essay. It's curious that none of Donner's canonical six books has women or gender as an explicit focus given that gender norms are by far his most frequently mentioned topic, appearing half a dozen times.[4] Although he refers in passing to prayer and finance and discusses intoxicants at some length, it's women's roles, dress, and status that ground his central argument that there is tremendous historical and contemporary diversity within Islamic law.[5] It's not coincidental that he both mentions gender frequently and argues for jurisprudential diversity. Although not unique to scholarship on Islamic law and gender, this point is central to that extensive literature.

So, then, why aren't there any books about gender and Islamic law on his list? Or even a primer on women and Islamic history? It's doubtful that an undergraduate or member of the broader public wanting to follow up would benefit more from a detailed technical account of early Islamic legal method than from a solid overview of the legal and cultural history of Muslim women's dress and its complex resonances in the modern world; or from the variety of views on sexual violence, which have contemporary ramifications; or

4. Donner mentions "the veiling and seclusion of women" ("Who's Afraid of Shariah Law?," 58), "the vexed question of veiling" (60), male guardianship of female relatives in the context of marriage (60), the "wide range" of juristic views on veiling (62), conflict between "liberal attitudes toward women" and "restrictive views on women" (65), and, again, "seclusion of women," with a shift from women "mostly unveiled" to "veiling [now] increasingly prevalent" (66). In addition to copious beginner-friendly, academically sound publications on veiling as well as marriage and family law, Donner could also have recommended books by women scholars on prayer—e.g., Marion Katz's survey *Prayer in Islamic Thought and Practice*—or alcohol—Kathryn Kueny, *The Rhetoric of Sobriety: Wine in Early Islam* (Albany: SUNY Press, 2001).

5. Ironically, premodern legal treatments of veiling show minor disputations alongside fairly consistent norms, except for rules pertaining to enslaved women. Diversity is important to highlight for general audiences, but in the classroom, when topics like this come in for sustained engagement, we owe our students more nuance, including acknowledging basic shared patriarchal rules and assumptions.

from the complex ways Muslim jurists managed marriage and divorce; and so on.

Donner's list—which, to be fair, I've probably spent more time dissecting than he did assembling—illustrates a common pattern: scholarship on women and gender is, paradoxically, treated as irrelevant to the core work of Islamic (legal) studies, and hence not worth bothering about, even as gender is acknowledged as central to processes of law, identity formation, and Muslim heritage. Put differently, though as *subject matter* it's acknowledged as relevant, gender isn't taken seriously within Islamic studies *as a field of scholarly enquiry* requiring expertise. This, of course, allows others to ignore the work of specialists, usually not men, and incorporate their analyses and insights into topical overviews as if they were obvious.

2

Citing Islamic Studies

IN 1992, THE YEAR Annemarie Schimmel retired after twenty-five years on the faculty at Harvard University, two books appeared that have dramatically shaped subsequent conversations in and beyond academia. The first was Leila Ahmed's *Women and Gender in Islam: Historical Roots of a Modern Debate*. Ranging from ancient Mesopotamia through Egypt in the 1980s, it treated Near Eastern and Mediterranean marriage norms, the advent of Islam, the formation of the Muslim scholarly tradition, European invasion and occupation of the Middle East and the concomitant effects on Muslim gender debates, and the emergence of both Arab feminism and modern Islamist movements. Ahmed, then a professor of Near Eastern studies and women's studies at the University of Massachusetts in Amherst, observed that standard histories either ignored women and gender entirely or treated them fleetingly. She pointed to Ira Lapidus's "recent authoritative tome on the history of the Islamic peoples," which "makes no reference to women or the construction of gender prior to the nineteenth century and devotes only a small number of pages to women after 1800."[1] Lapidus's survey was published in 1988.[2] Few books then dealt with women in Muslim histories and societies and even

---

1. Ahmed, *Women and Gender in Islam*, 2.

2. Ira Lapidus, *A History of Islamic Societies* (Cambridge: Cambridge University Press, 1988).

fewer addressed gender, the socially constructed roles of men and women and the symbolic understandings of masculinity and femininity in the authoritative Muslim tradition or in past Muslim societies.

That was in the process of changing. Ahmed's book, published by Yale University Press, was unique in its scope but reflective of the zeitgeist, which was increasingly attuned to women and gender in the Muslim past and present—and to Islamic texts and tradition. The same year, amina wadud published *Qur'an and Woman* with a Malaysian press.[3] Like Ahmed, who pursued Oriental Studies as she earned her doctorate in English from Cambridge University, wadud had formal philological training, earning an MA in Near Eastern studies and a PhD in Arabic and Islamic studies from the University of Michigan. And, like Ahmed, wadud was pushing back against Muslim patriarchy while rejecting white feminist condescension toward Muslim women. Informed in part by extensive collaboration with the Kuala Lumpur group Sisters in Islam, wadud bypassed centuries of male-centered scriptural interpretation and returned anew to the Qur'an itself, "rereading" it, as the subtitle of the second edition published by Oxford University Press (1999) would proclaim, "from a woman's perspective."[4]

Throughout the 1990s, the parallel streams of work reflected in *Women and Gender in Islam* and *Qur'an and Woman* grew from a trickle to a deluge. Historians, anthropologists, and textual scholars

3. This absence of capitalization is wadud's preferred rendering. I use it when I talk about her in my own voice. In quotations from other works or when citing her publications, I follow their capitalization. Now identifying as nonbinary, wadud uses both *she* and *they* pronouns. I use she/her throughout.

4. After returning from Malaysia, wadud joined the faculty at Virginia Commonwealth University, where she earned tenure and, later, promotion to full professor. See Wadud, *Inside the Gender Jihad*; Kecia Ali, Juliane Hammer, and Laury Silvers, eds., *A Jihad for Justice: Honoring the Work and Life of Amina Wadud* (2012), open access at https://hdl.handle.net/2144/24691; and Kecia Ali, "The Making of the 'Lady Imam': An Interview with amina wadud," *Journal of Feminist Studies in Religion*, 35:1, 2019: 67–79.

attended to Muslim women's complex pasts and presents. Muslim women advocates of gender justice inside and outside the academy drew directly on scripture and accounts of early Muslim history to advocate for more egalitarian interpretations. Sometimes, the streams crossed, as in the work of Fatima Mernissi.[5] Initially, secular feminism shaped Mernissi's studies such as *Beyond the Veil* (1975), an exploration of patriarchy in Moroccan society and psyche. Mernissi had written off Islamic tradition as unremittingly patriarchal in her pseudonymous *Woman in the Muslim Unconscious* (1984). However, as Islamist ideas made substantial inroads in North Africa and the Middle East as the decade progressed, she shifted to constructive engagement with Muslim texts, first in a revised edition of *Beyond the Veil* (1987) and more fully in *The Veil and the Male Elite* (1991). Those of her books published initially in French were swiftly translated into English and widely read and cited. Not only did the general tone of Mernissi's work change, so did her sense of the relationship among Qur'anic and prophetic sensibilities on the one hand and, later interpretive and historical interventions on the other. The polemic by "Fatna Sabbah" had conflated scripture, interpretation, and social practice, while Mernissi's scholarly work under her own name began to engage religio-legal texts more directly and with more nuance, culminating in her argument for an early egalitarianism quashed by subsequent patriarchal pressures.[6]

5. On Mernissi, see Raja Rhouni, *Secular and Islamic Feminist Critiques in the Work of Fatima Mernissi* (Leiden: Brill, 2010).

6. Fatima Mernissi, *Beyond the Veil: Male-Female Dynamics in Modern Muslim Society* (Cambridge, MA: Schenkman Publishing Co., 1975), revised edition (Indianapolis: Indiana University Press, 1987); Fatna A. Sabbah, *Woman in the Muslim Unconscious*, trans. Mary Jo Lakeland (New York: Pergamon Press, 1984); and Fatima Mernissi, *The Veil and Male Elite: A Feminist Interpretation of Women's Rights in Islam*, trans. Mary Jo Lakeland (Reading, MA: Addison-Wesley, 1991). *Woman in the Muslim Unconscious* was eventually republished as Fatéma Mernissi (Fatna Aït Sabbah), *La femme dans l'insconscient musulman* (Casablanca: Le Fennec, 2021).

In the ensuing decades, the study of Islam and gender has grown to encompass studies by Muslims and non-Muslims of women's and gender histories and contemporary realities as well as analyses of Islamic scripture and interpretive texts. It is challenging to map the complex and shifting alignments among the intellectual trends and scholarly networks. Do the ethicists belong alongside the philologists? Should the theologians and the historians keep company with each other, or with the sociologists? Scholars who study women and gender generally reject any pretense of disinterested objectivity and operate with a range of political, social, and religious commitments. Muslim feminists who engage the tradition constructively do not forgo analytic clarity or intellectual honesty. Who engages which scholars' works, however, remains complicated and contested. Within this extensive literature, debates are both heated and intricate. And still, as Chapter 1 discussed, much of it remains siloed off from other scholarly conversations or engaged perfunctorily.

Although the intellectual landscape for the study of women, gender, and Islam looks considerably different now than it did at the outset of the 1990s, you wouldn't know it from the way many men continue to write about the tradition. Decades after Leila Ahmed noted Lapidus's neglect of women and gender, *What Is Islam?* (2016) by Shahab Ahmed (no relation) pays even less attention to those topics. In 546 pages of main text, just three pages address gender, specifically, reformist thought on women's rights and scriptural interpretation.[7] Even here, Ahmed avoids references to specific women's ideas and lives and barely engages any women's writings. He omits all mention of wadud's influential work on the Qur'an. He never mentions Leila Ahmed's work either, even though she writes cogently about his book's central themes, including the tensions between textual norms and lived experience and how people navigate among competing understandings of what is Islamic. Like *Qur'an and Woman, Women and*

---

7. Ahmed, *What Is Islam?*, 511–513.

Gender in Islam is absent from his text, nowhere in his notes, missing from his 45-page bibliography. Meanwhile, he devotes eight pages to an updated edition of Lapidus's *History*.[8]

Though it has been repeatedly hailed as a monumental achievement, with respect to its citational politics *What Is Islam?* is frustratingly typical. Men often bypass with impunity women's publications on relevant topics, especially on women and gender.[9] Men who write about minor marriage, illicit sex, marital violence, family law in minority contexts, and the sexual use of enslaved women and girls roundly ignore the work by women colleagues who have initiated these conversations, publishing blogs and articles and books that cite and analyze classical legal and exegetical texts as well as scripture. Instead, they return to the texts directly, often repeating our analyses or making interpretive moves that have already been carefully assessed and rejected. They overlook the women historical figures who have been instrumental in social debates over women's roles since the late nineteenth century, eschewing the substantial historiography, mostly by women, on those contributions. In doing so, they again miss the vibrant, careful, important work others have performed.

I am not suggesting that everyone in the field must become an expert on gender. As Lena Salaymeh notes: "Not every scholar of Islam is qualified to produce scholarship about Muslim women."[10] Rather, I contest the implicit presumption that because one is knowledgeable about specific histories or geographies or fields of inquiry, one can opine on gender as it intersects that topic—and that one can do so without crediting or referencing foundational work on gender, often done by women. By not crediting or directing readers to that work, authors perpetuate these exclusions, with

8. Ibid., 216–223.

9. Ahmed also inexplicably fails to cite Kathryn Kueny's *Rhetoric of Sobriety*, a study of discourses on wine drinking that is germane to one of his major areas of focus (Ahmed, *What Is Islam?*, 58 and passim).

10. Salaymeh, "Imperialist Feminism and Islamic Law," 99.

unfortunate consequences for the field and potentially significant impact on scholars whose contributions go unrecognized, including but not only in the form of citation.

Citing the work of others

Citation is a form of curation. Curation collects, selects, and presents from a larger body of available work and resources. Notes and bibliographies reflect some of what an author chooses to gather and read. Some omissions stem from others' prior acts of curation, meaning there are things one simply doesn't know about. Decisions about whether to include or leave out work one does know about are shaped by ongoing scholarly conversations. Peer review shapes citational practice in advance, under real or perceived pressure to cite purportedly classic works or the new It Book.[11] It also shapes citational practices after the fact, in reviewers' and/or editors' insistence on remedying some exclusions and their willingness to let other absences remain. Defining the literature, and hence the scholars, one will engage involves both framing—what's relevant?—and culling—what's inessential? Choices about what to include are choices about what to exclude, shaped by what others presume, or what we think they presume, important.

Citation serves at least three interlinked purposes. First, citation *attests*: the evidence exists and says what we say it says. If I assert that a given jurist holds a specific position, I must cite my source so others can verify whether I fairly represent its contents. That such checking is often impractical, as with archival holdings, makes citation no less obligatory. Second, citation *credits*. Our references acknowledge previous work on which we rely, whether for factual discoveries, for concepts central to our analyses, or for findings that we're extending or comparing to our own. Third, and

---

11. See the Conclusion for more discussion of peer review.

related, citation *situates*. What and whom we cite reveals whom we see as our teachers, interlocutors, adversaries, and audiences. Citation, which Sara Ahmed (still no relation) calls "a rather successful reproductive technology," places our work in ongoing conversations.[12] It directs readers to resources: technical and theoretical publications for specialists, introductory and foundational works for lay audiences and generalists. Our citations signal earlier findings we dispute or work on which we build. When we fail to cite relevant works, we give both their authors and our readers short shrift.

Gender bias in citation pervades academia.[13] Men cite their own work more often than women cite their own work.[14] Men cite work by other men disproportionately compared to women's work.[15] These gendered disparities are also often racialized.[16]

Citational inequalities widen over time as work that has been cited continues to get cited. This is, as Victor Ray observes, a form of "path dependency." Writing about racial, and also gendered,

12. Sara Ahmed, "Making Feminist Points." September 11, 2013, https:// feministkilljoys.com/2013/09/11/making-feminist-points/.

13. Studies to date have used binary gender divisions in counting citations.

14. One research group examined 1.5 million research papers published over more than two centuries and found a "substantial gender gap in self-citation in most fields." Molly M. King, Carl T. Bergstrom, Shelley J. Correll, Jennifer Jacque, and Jevin D. West, "Men Set Their Own Cites High: Gender and Self-citation across Fields and over Time," *Socius*, 2017. See also Lutz, "The Erasure of Women's Writing," 620, and Baker, "Are You Reading Enough Academic Women?," in *Sexism Ed*, 8–12.

15. Michelle L. Dion, Jane Lawrence Sumner, and Sara McLaughlin Mitchell. "Gendered Citation Patterns across Political Science and Social Science Methodology Fields," *Political Analysis* 26:3, 2018: 312–27, discussed in Rachael Pells, "Understanding the Extent of Gender Gap in Citations," August 15, 2018, https://www .insidehighered.com/news/2018/08/16/new-research-shows-extent-gender-gap -citations. See also Lutz, "The Erasure of Women's Writing," 620.

16. Christen A. Smith and Dominique Garrett-Scott, "'We are not named': Black Women and the Politics of Citation in Anthropology," *Feminist Anthropology*, 2:1, 2021: 18–37.

exclusions in law literature, Ray observes that "Inequality is reproduced (and whiteness is institutionalized) by citation patterns as
earlier periods of overt exclusion are legitimated by an almost ritu-
alistic citation of certain thinkers."[17] There's a similar pattern of
gendered, and also (religio-)racial,[18] exclusions in literature on Islamic law. What else could explain why a scholar writing about
Islamic family law in the twenty-first century cites long-ago work
by J. N. D. Anderson (a white Christian British man) rather than
recent, well-regarded work by Ziba Mir-Hosseini (an Iranian Muslim woman)?[19] Richard Delgado, writing about the exclusion of
"minority scholarship" by white male colleagues writing about
civil rights, attributes this "strange absence" to "unconscious ac-
tion and choice" rather than "conscious malevolence or crass
indifference."[20] A similar strange absence exists in recent publications by men that address gender in the Muslim tradition while
ignoring relevant scholarship by people who are not men, especially Muslims, especially Muslim feminists.

17. Victor Ray, "The Racial Exclusions in Scholarly Citations (Opinion)," *Inside
Higher Ed*, April 27, 2018, https://www.insidehighered.com/advice/2018/04/27
/racial-exclusions-scholarly-citations-opinion.

18. Judith Weisenfeld offers the term religio-racial. See Weisenfeld, "The House
We Live in: Religio-Racial Theories and the Study of Religion," *Journal of the American Academy of Religion*, 88:2, 2020: 440–459.

19. For example, in a 2019 chapter by Abdullahi An-Na'im about "The Postcolonial Fallacy of 'Islamic' Family Law," only two of forty-four footnotes cite women's
work. Unlike numerous parvenus, whose work on women and gender in the Muslim
tradition is both recent and superficial, An-Na'im has been at this a long time, contributing important work to the field. Still, apart from Lynn Welchman's chapter on
Jordanian Law (1989) and an article on child custody by Aayesha Rafiq (2014),
everything is by men. There are sixteen citations to works by Wael Hallaq, including
for an overview of marriage law; six to his own work; and four each to work by Jamal
Nasir (for an overview of dower and divorce) and J. N. D. Anderson. Abdullahi
Ahmed An-Na'im, "The Postcolonial Fallacy of 'Islamic' Family Law," in Shazia
Choudhry and Jonathan Herring, eds., *The Cambridge Companion to Comparative
Family Law* (Cambridge: Cambridge University Press, 2019), 254–79.

20. Quoted in Ray, "Racial Exclusions."

Citation failures, as Meena Krishnamurthy and Jessica Wilson argue in terms that broadly apply to Islamic studies as well, have both moral and philosophical dimensions.[21] As to the former, they note that "citations of an individual's work have concrete positive bearing on a variety of professional outcomes" and "failure to cite work that is clearly relevant to the topic at hand is concretely injurious to the individual authors of that work." Not only are reputations built in part from scholars encountering others' works in their reading and research, even in the humanities we cannot wish away the growing, pernicious impact of citation indices and metrics. Choices individual scholars make about whom to cite will ultimately have impact on others' prospects for tenure and promotion. Moreover, "citation failure is most clearly a problem for members of . . . disadvantaged categories" in ways that are "exacerbated in cases where the disadvantaged individual is comparatively junior or is not a member of the 'in-crowd' working on a given topic (membership in which strongly tracks advantageous demographic categories) whose work must be cited by anyone working on the topic at hand." Beyond harm to individuals, failures to cite appropriately perpetuate unjust hierarchies.

As for the philosophical, or what Sarah Imhoff terms intellectual, harms of such omissions, an author's failure to cite a "clearly relevant work" suggests that they haven't read it, which "can lead to any number of philosophical wrong turns." Additionally, according to Krishnamurthy and Wilson, "the failure to properly cite individuals or groups of individuals whose work is relevant to the topic at hand can lead to a distorted presentation of a given dialectic and/or to the reinvention of existing wheels." The harms are magnified when work flawed in these ways, "especially when disseminated by influential individuals," shapes the field. That is certainly the case for some of the books discussed in this chapter—which,

---

21. Meena Krishnamurthy and Jessica Wilson, "What's Wrong with Current Citation Practices in Philosophy?," https://whatswrongcvsp.com/2015/12/14/whats-wrong-with-current-citation-practices-in-philosophy/.

when they become the new standard, means their failures of engagement solidify the exclusions.

In what follows, I assess these significant gendered imbalances using qualitative and quantitative methods.[22] I count and calculate percentages of women mentioned as historical agents and as scholarly authorities in the body of the text and/or in indexes as a proxy for appearance in the main text. (Those who go unnamed in the main text are typically excluded from indexes, although being named in the text is not a guarantee of appearing in the index.)[23] I analyze the presence or absence of works by women in citations and bibliographies of articles and books, making allowances for premodern texts versus modern scholarship. I also consider *where* women are cited or engaged: in discussions of American Muslim life? Islamic legal thought? I also ask *which* women appear: are they North American or European? White? Muslim? Qualitatively, I consider how authors repeatedly undermine women's importance by how they frame their work and words, compared to how they frame men's historical and scholarly contributions. Drawing on the subset of books from this chapter and other work discussed earlier, I show the cumulative and mutually reinforcing "microdynamics" at work.[24]

Quantitative analysis is, to be sure, an imperfect way of assessing a book's citational practices. In theory, a book could cite many men superficially while engaging a few women's writings in depth. In such a case, a numerical ratio would understate women's presence. In actuality, however, ratios of women cited and named in indexes usually overstate women's prominence considerably. A woman mentioned briefly once, as a preponderance of women in these books are, counts the same as a man named repeatedly and

22. I discuss my methodology in more detail in the appendix.

23. For instance, in *Marriage and Slavery in Early Islam*, my notes cite both Baber Johansen and Shaun Marmon on the legal-conceptual treatment of enslaved women, but I name only the former in the text. Thus, he appears in my index, but she does not.

24. Annette Yoshiko Reed (@AnnetteYReed), Tweet, June 29, 2020, https://twitter.com/AnnetteYReed/status/1277597651026886657.

whose work and ideas are discussed at length. If ratios become rules, will we see more superficial engagement? Perhaps. The Leiden Manifesto on research metrics points both to the usefulness and the limits of quantitative indicators for assessment. In part because of the likelihood that any single metric will be gamed, it advocates "a suite of indicators."[25] But even multiple measures cannot do everything we want them to do.

There are perils to relying on numbers beyond the possibility of their being misleading. Carrie Mott and Daniel Cockayne counsel us to "be wary of strategies that further attune us to the quantification of the neoliberal university and regimes of accounting."[26] In *Data Feminism*, Catherine D'Ignazio and Lauren Klein warn against the fantasy of massive, quantitatively exhaustive accounts.[27] My aim is more modest: to demonstrate a serious problem. Numbers are not a purely objective measure, as someone must choose *what* to count, but they make disparities starkly clear in a way that purely qualitative accounts may not.

To evaluate present-day imbalances, one must acknowledge past inequities, including disparities in our broader source corpus, both literary and documentary. Nearly all literary sources for premodern Islam were written by men.[28] Female jurists, preachers, Sufis, and poets existed, but very few wrote books that have survived. Of those extant texts, an even smaller subset has been

---

25. Dana Hicks, Paul Wouters, Ludo Waltman, Sarah de Rijcke, and Ismael Rafols, "Bibliometrics: The Leiden Manifesto for research metrics," *Nature*, 520, 2015: 429–431, https://doi.org/10.1038/520429.

26. Carrie Mott and Daniel Cockayne, "Citation Matters: Mobilizing the Politics of Citation toward a Practice of 'Conscientious Engagement,'" *Gender, Place & Culture: A Journal of Feminist Geography*, 7, 2017: 954–973 at 962.

27. Catherine D'Ignazio, and Lauren F. Klein, *Data Feminism* (United Kingdom: MIT Press, 2020).

28. Scholars who have explored women's participation in the premodern Muslim scholarly tradition, as well as the social and institutional constraints that have shaped that participation, include Omaima Abou Bakr, Marion Katz, Asma Sayeed, and Saadia Yacoob.

edited, published, or translated. Documentary sources reflect similar if less extreme imbalances. Most rulers and significant political figures were men; likewise, madrasa students, judges, and scribes. Women show up frequently in court records and contracts, but not in equal numbers with men.[29] Moreover, lopsidedness is baked into secondary scholarship, via the path dependency Ray warns about and the historical reality that most early twentieth-century Orientalists were men.

Given these unbalanced legacies, authors today choose to either further entrench such erasures or to mitigate them. In *Islam Is a Foreign Country*, a study of American Muslim knowledge seekers, Zareena Grewal theorizes about how tradition is formulated and sustained. She writes that "[e]lements of the past are mediated into the present by custodians, individuals in the present who decide which aspects of the past are nonessential to the tradition's future and may, therefore, be deleted or deemphasized."[30] Islamic studies scholars are custodians of an academic tradition. What and who we include helps determine what is essential. What and who we omit helps decide what is nonessential.

Books about the early centuries of Islam tend to omit women, whether as historical figures or as modern scholarly authorities.

29. Many social and legal historians, including Maya Shatzmiller, Amira El Azhary Sonbol, Judith Tucker, and Amalia Zomeño, have mined this documentation to excellent effect.

30. Grewal, *Islam Is a Foreign Country*, 200. "Custodians" clearly alludes to Muhammad Qasim Zaman's *The Ulama in Contemporary Islam: Custodians of Change* (Princeton, NJ: Princeton University Press, 2002). Grewal also draws on formulations by Talal Asad, who engages Alasdair MacIntyre. When I tweeted this passage from the book, suggesting that we can now start citing Grewal on tradition and not MacIntyre and Asad, a junior scholar objected nearly instantaneously: was I seriously considering forgoing those luminaries? I pointed out that they're cited and engaged in her text and notes. He conceded that we could *add* Grewal but objected that we can't just leave these men out. He prefers to keep citing everyone. This is path dependency. If we're all citing MacIntyre, we can never stop citing MacIntyre! Although there appears to be a statute of limitations. Despite MacIntyre's clear engagement with Aristotle, we apparently needn't go back quite that far.

Najam Haider's *The Origins of the Shi'a* (2011), for instance, names more than two hundred men in its index and just five women, three from Muhammad's household and two modern scholars.[31] Farhad Daftary's *A History of Shi'i Islam* (2013) also has five women in its index along with more than five hundred men. Of the five, four are mothers, daughters, and/or wives of Imams. The last is a Yemeni queen.[32] His index has more men named Ja'far than women. Daftary includes work by contemporary women academics in his bibliography, but none appears in the index although many of their male peers do. This suggests that he does not name them or engage their work in the main text as he does scholarship by men. Certainly, that is the case for his all-male historiographical overview.[33]

Work on Islam's formative centuries can be more inclusive than Haider's and Daftary's books suggest.[34] Maria Dakake's *The Charismatic Community* (2007), also on early Shi'i identity, indexes fewer men (121) and more women (nine) than the books by Haider or Daftary.[35] The overall numbers are too small to draw

31. Najam Haider, *The Origins of the Shi'a: Identity, Ritual, and Sacred Space in Eighth-Century Kufa* (New York: Cambridge University Press, 2011). He names Aisha, Fatima, Umm Salama, (Laura) Veccia Vaglieri, and Maria Dakake.

32. Farhad Daftary, *A History of Shi'i Islam* (London and New York: I.B. Tauris, 2013). Though he names fewer women, Daftary's approach echoes Moojan Momen's introduction to Shi'ism, in which, of the hundreds of named individuals, there are eleven women, of whom ten are mothers, daughters, and/or wives of prophets or imams. Momen, *An Introduction to Shi'i Islam* (New Haven, CT: Yale University Press, 1985).

33. Daftary, *A History*, 16–24. His discussion of Zaydi studies cites an overview by Sabine Schmidtke, but he names her only in the note.

34. My own work on this early period is nothing to write home about. Roughly one in eight (13%) named individuals in the index to my biography of ninth-century jurist and legal theorist Muhammad ibn Idris al-Shafi'i (*Imam Shafi'i: Scholar and Saint* [Oxford: Oneworld, 2011]) is a woman. In my study of formative-era Sunni law, *Marriage and Slavery in Early Islam*, that figure is three in ten (30%). Nearly all (*Imam Shafi'i*) or all (*Marriage and Slavery*) of the Arabic sources I reference are by men.

35. Maria Massi Dakake, *The Charismatic Community: Shi'ite Identity in Early Islam* (Albany: SUNY Press, 2007).

statistically meaningful conclusions, but the differences are stark. About one of every fifteen people Dakake includes is a woman. For Haider, it's one in forty. For Daftary, one in a hundred. Both Haider and Daftary cite Dakake's book, and Haider includes her in his index. Some women she mentions, though, including the central figure of Zaynab, do not appear in either man's index or, as far as I can tell, in the main text of their books. Leaping straight from Zayn al-'Abdin to 'Urwa b. al-Zubayr (Haider) or *ziyara* (Daftary), these scholars write Zaynab bint Fatima bint Khadija out of the origins and history of Shi'ism.

Whatever the rationale for major gendered disparities in scholarship on premodern eras, in work on the modern period, or writing that uses the classical tradition to address contemporary concerns, such omissions are less justifiable. And when texts frame questions about defining and studying Islam or the Muslim world in ways that overlook women's participation in, scholarship on, and critical engagement with Muslim tradition and history, they make an unforced error. Strikingly, this gendered dismissal sometimes happens even in works that take gender as a subject of analysis and that focus on women and the family as a way of engaging questions about colonialism, identity, and legal reform.

I know how easy it is to unwittingly sideline women as subjects and as scholars. My book *The Lives of Muhammad* (2014) devotes five of its six chapters to the modern era.[36] Two chapters foreground representations of Muhammad's marriages and wives. Writing inclusively should have been easy. But by defining my source corpus as biographies of Muhammad, I guaranteed that women, especially Muslim women, would be underrepresented as thinkers and authors. As I realized belatedly, Muslim women seldom write about the Prophet directly. Instead, they recount his life by focusing on the women of his household. By initially excluding books about the Mothers of the Believers, I inadvertently excluded

---

36. Kecia Ali, *The Lives of Muhammad* (Cambridge, MA: Harvard University Press, 2014).

most women biographers, and those who were left were mostly white and non-Muslim. What seemed methodologically obvious—to understand the changing biography of the Prophet, I would study biographies of the Prophet—led to a focus on men's writing and men's ideas, including men's ideas about women. My epiphany came too late to overhaul the book. Among the 261 people named in my index, there are four men for every woman. That ratio obviously isn't the full story. The figures below don't tell the whole story of any of the books I discuss here, either. But a mix of quantitative and qualitative indicators shows how they engage or, far too often, fail to engage women as historical subjects, scholarly specialists, and intellectual interlocutors.

Sampling the literature

Nine books published between 2014 and 2018 by tenured men from humanities departments, law schools, and divinity schools in the United States and Canada give an impression of the field.[37] Because books remain still the main criterion for academic recognition in fields that comprise Islamic studies, I have focused on them rather than journal articles.[38] These books attempt to speak broadly about Muslims, Islam, and Islamic studies. Three aim to survey and shape how Muslims engage Islam's legal-ethical tradition: Khaled Abou El Fadl's *Reasoning with God: Reclaiming Shari'ah in the Modern Age*; Jonathan A. C. Brown's *Misquoting Muhammad: The Challenge and Choices of Interpreting the Prophet's Legacy*; and Rumee Ahmed's *Sharia Compliant: A User's Guide to Hacking Islamic Law*.[39] Two

37. An exception: Shahab Ahmed (d. 2015) never attained tenure. He is, of course, beyond the reach of any professional repercussions.

38. I address my methodological choices further in the appendix.

39. Khaled Abou El Fadl, *Reasoning with God: Reclaiming Shari'ah in the Modern Age* (Lanham, MD: Rowman and Littlefield, 2014); Jonathan A. C. Brown, *Misquoting Muhammad: The Challenge and Choices of Interpreting the Prophet's Legacy* (London: Oneworld, 2015 [2014]); and Rumee Ahmed, *Sharia Compliant: A User's Guide to Hacking Islamic Law* (Stanford, CA: Stanford University Press, 2018).

treat the West African Islamic tradition: Rudolph Ware III's *The Walking Qur'an: Islamic Education, Embodied Knowledge, and History in West Africa* and Ousmane Kane's *Beyond Timbuktu: An Intellectual History of Muslim West Africa*.[40] One addresses Muslim identity and interpretation with a focus on the United States: Abdullahi An-Na'im's *What is an American Muslim? Embracing Faith and Citizenship*.[41] These geographically focused books, especially Ware's, also attend to larger questions about how to approach the study of Islam and Muslims, which is the central issue raised by the final three books: Shahab Ahmed's *What Is Islam? The Importance of Being Islamic*, Cemil Aydin's *The Idea of the Muslim World: A Global Intellectual History*, and Ahmad Atif Ahmad's *Pitfalls of Scholarship: Lessons from Islamic Studies*, comprising essays on Islamic legal studies and academic knowledge production.[42] Six of the nine were published by university presses, two by for-profit academic publishers, and one by a crossover press with a solid reputation in Islamic studies.[43] They have had vastly differing receptions. Some have sold exceptionally well, some have generated huge buzz and provoked sustained scholarly attention, and others have made quieter impacts in the field or gone largely unnoticed. Still, enough commonalties connect them, beyond the random chance of their having been published in a five-year period, that considering them together helps illustrate important dynamics.

40. Rudolph T. Ware III, *The Walking Qur'an: Islamic Education, Embodied Knowledge, and History in West Africa* (Chapel Hill: University of North Carolina Press, 2014) and Ousmane Kane, *Beyond Timbuktu: An Intellectual History of Muslim West Africa* (Cambridge, MA: Harvard University Press, 2016).

41. Abdullahi Ahmed An-Na'im, *What Is an American Muslim? Embracing Faith and Citizenship* (New York: Oxford University Press, 2014).

42. Shahab Ahmed, *What Is Islam? The Importance of Being Islamic* (Princeton, NJ: Princeton University Press, 2016), Cemil Aydin's *The Idea of the Muslim World: A Global Intellectual History* (Cambridge, MA: Harvard University Press, 2017), and Ahmad Atif Ahmad *Pitfalls of Scholarship: Lessons from Islamic Studies* (New York: Palgrave Macmillan, 2016).

43. Full disclosure: as of this book, I have published with four of these eight presses.

All but one of these authors identify with or position themselves in their books within a broad Islamic tradition. Some signal their religious commitments explicitly. For instance, Abou El Fadl declares: "I wrote this book as a Muslim who is also an academic scholar and not as an academic scholar who happens to be Muslim."[44] Ware affirms: "I am a practicing African American Muslim."[45] *Sharia Compliant* by Rumee Ahmed (yet again, no relation) begins with "A Letter to My Muslim Readers," in which he refers to "our community" and "our tradition." In other cases, the link is less direct. Shahab Ahmed dedicates his book to his parents, "who raised me in the Islam of their cosmopolitanism and in the cosmopolitanism of their Islam."[46] And although he refers to his Egyptian identity repeatedly, Ahmad Atif Ahmad (Ahmad with a second *a*!) only indirectly situates himself as part of a post-9/11 population of Muslims subject to "American xenophobia and nativism."[47] Only Aydin, a historian working in a discipline where such disclosures are uncommon, makes no such implicit or explicit claim of Muslimness.

Someone might object that my focus on Muslim men's writings unfairly stigmatizes them by holding them to different standards than non-Muslim men. As my earlier analysis of state-of-the-field overviews and discussion of Fred Donner's essay show, the problem is in no way confined to those who explicitly claim Islam in their work or to those from Muslim backgrounds.[48] I choose these books partly because Muslim women who write about the Islamic tradition are often presumed to be compromised in some way by religious commitments. For instance, as the last chapter showed, Muslim women analyzing, performing, or theorizing Qur'anic interpretation are seldom included in edited volumes,

44. Abou El Fadl, *Reasoning with God*, xiii.

45. Ware, *Walking Qur'an*, 12. See also Kane, *Beyond Timbuktu*, 3–5; An-Na'im, *What Is an American Muslim?*, 1 ("As an American Muslim").

46. Ahmed, *What Is Islam?*, vii. See also Brown, *Misquoting Muhammad*, 13–14.

47. Ahmad, *Pitfalls of Scholarship*, 157.

48. See Chapter 1 and, prior to this chapter, "DUDE."

anthologized, or discussed in state-of-the-field essays, while some "professed Muslim" men are.[49] Unlike Muslim women's writings, Muslim men's scholarship is often lauded despite, or occasionally because of, its expressed religious commitments.

Some of these nine books ignore women and gender almost entirely, including those by Ahmad Ahmad and Shahab Ahmed. Others say a lot about gender while ignoring women as historical actors and/or excluding women's scholarship, such as those by Khaled Abou El Fadl, Cemil Aydin, and Jonathan Brown and, to a lesser extent, Rumee Ahmed and Abdullahi An-Na'im. Others fall in the middle, talking about women in some sections and ignoring them elsewhere (Ousmane Kane's book) or actively discussing gender, including masculinity, in places (Rudolph Ware's book). When these authors mention women and/or women's scholarly works, most downplay their significance through a variety of textual and rhetorical strategies. Although they differ from each other in many ways, the named individuals in each book are at least 85% male.

More than nine of every ten people named in the books on the Muslim legal and ethical tradition are men. Abou El Fadl's *Reasoning with God* indexes 127 men and just eight women, about one woman for every sixteen men. Brown's *Misquoting Muhammad* has two dozen women and nonbinary people in its index and ten times as many men, roughly the same ratio as those named in the main text.[50]

49. The phrase "professed Muslim" is from Rippin, "The Reception of Euro-American Scholarship on the Qur'an and *tafsir*." In this piece, which names and quotes only men, save a passing mention of Jane Dammen McAuliffe that diminishes her expertise and authority, Rippin includes some men who engage the Qur'an as insiders, such as Pakistani Fazlur Rahman, Iranian Abdolkarim Soroush, and Egyptian Nasr Hamid Abu Zayd. However, he excludes American theologian amina wadud, U.S.-based Pakistani scholar Asma Barlas, French-Moroccan Asma Lamrabet, and Tunisian Olfa Youssef, who brings linguistic and psychoanalytic tools to bear on Qur'anic polysemy.

50. This figure excludes individuals from the exclusively male scholarly lineages reproduced, those mentioned in the appendices (all men, save Aisha), and those who appear in the glossy inset section's photo captions. Though some women and girls are pictured, only men are named.

In his substantially shorter *Sharia Compliant*, which has no index, Rumee Ahmed has the same proportion in the main text: half a dozen named people who aren't men and sixty-one who are. The books centering on America and West Africa mostly have a higher percentage of women, if judged by the most generous metrics. Though the index names only men, about five men for every woman appear in the main text of *What Is an American Muslim?*[51] The *Walking Qur'an* names around seven men for every woman in the index. In *Beyond Timbuktu*, there are eleven women and nearly fifteen times as many men in the index, only a bit higher of a proportion than in *Reasoning with God*, but the glossary includes roughly one woman for every four men. In both Ware's and Kane's studies, the inclusion of women alongside men as participants in the West African Muslim scholarly tradition is a recurrent theme. "All my mother's sisters," Kane writes in his prologue, "received Islamic education."[52]

The books by Shahab Ahmed and Aydin, which interrogate the terms "Islam" and "the Muslim world," name very few women. Of the nearly five hundred people indexed in Ahmed's *What Is Islam?*, less than one in a dozen is a woman. There are more men under the letter A than women in the entire index. Aydin's *The Idea of the Muslim World* names only four women, none of them Muslim, among the nearly two hundred people in its index. Two other women are named in passing in the main text, but the only woman mentioned more than once in the entire book is Queen Victoria. Aydin's *Aeon* magazine précis of his argument that the idea of a unified Muslim world is a modern invention names twenty-seven men and no women.[53] It feels true to the book.

51. This figure excludes names (mostly last names) from court cases or (men's) titles without personal names listed, e.g., Aga Khan IV or Shaykh al-Azhar. This tally also excludes informants, mostly women, given first-name pseudonyms, from a study conducted by (then-student) research assistant Shehnaz Haqqani, as well as first-named informants from journalistic sources.

52. Kane, *Beyond Timbuktu*, 4.

53. Cemil Aydin, "What Is the Muslim World?," August 1, 2018, https://aeon.co /essays/the-idea-of-a-muslim-world-is-both-modern-and-misleading.

Ahmad's book of reflective essays on Islamic (legal) studies
within its humanities context invokes scores of thinkers, writers,
and public figures, ranging from well-known to obscure, in 162
pages of main text. Although a few works by women appear in the
notes and bibliography, he names only two women, both white
and non-Muslim, in the main text: Hannah Arendt, in a blink-and-
you-miss-it reference, and Georgie D. M. Hyde, author of a book
about the Egyptian educational system. Hyde is the only named
woman whose ideas are engaged in the body of the book.[54] She
does not appear in the all-male index.

These books, then, range from a high of 98–100% male in their
references to individuals (Ahmad's, Aydin's, and An-Na'im's indexes) to a low of around 85% male (Ware's and An-Na'im's texts).
The people named by Abou El Fadl, Kane, Shahab Ahmed, Rumee
Ahmed, and Brown are 90–95% male. But even if ratios cluster in
a small range, these books vary considerably in approach and feel.

At one end of the spectrum, Shahab Ahmed's *What Is Islam?*
persistently avoids questions of women and gender. The tome has
garnered substantial attention from Islamic studies scholars,
because of both its field-defining ambition and its release nearly
simultaneously with its author's premature death. In his study,
subtitled "The Importance of Being Islamic," Ahmed contends
that scholars of Islam should expand their focus beyond a narrow
law-centric Arabic intellectual tradition. This frame should have
provided ample opportunity to engage women's scholarship, as
feminists have been among those rethinking how to interpret,
appraise, and reshape canons. Ahmed ignores this literature. The
scant three pages he devotes to the issues appear in the index
as the sole entry under "feminism," "gender, equality of," and

54. Ahmad, *Pitfalls of Scholarship*, Arendt (18) and Hyde (37). The notes and
bibliography contain a handful of references to other women's work. None are
named in the text, even when quoted there. The notes ratio (5 / 147) is legitimately
terrible, but the bibliography (7 / 82) is less skewed than it might seem because numerous entries are premodern Arabic texts.

"women, rights of." Even apart from questions of gender, not a single Muslim woman appears as a historical actor or cultural producer over the centuries he discusses.

Such omissions limit the accuracy and reach of his analyses. As Taymiya Zaman notes, Ahmed's failure to consider how poets' genders shaped their work undermines his "universalizing argument about how poetic social words shaped Muslim selves." Ignoring the gendered "relations of power" in his account of how the stories of Yusuf and Zulaykha and Layla and Majnun resonate leads him to make unsustainable claims, by "assum[ing] that Muslim male experiences of love and desire are inclusive of female experiences or, if women's experiences are different, this is not worth exploring." And "ignoring premodern women's negotiations of laws written by men diminished the latitude of an argument that emphasizes lived experience in its definition of Islam."[55] These are all subjects that women have written about at length. Taking that scholarship seriously would have led to more methodologically careful and substantively nuanced accounts of the Muslim tradition instead of "a selective argument reliant on a partial reading of the Muslim past . . . that replicates silences in the archive and attenuates the dynamism of historical forces in its need to construct a past that can serve as a contrast to a disenchanted present."[56]

If Ahmed follows in a long line of predecessors in mostly omitting women, gender, and feminism, *The Idea of the Muslim World* reminds readers at regular intervals about gender's relevance to modern Muslim history and thought. Aydin mentions "women's rights, education, and economic activity" and publications "with essentializing titles such as . . . *Women's Rights in Islam*" and "'Women according to Islam.'"[57] He notes mid-twentieth-century

---

55. Taymiya R. Zaman, "An Islam of One's Own: Review of Shahab Ahmed's *What Is Islam? The Importance of Being Islamic*," in *Comparative Studies of South Asia, Africa and the Middle East*, 40:1, 2020: 214–218 at 217.

56. Ibid., 218.

57. Aydin, *The Idea of the Muslim World*, 8, 9–10, 75.

Islamist Abul Ala Maududi's youthful Urdu translation of turn-of-the-century Egyptian writer Qasim Amin's *The New Woman*.[58] He invokes a late nineteenth-century Ottoman reformer who avers that Muslims "need not imitate blindly European dance or marriage principles" to be civilized.[59] Aydin points out major historical shifts that revolve around gender norms, including "the British empire['s] . . . codifying *sharia* for personal and family law and implementing it among Muslim subjects," "modernizing Muslim leaders' [investment] in . . . education for women," and Turkey's ban on "the veiling of women in public spaces."[60] Still, notwithstanding Aydin's inclusion of feminists among the diverse actors who are part of the story of the emergence of the idea of the Muslim world, the book ignores the myriad ways women's organizations, political activities, and print culture intersect with its narrative.[61] Like Donner, Aydin uses veiling as a proxy for other socio-political changes. It is central enough that his précis notes of several male leaders: "None of them wanted to veil women."[62] But his book fails to grapple at any length with the gender discourses of its prominent male subjects, nor does it even mention the copious writings of their women contemporaries.

Although gender needn't be the main story, gendered norms and laws are obviously a charged arena for negotiating identity in modernity. Even a bit more engagement with the activities of feminists and other women writers and social actors could deepen Aydin's analysis of, for example, narratives of Muslim decline or the push-pull attraction of Western gender norms, at once compelling and repugnant. Instead, key points are mentioned as though they were simply common sense, not the hard-won revelations of

58. Ibid., 152. Samira Sidhom Peterson has translated Amin's books *The Liberation of Women* and *The New Woman* into English. The classic discussion of Amin's writings is Ahmed, "The Discourse of the Veil," in *Women and Gender in Islam*, 144–68.

59. Aydin, *The Idea of the Muslim World*, 45.

60. Ibid., 200.

61. Ibid., 224.

62. Aydin, "What Is the Muslim World?"

a generation of scholars of Muslim women's history. Aydin's decision to omit detailed consideration of women and gender leads not only to the absence of key figures such as Egyptian Feminist Union founder and prominent nationalist Huda Sha'rawi, but also to a lack of engagement with the extensive literature by women about women in the late Ottoman era, especially in Egypt. He neither draws upon it for his own analysis nor directs readers to foundational works in the field. Although he is assiduous in citing women historians' scholarship on broader themes of Muslim modernity and colonialism, his exclusion of women as historical actors results in the disproportionate exclusion of women scholars, who disproportionately study these figures. Such omissions occur partly because that scholarship is largely grounded in the question of gender, which receives only superficial if repeated mentions.[63]

Ware's *The Walking Qur'an*, by contrast, engages directly with questions of gendered pedagogy and religious manifestations. The formation of both male and female Muslim students figures centrally in two chapters. The paucity of named women owes partly to the historical era. The European invaders, adventurers, and administrators Ware discusses are men. Additionally, his focus on "ordinary Qur'an schooling [for] girls in West Africa" seldom yields named individuals, while records from colonial-era boys' schools name students and preserve their recollections of schooling. When reading Ware's book, I found myself wanting more attention to the lives and legacies of the "accomplished female scholars" who do appear, such as Ruqayya Niass.[64] Ware's discussion of her poetry instructing girls is resonant and provides a vital lens on the presumptions about what girls would have learned in school.[65]

63. An exception is the MA thesis by Ansev Demirhan: "Female Muslim Intellectuals: Understanding the History of Turkey's Woman Question through the Construction of Islamic Tradition," University of North Carolina—Chapel Hill, 2014, https://cdr.lib.unc.edu/concern/dissertations/vd66w087g.

64. Ware, *The Walking Qur'an*, 247. See also 174–76.

65. Comparisons to the work of Nana Asma'u, mentioned briefly in the introduction (Ware, *The Walking Qur'an*, 5), could have been fruitful. See Jean Boyd and

Along with her sister Mariama Niass and Khadija bint Muhammad al-'Aqil, Niass is the subject of a paragraph in the conclusion affirming that "not all of the exceptional West African intellectuals were men."[66] Despite the relatively low ratio of women in Ware's index, including women academics named in main text and in the notes, the study is balanced.

Unlike some of his colleagues, Ware has gender on his mind. He notes the way gendered binaries align in scholarly attention to various topics. Africa, associated with embodiment and spirit possession, is feminized. Islam, associated with Arabic and with texts, is masculinized.[67] He argues for centering West Africa within Islamic studies, as a locus of historically widespread Islamic ways of learning and knowing and a corrective to the text-centrism of academic Islamic studies.[68] Building on his analyses, I would suggest that the abjection of feminized topics explored in the previous chapter helps account for the marginalization of the study of African Islam within Islamic studies.[69]

Although Asma'u, Mariame Niasse, and a handful of other women also show up in Kane's "intellectual history of Muslim West Africa," which also mentions the gendered practices of modern reformist groups such as Yan Izala and Yan Taru, overall there are far fewer women.[70] Between West African scholars from the seventeenth century onward and the colonial and post-colonial figures who write about them, the historiography Kane offers is replete with men. One paragraph in his account of Timbuktu

---

Beverly Mack, *One Woman's Jihad: Nana Asma'u, Scholar and Scribe* (Indianapolis: Indiana University Press, 2000) and Mack and Boyd, eds., *Collected Works of Nana Asma'u: Daughter of Usman 'dan Fodiyo (1793–1864)* (East Lansing: Michigan State University Press, 2012). The latter stretches to nearly 800 pages.

66. Ware, *The Walking Qur'an*, 247.

67. Ibid., 4–5.

68. Ibid., 14.

69. See also Kane, *Beyond Timbuktu*, 7.

70. Ibid., 71–72, 176–77.

studies names fourteen men and no women.[71] The proportion of named women in the book overall is similar to that found in works on the formative, classical, and medieval eras.

Shifting from West Africa to America: in his thematic exploration of American Muslim identity, Abdullahi An-Na'im addresses women and gender repeatedly but intermittently. His discussion of how the American legal system could accommodate shariah mentions Muslim women's potential vulnerability to coercion but cites nothing by Muslim women who, individually and through community organizations, have made this point repeatedly in debates over so-called shariah tribunals or councils. As Brittney Cooper points out in her study of Black women intellectuals, treating people as activists rather than as thinkers or theorists diminishes their contributions to scholarly debates.[72] But An-Na'im excludes not only active campaigners; he also excludes a substantial body of work by Muslim women academics exploring the challenging interactions of civil and religious laws. He names no women and discusses no women's work on this topic in the main text. He cites no women's scholarship on Islamic or religious law at all in this chapter, including on its implementation in the comparative contexts he describes.[73] By choosing not to engage this literature, An-Na'im leaves unanswered the substantial concerns raised by others about how the kinds of organizations and procedures he outlines would affect Muslim women's lives in practice.

71. Ibid., 31–32.

72. Brittney C. Cooper, *Beyond Respectability: The Intellectual Thought of Race Women* (Champaign: University of Illinois Press, 2017). On the tendency to treat women's work as empirical rather than theoretical, see also Smith and Garrett-Scott, "'We are not named'" and Lutz, "The Erasure of Women's Writing."

73. An-Na'im, "Identity and Citizenship: Beyond Minority Politics," in *What Is an American Muslim?*, 1–34. Only one endnote for the pertinent sections ("Islam, the State, and Politics," "Sharia in Secular Courts," and "Sharia and Religious Self-Determination" [200 nn. 26–41]) cites work by a woman, and it is unrelated to Muslims or Islam. An-Na'im, *What Is an American Muslim?*, 200 n. 35.

An-Na'im's topical citational disparities are pronounced, sharply sidelining American Muslim women's engagements with tradition. In the chapter on American Muslim life, An-Na'im names his seven women interlocutors, most of whom are American Muslims, and cites women's work in about half the chapter's notes. He still names several times more men than women in the text and the total number of works by women cited is substantially lower than the number of works by men.[74] But in comparison to the rest of the book, this chapter stands out dramatically. For instance, although the next chapter uses marriage and divorce to make a larger case about religious identity and community belonging, topics that women in Islamic studies have written about extensively, An-Na'im cites only four works by women about Islamic family law, all about its implementation in North America, written by law students, lawyers, and a sociologist. He cites no work by any woman specialist on Islamic law. He names no Muslim woman thinker, activist, or organizer who works on these issues. One particularly notable omission is the study on American Muslims and marriage contracts that Najeeba Syeed and Asifa Quraishi-Landes wrote for a project An-Na'im himself directed.[75]

In writing as a Muslim speaking from within the tradition, but failing to engage work by women doing the same, An-Na'im is sadly representative. Very similar patterns emerge in Brown's, Rumee Ahmed's, and Abou El Fadl's sweeping prescriptive books on the Sunni legal tradition, even though they differ dramatically in other ways from An-Na'im's and from each other.

74. An-Na'im, "Religious Self-Determination for American Muslims," in *What Is an American Muslim?*, 67–113. He cites thirteen works by women and twenty-two by men.

75. An-Na'im, "Legal Dimensions of Religious Self-Determination," in *What Is an American Muslim?*, 114–158. Initially published in 2004, the study has been republished as Najeeba Syeed and Asifa Quraishi-Landes, "No Altars: A Survey of Islamic Family Law in the United States," in Kecia Ali, ed., *Half of Faith: American Muslim Marriage and Divorce in the Twenty-first Century* (Boston: OpenBU, 2021), 80–110, https://hdl.handle.net/2144/420505.

Brown's *Misquoting Muhammad* is a historical treatment of the Sunni scholarly tradition, grappling with its methods and its applicability to Muslims today. It uses controversial topics to illustrate the dynamism and adaptability of this tradition, including women's leadership of prayer, minor marriage—specifically, that of Muhammad to Aisha—and male marital violence. But despite its substantial attention to gender, individual women are largely absent. Brown names thirty women in the body of the book—if one counts the five who fleetingly appear in an account of a modern Egyptian scholar's comments.[76] Muslim women typically appear as historical agents, thinkers, or scholars only in brief cameos. Just five people who aren't men are treated in some way as producers of Islamic religious knowledge. Aisha bint Abi Bakr, the prophet's wife/widow and a community authority, is mentioned repeatedly, usually in connection with her age at marriage, and Fatima bint ʿAbbas, a medieval jurist and preacher, is mentioned once. Among the modern figures, the "esteemed and pious" Egyptian Qurʾan scholar Aisha ʿAbd al-Rahman appears only as she figures in the thought of a man who is Brown's concern.[77] Moroccan hadith scholar Khadija Battar, "who wrote a detailed critique of Bukhari's *Sahih* using traditional Muslim sources, merely gets a half sentence and an endnote."[78] Finally, amina wadud is mentioned a few times, more often with regard to her leadership of a public mixed-gender Friday prayer than to her egalitarian commentary on the Qurʾan. Brown names more Church Fathers, more medieval Christian clerics, more Greek philosophers, more ancient historians, more Enlightenment thinkers, and more rabbis than he does Muslim women scholars.

76. Brown, *Misquoting Muhammad*, 137–138, 139. Muhammad al-Ghazali draws lessons about leadership from Golda Meir, Indira Gandhi, Margaret Thatcher, and the Queen of Sheba and discusses Aisha ʿAbd al-Rahman's piety and accomplishments.

77. Ibid., 139.

78. Scott C. Lucas, "The Anxiety of Misquotation," *Los Angeles Review of Books*, February 28, 2015, https://lareviewofbooks.org/article/anxiety-misquotation/.

Just under one in ten of the people Brown names are women, but they are substantially less represented in the text of the book than this number suggests. Of the five women and nonbinary people who appear more than once, three are members of Muhammad's seventh-century household and the other two are modern Westerners.[79] Despite his repeated affirmation that "women have always been present among the ranks of the ulama," Brown excludes traditionally educated Muslim women alongside their Western-trained academic counterparts, thereby helping keep "their role . . . invisible."[80] 'Abd al-Rahman, who in addition to her scholarship on the Qur'an also wrote about Muhammad's wives and household, could easily have received more attention. Considering her treatment of polygyny alongside that of Muhammad 'Abduh, for instance, would have provided a useful lens onto women's diverse and divergent perspectives—and provided a potential contrast with the wide-ranging and long-running debate in Egypt's women's press in the central decades of the twentieth century, in which notable figures such as Malak Hifni Nasif participated.[81] Not only do Muslim women seldom appear as thinkers or historical actors in *Misquoting Muhammad*, even the chapters on the modern era rarely cite them as authors of secondary literature. Again, this is a mutually reinforcing dynamic, since women have tended to write more about women.

While Brown's book is replete with non-Muslim historians and philosophers, these too are nearly all men. Three non-Muslim women appear in the main text: Arendt (again), Gayatri Spivak,

79. They are Aisha, Fatima, Khadija, Lady Montagu, and amina wadud.

80. Brown, *Misquoting Muhammad*, 198. As Omaima Abou Bakr observes, too often people point to the existence of a tradition of women's learning and the existence of women scholars as though this history obviates the need for change today. Quoted in Katz, "Textual Study of Gender," 103.

81. One classic study is Beth Baron, *The Women's Awakening in Egypt: Culture, Society, and the Press* (New Haven, CT: Yale University Press, 1994). Margot Badran, *Feminists, Islam, and Nation: Gender and the Making of Modern Egypt* (Princeton, NJ: Princeton University Press, 1995) is also relevant.

and Maribel Fierro, an Islamicist focused on medieval Andalusian history and law who is partly responsible for Spain's significant, and largely female, cohort of scholars in this area. Brown engages no feminist historiography, which grapples usefully with the crucial questions about context and change he raises, as well as the question of whose perspectives and experiences matter. Taking this literature seriously would have required him to justify the choice to focus on the ulama without considering their women critics and competitors.

Although his endnotes cite perhaps a dozen-and-a-half books and articles by women Islamic studies scholars (construing the field of Islamic studies broadly), Brown overwhelmingly fails to cite or engage Muslim women colleagues who have written about slavery and concubinage, minor marriage, illicit sex, and domestic violence. Neglecting this work means he commits the intellectual errors that Krishnamurty and Wilson describe. He repeats things others have already said, failing to advance the conversation, or he makes statements without addressing the critiques that have already been levied against those positions. For instance, in examining wadud's Qur'an commentary on husbands hitting their wives, Brown notes her oppositional stance and signals its departure from standard approaches—a point made by others earlier in work he either did not consult or chose not to cite.[82] Likewise, in discussing wadud's leadership of a public mixed-gender prayer, he gives only cursory attention to the ways a variety of Muslim women thinkers engaged the event and the larger question of

---

82. See, e.g., Juliane Hammer, *American Muslim Women, Learning, and Authority: More than a Prayer* (Austin: University of Texas Press, 2012), 69. Although Hammer's book appears in Brown's bibliography, he does not cite it, or any of the other secondary literature that addresses wadud's interpretation, in the notes to his discussion of her ideas (*Misquoting Muhammad*, 286–89). Had he consulted the open access Festchrift for wadud, he would have encountered my essay making that argument (and quoting Taylor Swift before it was trendy). See Kecia Ali, "Just Say Yes: Law, Consent, and Muslim Feminist Ethics" in Ali, Hammer, and Silvers, eds., *A Jihad for Justice*, 121–34.

woman-led prayer. His assertion that women praying in front of men is impossible because of the seductiveness of prostration is one that various thinkers had already rebutted.[83]

Misquoting Muhammad has 530 notes, including citations of premodern texts. Thirty-five, about one in every fifteen, cite works by women and nonbinary people, either on their own or in conjunction with works by men. These citations are unevenly distributed, from none in Chapter 1 up to nearly one in four in Chapter 7. Most of the other chapters hew to the low end of that range, with only Chapter 4 having more than one in ten of its notes including work by non-male scholars. Six of every seven of European language works in the bibliography (230 / 268) have only men authors or editors. (Among the one in seven works authored, co-authored, edited, or co-edited by people who aren't men is Ayesha Chaudhry's *Domestic Violence in Islam* [2013], which Brown never cites though it bears directly on a topic he discusses at length.[84]) Only one of the 216 Arabic and Persian language sources is by a woman, the aforementioned Battar. While one obviously cannot alter the percentage of classical Islamic texts written by women, there are numerous modern sources in those languages on the topics about which Brown writes. Overall, more than nine out of ten works in the bibliography are by men, though the percentage of modern academic works is lower.

It is unsurprising that Brown's "paean to an intellectual and religious tradition" that is predominantly male focuses near-exclusively on men's texts.[85] It is disconcerting to find the same pattern in Rumee Ahmed's *Sharia Compliant*, a book that otherwise has a

83. See Laury Silvers, "Islamic Jurisprudence, 'Civil' Disobedience, and Woman-Led Prayer," *The American Muslim*, May 13, 2005 (http://www.theamericanmuslim .org/tam.php/features/articles/islamic_jurisprudence_civil_disobedience_and _woman_led_prayer/) and Hammer, *American Muslim Women*, 52.

84. Ayesha S. Chaudhry, *Domestic Violence in Islam* (New York: Oxford University Press, 2013).

85. Brown, *Misquoting Muhammad*, 13. Note, though, that he names and engages numerous men who are not ulama.

very different relationship to the gendered politics of the Muslim tradition. Writing for a nonspecialist audience, Ahmed observes that jurisprudence (*fiqh*) has always been subject to interpretation and open to change. He encourages ordinary "*fiqh*-minded Muslims" to "hack" Islamic law—that is, to make and argue for claims that resonate with their own deeply held ethical beliefs, even if they diverge from the doctrines and rationales of traditionally trained scholars. For instance, Ahmed advocates "hacking" illicit intercourse (*zina*) to mean nonconsensual sex rather than sex outside the confines of a legally recognized relationship. In making this argument, though, Ahmed obscures generations of feminist activism and scholarship exploring the scriptural and legal roots of the current definition, its legislative manifestations, and its human consequences. Framing zina as gender-neutral hides the ways the standard definition disadvantages women in theory and practice. The entire section is written as though zina and rape affect men and women in the same way.[86] Although women are those disproportionately punished for illicit sex in modern countries that purport to apply shariah, as work by Sarah Eltantawi on Nigeria and Asifa Quraishi-Landes on Pakistan has shown, the book's single example of someone accused of committing zina is a man from Muhammad's community.[87] Readers are thus left unaware of the deeply

---

86. Ahmed, *Sharia Compliant*, 213–224.

87. Ibid., 219. Although their work is cited in the endnotes, the text would have benefited from more engagement with Hina Azam's meticulously researched *Sexual Violation in Islamic Law: Substance, Evidence, and Procedure* (New York: Cambridge University Press, 2015) on the development of laws around zina in Muslim jurisprudence, with attention to the modern situation in Nigeria and Pakistan, and Sarah Eltantawi's *Shariah on Trial: Northern Nigeria's Islamic Revolution* (Berkeley: University of California Press, 2017), which addresses history, colonialism, and ordinary Nigerians' ideas about Islamic law, devoting considerable attention to a zina prosecution that became a global spectacle. Significantly earlier, and important for the debates that followed, is Asifa Quraishi[-Landes]'s "Her Honor: An Islamic Critique of the Rape Laws of Pakistan," first published in a law journal in 1997 and more widely known from its inclusion in Gisela Webb, ed., *Windows of Faith: Muslim*

gendered dynamics surrounding zina. These matter for any attempt to craft effective solutions.

Of these nine books, Ahmed cites by far the highest proportion of women's publications.[88] Yet relegating his references to endnotes obscures women's contributions and impoverishes his arguments. Though published by a university press, *Sharia Compliant* has no index, bibliography, or numbered notes. Instead, bolded sentence fragments introduce discursive notes. This is a technique used in trade books where it is feared that reference markers, never mind footnotes, will alienate readers. Because the main text carries no note numbers or marks, the general reader, for whom a conventional scholarly apparatus was presumably abandoned, will miss that these conversations about how to reform and reshape Islamic law have been ongoing for years, and that women have been central to these debates. Unless they peruse the notes carefully, readers won't know that many of the ideas *Sharia Compliant* presents, especially the critiques of conventional understandings of topics like consent, have been formulated by women over the past decades.

When Ahmed mentions Muslim feminist legal interpretation, he seldom names specific thinkers and scholars. Even setting aside the classical jurists he discusses, the modern Muslim thinkers Ahmed names in the main text are mostly men. When he mentions the transnational collective Musawah, he connects it neither to Ziba Mir-Hosseini, whose work on Islamic law he mentions elsewhere, nor to its other co-founders or members. He signals the work of scholars associated with the American organization

---

Women Scholar-Activists in North America (Syracuse, NY: Syracuse University Press, 2000), 102–35.

88. Of 153 citations, eighty list works by men, thirty-two works by women and nonbinary people, and seven works co-authored/co-edited by men and women. Works by women and nonbinary people constitute one fifth (20.9%) of the total, or one fourth (24.8%) if one removes works without named authors (twenty-four items). If one adds in work written or edited jointly by mixed-gender teams, those percentages rise to 25.5% and 30.2% respectively. If one omits works in Arabic first written before 1900, about one in three cited works has a non-male author.

Al-Rawiya as a basis for woman-led prayer, but never names its founder, al-Azhar-trained Reima Yosif, who parses the arguments for and against its permissibility.[89] Recognizing organizations and collectives, not just individual geniuses, yields a fuller picture of Muslim reformist thought and women's contributions to it. Yet naming men but omitting women thinkers in favor of crediting women's nonprofits distorts and downplays women's intellectual contributions. Apart from Mir-Hosseini, no woman is named until two thirds of the way through the book.[90] Just as Brown asserts women's inclusion among the ulama but doesn't himself include them, Ahmed invokes "feminist ulama" half a dozen times without defining the category; naming anyone specific in conjunction with it; situating such scholars intellectually, institutionally, or socially; or referencing publications by or about them.[91] The idea that hackers following Ahmed's approach can sidestep the issues that Islamic feminist thinkers have been grappling with for decades seems, in Saadia Yacoob's term, "untenable."[92]

Ahmed's failure to directly engage women's work echoes in the book's scholarly reception. In his roundtable review of *Sharia Compliant*, Anver Emon uses the case of illicit sex to discuss Ahmed's approach. He includes only men: besides Ahmed, the ninth-century jurist al-Shafi'i, late nineteenth century reformers Muhammad 'Abduh and Jamal al-Din al-Afghani, and Kwame Anthony Appiah. Emon avoids the words "woman," "women," "female," and "gender." Instead, he follows Ahmed's example by deploying gender-neutral words: individual, humanity, adult. In critiquing the extant "hierarchy of expertise," with the aim of decentering "elitism,"

---

89. Reima Yosif, "Can Women Lead Women/Men in Salah/Jum'a?," January 20, 2015, https://youtu.be/OkHPOtp7GN0.

90. In the main text, Ahmed names Ziba Mir-Hosseini (26, 152), Ayesha S. Chaudhry (144), 'A'isha (145), Suzanne Mubarak (161), Farhat Hashmi (201), and Amina Wadud (209).

91. Ahmed, *Sharia Compliant*, 112, 113, 148, 151, 180.

92. Saadia Yacoob, "Hacking and Intentionality," *The Immanent Frame*. May 1, 2018, https://tif.ssrc.org/2018/05/01/hacking-and-intentionality/.

Emon cites none of the women scholars or activists or scholar-activists who have been working on these issues for decades. Discussing women's bodies while ignoring women's voices, Emon and Ahmed reproduce in practice what they deplore in their analyses. When Donner recommends Ahmed's book rather than any of those by the women scholars Ahmed draws on, the cycle continues.

A similar failure to cite and engage women's scholarship plagues the work of Khaled Abou El Fadl, whose publications on Wahhabi misogyny have been resources for Muslim women pursuing gender equity. Abou El Fadl passes over in silence egalitarian-minded Muslim women scholars and thinkers in *Reasoning with God*.[93] His omission of Muslim feminist scholarship on law is particularly frustrating given his glowing praise for some examples of it in other contexts. In a cover endorsement, he calls the collection *Men in Charge? Rethinking Authority in Muslim Legal Tradition* (2015), edited by Ziba Mir-Hosseini, Mulki Al-Sharmani, and Jana Rumminger, "the best treatment of women and Islamic law that I have read in the past twenty years," and avers that "it is difficult for me to take seriously any student or scholar dealing with the subject of guardianship of men over women in Islam unless, or until, they have read and digested this book."[94] Yet while foregrounding the legal and customary patriarchy and misogyny that contributors to *Men in Charge?* have been publishing about for years, he cites none of them.[95] In fact, he cites little by women of any background or stripe on the Muslim legal tradition. In sixty-five pages

93. He twice gives overlapping lists of four women "native informants." Unlike some of the anti-Muslim or "ex-Muslim" men he mentions, he discusses none of these women's works in the main text, though he does list some of their publications in the notes (e.g., Abou El Fadl, *Reasoning with God*, 422, n. 7 and 439, n. 19).

94. Mir-Hosseini, Al-Sharmani, and Rumminger, eds., *Men in Charge?*.

95. *Men in Charge?* appeared about six months after *Reasoning with God*, so Abou El Fadl cannot be faulted for failing to cite its chapters. However, he could have drawn on many relevant earlier publications by its contributors.

of densely packed endnotes, I found only a dozen publications by women on Islamic law.

The same pattern obtains when he discusses Qur'an 4:34 and conjugal violence: he turns back to texts and bypasses extant interpretive work. He includes Laleh Bakhtiar's rendering in the notes but cites none of the copious feminist and gender-minded literature engaging the verse or its interpretation.[96] In a glowing foreword to wadud's *Inside the Gender Jihad* (2006), Abou El Fadl waxes eloquent about how patriarchy "erases and marginalizes women."[97] His own work, unfortunately, also erases and marginalizes women. He engages a variety of men in the text but Bakhtiar appears only in the notes, wadud and Mir-Hosseini are nowhere to be found, Chaudhry and her monograph on marital violence go unmentioned, and so on. Erasure, as he correctly points out, need not be "purposeful and sinister" or motivated by "animosity" to hurt women.[98] Beyond the ethical harms of citational failures, there is also the wasted effort that Krishnamurty and Wilson signal. By largely repeating points about the interpretation of Q. 4:34 that others have already raised and failing to engage work such as Chaudhry's that considers scholars' patriarchal cosmology, Abou El Fadl misses opportunities to advance the scholarly conversation.

Deferring to expertise

Beyond the failures to cite women's intellectual work at all, and the strikingly gendered topics on which their work is consulted, dramatic disparities appear in how women's scholarship shows up in these publications. Women scholars are less likely to be named and more likely to have their contributions diminished as simple

---

96. Instead, he cites pages from his own *The Search for Beauty in Islam* (Lanham, MD: Rowman and Littlefield, 2006). Abou El Fadl, *Reasoning with God*, 450 nn. 25–26.

97. Khaled Abou El Fadl, "Foreword," in Wadud, *Inside the Gender Jihad*, xii.

98. Ibid., xii.

case studies rather than treated as serious analyses with theoretical import. Sexism sometimes emerges despite putatively inclusive language, as with Rumee Ahmed and Emon's discussions of zina, or alongside acknowledgment of gender imbalance.[99] Other rhetorical tactics further downplay women's importance and authority. As anyone who has been introduced by her first name in a context where her male colleagues are accorded their earned titles knows, women's expertise can be diminished by how they are presented.[100]

Let us begin with the gendered relegation of scholars to the notes, a widespread practice of which I've also been guilty.[101] In his chapter on American citizenship, An-Na'im routinely attributes men's ideas to them: "As Richard Bellamy argues"; "to paraphrase Ulrich Preuss"; "According to Chief Justice Roger Taney." (These are just the first three men named in the chapter.) Although An-Na'im doesn't introduce every man's ideas in this fashion, he credits in the chapter text *none* of the few women whose work he draws on, even when he quotes their words. Instead, while citing their work appropriately in the endnotes, he seamlessly incorporates their ideas into his own narrative and argument. There is nothing inherently wrong with quoting or paraphrasing other scholars, naming them only in references. The problem is not the stylistic choice but the gendered disparity.

Another example of how gender shapes the presentation of scholarly work appears in a paragraph in *Pitfalls of Scholarship* about Ann Taves's *Religious Experience Reconsidered*.[102] Ahmad

99. See, e.g., Ahmad, *Pitfalls of Scholarship*, 49, 90, 148.

100. For an overview of linguistic gender bias and its effects, see Michela Menegatti and Monica Rubini, "Gender Bias and Sexism in Language," Oxford Research Encyclopedia: Communication (2017), https://doi.org/10.1093/acrefore/9780190 228613.013.470.

101. See, e.g., Ali, *Sexual Ethics in Islam*, 79–85.

102. Ann Taves, *Religious Experience Reconsidered: A Building-Block Approach to the Study of Religion and Other Special Things* (Princeton, NJ: Princeton University Press, 2009).

manages to avoid naming either Taves or her prize-winning book. In effusive language ("accomplished," "ingenuity," "insights"), he recognizes the "interdisciplinarity" and contemporary "flavor" of the "work," but relegates author and title to the endnotes. He downplays Taves's originality, emphasizing that the book is "drawing on earlier ideas and work," as if this were not what all responsible scholarship does. He specifically credits William James as her predecessor and influence, remarking in the main text on James's specialized knowledge of "medicine and philosophy." Ahmad's slighting of Taves contrasts sharply with the following paragraph's treatment of a book chapter by Michael Montoya, whom he names. Ahmad gives its title and summarizes Montoya's key findings. For one of those findings, he writes, "as one of his citations has it." That "citation" is Hannah Landecker, whom Ahmad only names in the endnote. To recap, Taves (unnamed) draws on work of other scholars (James, named). Montoya (named) draws on work of other scholars (Landecker, unnamed). Gender bias, rather than notability bias, best explains Ahmad's selective naming.[103]

Loaded language can also minimize and denigrate women's actions in other ways. Brown mentions "a female graduate of Cairo's law faculty" who objected to the policy that barred her from becoming a prosecutor or judge. In 1950, Aisha Ratib had argued in a letter to the Minister of Justice that the rule was out of step with

103. Ahmad Atif Ahmad, *Pitfalls of Scholarship*, 44. Despite the fact that Wikipedia requires, on average, a higher degree of notability from academic and other women than from men, as of February 27, 2019, Montoya had no Wikipedia page while Taves and Landecker did. On Wikipedia and gender, see Julia Adams, Hanna Brückner, and Cambria Naslund, "Who Counts as a Notable Sociologist on Wikipedia? Gender, Race, and the 'Professor Test,'" *Socius: Sociological Research for a Dynamic World*, 5:1, 2019: 1–14, https://journals.sagepub.com/doi/pdf/10.1177/2378023118823946 and Claudia Wagner, Eduardo Graells-Garrido, David Garcia, and Filippo Menczer, "Women through the Glass Ceiling: Gender Asymmetries in Wikipedia," *EPJ Data Science Journal* 5:5, 2016: 1–24, https://link.springer.com/article/10.1140/epjds/s13688-016-0066-4.

the significant roles played by Muslim women like Aisha.[104] Brown uses her case as an entrée into Egypt's shift to a "European-inspired judiciary" and "enduring" debates over whether women can hold public office, including head of state. The issues are significant, but Ratib isn't. Brown never names her, resorting to phrases like "the letter's author." He uses derivatives of "complain" three times to describe her letter. Once the minister hands it off to the ulama, however, Brown dignifies it as a "controversy" over women's capacity to hold public roles.[105] He then explores at length the responses and related ideas of several men, all of whom he names, over the next six decades. By then, Ratib has lost any residual agency, even grammatical. Neither she nor her letter is the subject of Brown's summary sentence: "The debate sparked over six decades ago with a female law graduate's petition to apply for a judgeship continues in Egypt and elsewhere to this day."[106] Compare with this alternative: "By advocating for her own and other women's right to apply for judgeships, law graduate Aisha Ratib sparked a lasting debate that continues in Egypt and elsewhere to this day." In Brown's account, the debates only matter when they are among men.

The diminishment of women's stature can manifest not only by leaving women entirely unnamed or relegating their names to the endnotes, but also by downplaying their credentials or accomplishments relative to men when they are named. For example, in An-Na'im's brief final chapter, "Imagined and Re-imagined Communities," the chapter title alludes to Benedict Anderson, who appears in the text as having "famously said" certain things about communities. Meanwhile, Margot Badran shows up allowing women's exclusion from a Washington D.C. mosque to be "reported by" her. A senior scholar of Egyptian women's history and global Muslim feminism becomes a mouthpiece for empirical

104. See Nadia Sonnenveld and Ahmed Tawfik, "Gender, Islam and Judgeship in Egypt," *International Journal of Law in Context*, 11:3, 2015: 341–360.

105. Brown, *Misquoting Muhammad*, 131–32.

106. Ibid., 140.

information on American Muslim practice, a participant-witness rather than an analyst.

Sometimes authors pair rhetorical deference toward men and their ideas with dismissiveness of women and their ideas. When, for example, Shahab Ahmed criticizes men's law-centric models, he names them and praises their qualifications. For example, he introduces "Khaled Abou El Fadl and Mohammad Fadel" as "two deeply thoughtful and learned liberal reformist Muslim academics in North America (and both professors of law)." He lays out their arguments with illustrative quotations from their published works. Only then does he object forcefully to their "truncated, law-centered construction put forward as reformed, liberal and modern normative Islam."[107] Unflattering, yes, but substantive.

In contrast, Shahab Ahmed's brief discussion of feminism and women's rights remains vague and superficial, the main text devoid of specific thinkers, works, or ideas. Treating reformist approaches to topics women have written about extensively, such as polygyny in the Qur'an, he cites only the scriptural passages and none of the extensive body of interpretation, or secondary scholarship on those interpretations, in English, French, Arabic, and other languages. A lone footnote acknowledges that "there is now a large body of literature on the subject" of Islamic feminism. Ahmed gives just two examples, an essay on Qur'an interpretation by Karen Bauer, offering a "clear and concise survey of the issues and schematization of the various interpretive positions," and my own "thoughtful monograph," *Sexual Ethics and Islam.* The next note is twice as long. It quotes approvingly and at length from Ebrahim Moosa's "bracing criticism" (Ahmed's term) of Muslim feminists' methodology. Moosa's essay appeared in 2003, and thus engages neither my book (2006) nor Bauer's essay (2009), both of which treat the issue Moosa, who was first reader for my dissertation, raises at some length. Indeed, my book cites Moosa's

---

107. Ahmed, *What Is Islam?* 126–127.

essay and builds on its argument.[108] In short, the critique Ahmed levies against the limited feminist scholarship he deigns to mention is off base. And although his indexer routinely includes footnotes with substantive content under the names of authors discussed, neither Bauer nor I appear in the index, illustrating again the interplay of stylistic choices and quantitative measurements.[109]

In relegating scholarship on gender, and the women who write it, to a footnote, Ahmed does not disagree so much as dismiss. In doing so, he follows a well-trodden path. In our survey of 831 book reviews published in the *Journal of the American Academy of Religion* from 2006 to 2020, Lolo Serrano and I showed that men authors of books under review were significantly more likely than women to be described with terms such as "distinguished," "esteemed," or "eminent," reflecting "reviewers' attribution of academic significance and professional standing" to them beyond the specific publication under review.[110] Numerous examples in this vein came from Islamic studies, including one reviewer's

---

108. Ibid., 512, nn. 225–226. Karen Bauer, "*The Male Is Not Like the Female* (Q 3:36): The Question of Gender Egalitarianism in the Qur'an," *Religion Compass* 3:4, 2009: 637–654 at 644. My citation of Moosa's essay (Ali, *Sexual Ethics*, 191 n. 41) references a different point, but "'If you have touched women': Female Bodies and Male Agency in the Qur'an" (in *Sexual Ethics and Islam*, 112–134) explores precisely the topic on which Ahmed quotes Moosa: the tendency to overstate Qur'anic egalitarianism or, perhaps more precisely, to discount its patriarchal interpretations.

109. Ahmed did not compile or review the index himself. However, had he put us in the text, we would appear in the index.

110. Ali and Serrano, "The Person of the Author," 566. Although we did not investigate the phenomenon in our article, specific publications can also be described in gendered ways. In Ahmed's *What Is Islam?*, men write "panoramic" histories (9) and "state-of-the-art" monographs (9) and "magnificent" (41) and "classic" (10, 458) studies. Women's books are occasionally "thoughtful" (398, and 512 n. 225) or, at best, "valuable" (103, n. 2) Similar if less pronounced patterns manifest in other books—for instance, Khaled Abou El Fadl refers to a man's "masterful" study (*Reasoning with God*, 63). Rudolph Ware, whose *The Walking Qur'an* I discuss below, applies these epithets in more balanced ways, deeming women's publications "pathbreaking" (4), "extraordinary" (4), and "pioneering" (6) while offering similar encomia for men's work.

posthumous description of Shahab Ahmed himself as "quite simply, the greatest Islamic studies scholar of my generation."[111] We also showed that praise of male authors could coexist with sharp criticism of their books, again with illustrations drawn partly from Islamic studies.[112]

Both patterns play out in Shahab Ahmed's book. His first chapter, which sets out the six questions he intends to address in his study, names many men, including Muslim authors spanning the centuries and modern academics. The first woman, Suʿad al-Hakim, appears seventy-five pages into the chapter's main text; the second and last, Margaret A. Mills, several pages later.[113] They, like some of their male academic peers, are simply mentioned along with an idea or publication. But Ahmed praises numerous men's standing over and above any particular contribution to scholarship. W. Montgomery Watt is "the archdeacon of Islamic studies" in his era. Wilfred Cantwell Smith is "one of the most important figures in the comparative study of religion." Gustave E. von Grunebaum is among "the Orientalist luminaries of the age." Clifford Geertz is "the acclaimed anthropologist," Adam Sabra is "that most erudite historian of the natural sciences and philosophy in Islam," and Fazlur Rahman "probably the finest modern student of Islamic intellectual history." Oleg Grabar is "the father of the modern study of Islamic art." William Chittick is "distinguished" and Walter Andrews, "eminent." The closest any woman comes to having her scholarly stature thus affirmed is when Ahmed introduces a long

---

111. Ali and Serrano, "The Person of the Author," 570.

112. Ibid.

113. Ahmed, *What Is Islam?*, al-Hakim (79) and Mills (86). The only other women named in the main text of this chapter, save the Victoria in the Victoria and Albert Museum (64), are the literary characters Layla and Zulaykha. However, the chapter is saturated with gendered and sexualized references that beg analysis. A quote mentions "virgin brides" for secret knowledge (23) and Ahmed discusses "the receptacle 'virgin-girls' of this material world" in Neoplatonic philosophy (56). A long quotation from Rumi includes the insult, "your sister's a whore!" which Ahmed avers is among the "occasional expletive[s]" we must forgive "Our Sovereign Master" (100).

quotation from "two of the leading historians of Islamic art." With her co-author Jonathan Bloom, Sheila Blair is named only in the footnote.[114]

Ahmed's habit of hyping only men's reputations extends beyond this chapter. Of the thirty-six women in his index, thirty-two are modern academics. (He introduces two others as the wives of important men. The remaining two are literary characters.[115]) None is described as eminent or distinguished or important or acclaimed, not even Patricia Crone or Wadad al-Qadi.[116] One cannot be properly shocked that he chose to forgo laudatory adjectives for Annemarie Schimmel when one is busy being shocked that she does not appear in the index at all. Although there are too many men listed to perform the same search for each, a random perusal of men's names in later chapters turns up various "distinguished" and "eminent" contemporary academics.[117] Like other authors discussed in this chapter, Ahmed extends to a subset of modern men the sort of honorifics he grants to historical Muslim men. In most of these books, the largely masculinized nature of ulama norms and practices goes unexplored. Authors lionize

114. Ahmed, *What Is Islam?*, Watt (6), Smith (7), von Grunebaum (7), Geertz (7), Sabra (14), Rahman (30), Chittick (42), Andrews (46), Grabar (87), and Blair and Bloom (47). The "Orientalist luminaries" Ahmed refers to are the sixteen men contributors to a volume von Grunebaum edited, *Unity and Variety in Muslim Civilization* (Chicago, IL: University of Chicago Press, 1955).

115. As part of an account of Saudi destruction of early Muslim sites, Ahmed mentions "what was suspected to be the house of the Prophet Muhammad's first wife, Khadijah bint Khuwaylid" (532–33). Qaya Sultan links her husband, the Ottoman "gentleman-traveler and litterateur" Evliya Çelebi, to her father, Sultan Murad IV (319). Neither they, nor so far as I can tell any other women, appear as historical actors or authors of anything other than modern scholarly work in the entire book.

116. I checked the main text on the pages listed in the index for each of these thirty-two women as well as the notes in the numerous cases where they were only mentioned there. *Nada.*

117. For instance, Bruce Lawrence is a "distinguished scholar" (172), Ahmed Karamustafa is an "eminent Muslim scholar" (137), and 'Abd al-'Aziz al-Duri is an "eminent historian" (458).

premodern figures, accepting and reinforcing their reputations as great scholars and thinkers, and valuing their activities and the texts they left. They and their legacies are explicitly signaled as important, classic, and masterful, casting a reflective glow over the men who study them today. Premodern men and their texts, and modern men and theirs, become the proper subject of Islamic studies, with implications for all analyses of being Islamic.

The attribution of prominence and stature to colleagues shapes the way they and their works are engaged.[118] As with the gendering of qualities such as rigor, difficulty, and empathy, notions such as importance and seniority tend to be coded masculine and applied to men. Novelist and essayist Ursula K. Le Guin writes that "greatness, in the sense of outstanding or unique accomplishment, is a cryptogendered word." Unless otherwise modified, it presumes masculinity and, often, whiteness.[119] One can "regender" *great* by applying it specifically to a woman or "degender" it by making explicit its application to people of all genders. Otherwise, LeGuin notes, "greatness in the abstract, in general, is still thought of as the province of men."[120] The same holds for *intellectual* and *thinker*.[121] (It is unsurprising that the two works with "intellectual history" in their titles are among those that attend least to specific women in their narratives.) The qualities that make for *great* scholarship

118. Ali and Serrano, "The Person of the Author," 570–71, drawing on Menegatti and Rubini, "Gender Bias and Sexism in Language."

119. On the gendered and racialized nature of descriptive terms used for scholars, see Daniel Storage, Zachary Horne, Andrei Cimpian, and Sara-Jane Leslie, "The Frequency of 'Brilliant' and 'Genius' in Teaching Evaluations Predicts the Representation of Women and African Americans across Fields," *PLOS ONE* 11:3, 2016, https://doi.org/10.1371/journal.pone.0150194. See also Baker, "Ban Brilliance," in *Sexism Ed,* 36–40.

120. Ursula K. Le Guin, *No Time to Spare: Thinking About What Matters* (Boston: Houghton Mifflin Harcourt, 2017), 70.

121. See Ali and Serrano, "The Person of the Author," 566–67. There are exceptions. For instance, Brown refers to wadud as an "American Muslim intellectual" (*Misquoting Muhammad,* 271) and Ware terms Aisha "one of the early Muslim community's most important intellectuals" (*The Walking Qur'an,* 7).

are understood as masculine: rigor, objectivity, and expertise. Culturally, all are considered the province of (usually white) outsiders and/or men.[122] All of this helps explain why some Muslim men's expertise is acknowledged, as is that of some white, usually non-Muslim, women. It also explains why Muslim women scholars, especially Black scholars or scholars of color, are so rarely treated as experts, except sometimes on lived religious experience, and often only their own. Men routinely treat other men's ideas as worthy of careful engagement, even if they disagree with their premises or methods, but seldom accord women, especially Muslim women and/or feminist scholars, the same consideration.

As Serrano and I argue in our study of book reviews, these "habits of gendered rhetorical deference further entrench professional sexism." By consistently nodding to other men's importance and achievements, in addition to citing their work, scholars reinforce the expectation that some people should be taken seriously and their ideas, even if objectionable, reckoned with. There are personal career costs borne by those who go uncited, and intellectual harms to the field, but also diffuse effects on the general climate in which Islamic studies scholars work: "Although one cannot draw a direct causal relationship between regular invocation of men's importance and pervasive impunity for gendered, sexual, and racist harassment and abuse, the well-documented instances of powerful male academics getting away with bad behavior undoubtedly owes something to others' calculations of their professional standing."[123]

In sum, though there is variation among them, these recent books largely reinscribe male authority. Ware's *The Walking Qur'an* fairly reflects its sources, engaging gender and acknowledging women publications appropriately, but naming fewer women

122. On this point, see Chaudhry, "Islamic Legal Studies."
123. Ali and Serrano, "The Person of the Author," 574. We draw from Mansfield et al., "It's Time to Recognize How Men's Careers Benefit from Sexually Harassing Women in Academia."

given its archival materials. The same is true to a lesser extent for Kane's treatment of modern Senegal and An-Na'im's account of American Muslim life. Typically, however, these works cite women's scholarship in ways that diminish their authority: relegating authors' names to the notes (even if, as in Rumee Ahmed's case, they are generously represented there), framing them as lesser contributions than they are, or failing to engage their core ideas. Still others downplay or ignore the relevance of women actors and gender to their topics. Some, as in Donner's survey chapter, make women's issues a centerpiece of their analysis while failing to engage relevant scholarship by women.

If these books' contents mostly shore up male authority quietly, their paratexts proclaim it loudly.[124] Cover blurbs aim to persuade readers of a book's importance. Editors seek them from scholars with appropriate expertise and desirable cachet. Of the eight books that carry endorsements, six offer only men's, two or three or four. Two include one woman's endorsement alongside two from men. Of twenty-four endorsements spread over eight books, just two are from women. Only one of the two is a scholar of religion: Leila Ahmed, who literally wrote the book on women and gender in Islam.

---

124. Most of these books lack a foreword, but the one to *Misquoting Muhammad* declares Brown "the foremost scholar of the Hadith" and uses the word "rigorous" twice in five lines to describe his work. Omid Safi, "Foreword," in Brown, *Misquoting Muhammad*, xiii–xiv at xiv.

Q: Why did the worker quit her job crushing cans?
A: Because it was soda pressing.

YOU KNOW WHAT ELSE IS DEPRESSING? The "Navigating Differences" statement released in May 2023 by dozens of overwhelmingly male, mostly American clergy along with a handful of academics offering what they call a "collective, non-partisan articulation of Islam's position on sexual and gender ethics."[1] Parroting right-wing and white evangelical Christian talking points about "LGBTQ ideology," its authors position themselves as a beleaguered minority whose religious freedom is under threat. The statement, which others have critiqued in detail, is a curious mix of vicious and vacuous, at once breathtakingly overconfident and deeply anxious.[2] Despite being intellectually risible, its loud silences are revealing about the ways the gender politics of academic Islamic studies intersect with those of American Muslim communities, attesting to the impact of Muslim feminist thought while demonstrating a persistent refusal to engage it.

At the most basic level, "Navigating Differences" illustrates how religion functions as a system for gendering. It attempts to recruit the magical power of *Islam says* to cudgel folks back into line.

1. All quotations, unless otherwise noted, are from the statement "Navigating Differences: Clarifying Sexual and Gender Ethics in Islam," posted at www.navigatingdifferences.com. Emphasis sometimes added.

2. See, e.g., Magda Mohamed, "Muslim Preachers and the New American Boogeyman: A Reaction to the Open Letter," May 24, 2023, https://magdagrams.substack.com/p/muslim-preachers-and-the-new-american, and Su'ad Abdul Khabeer, "Dr. Su'ad on Navigating Differences," https://www.canva.com/design/DAFkVwsizwI/LLF3Mn-14wH71F6aal7gdA/view.

Setting aside any other signatories for a moment, those who teach at universities should know better than to offer an assertion about "Islam's position on" pretty much anything other than monotheism.[3] It's doubtful any would accept such pabulum from their Intro to Islam students. But they cosign it here (even if nearly all use alternative affiliations instead of the institutions that employ them) because it covers a multitude of sins—or tries to. Just one missing word destabilizes the foundations of the entire edifice.

The first sentence under the subheading "Islam's Position on Sexuality and Gender" declares: "By a decree from God, sexual relations are permitted within the bounds of marriage, and marriage can only occur between a man and a woman." That sentence is built around an omission. On first reading, my mind automatically supplied the missing word: *only*. Its appearance in the concluding clause, "marriage can *only* occur between a man and a woman," leads the reader to assume its presence in the preceding clause: "sexual relations are" *only* "permitted within the bounds of marriage." But it isn't there. It isn't there even though its absence leaves a logical gap a mile wide. Sexual relations being "permitted *within* the bounds of marriage" says nothing about the whole wide world of *outside* of marriage. I can only speculate that the authors trust, or perhaps desperately hope, that readers won't notice the absence. Because, of course, marriage has not historically been the *only* way "sexual relations are permitted."

The signatories to this statement, who identify as "Muslim scholars and preachers," cannot affirm that "by a decree from God" sexual relations are *only* permitted within the bounds of marriage without traducing Qur'an, hadith, prophetic precedent, and "a chain of scholarly tradition spanning fourteen centuries." All those texts and all those scholars and the reported practice of the beloved Prophet

3. On similar generalizations in the "Open Letter to Baghdadi," see Kecia Ali, "Redeeming Slavery: The 'Islamic State' and the Quest for Islamic Morality," *Mizan: Journal for the Study of Muslim Societies and Civilizations*, 1:1, 2016: 41–66 at 47–49, 53.

treat sex with enslaved concubines as a permissible practice not "within" but without "the bounds of marriage."

Clearly aware of the loophole in their opening salvo, a few sentences later they try to close it with another grand pronouncement: "Moreover, premarital and extramarital sexual acts are prohibited in Islam." But if all "premarital and extramarital sexual acts are prohibited" then it necessarily follows that *only* marital sexual acts are permitted. The obvious and elegant solution would have been to put *only* in the earlier sentence and cut this one entirely. The fact that this sentence even exists attests to the gravitational pull of the missing *only*. This clumsy attempt to backfill the black hole points to the fundamental flaw in the drafters' method.

Since the authors cannot honestly claim that "by a decree from God" sexual relations are *only* permitted within the bounds of marriage, they silently differentiate between what is established "by a decree from God" and what is simply "prohibited in Islam." Presumably, the historical and geopolitical shifts that have led to abolition worldwide, the treaties and constitutions outlawing slavery, and the seismic shifts in the views of modern scholars on the subject mean the signatories consider the matter settled. Now that slavery is no longer legal, sex with enslaved women is no longer legal. Hence, it can be glossed over in silence, praying no one will notice. It suffices to proclaim that "premarital and extramarital sexual acts are prohibited in Islam."

I say "presumably" because the authors of this statement conceal their reasoning. They do not offer it for readers' evaluation. They do not allude at all—and who can blame them?—to the resurgent practice of and justifications for capture and enslavement by various Muslim groups.[4] They do not proclaim a modern consensus.

---

4. Most obviously, the Islamic State, but also Boko Haram and the Taliban. See Chapter 3 and sources cited there. On enslavement by Muslims of Muslims in Sudan, see Mende Nazer with Bernadette Brooten, "Epilogue," in Bernadette Brooten, ed., *Beyond Slavery: Overcoming its Religious and Sexual Legacies* (New York: Palgrave Macmillan, 2010), 309–318.

They do not reassure readers that their authorities have things well in hand. They fear that even the mere mention of concubinage, the third rail of Muslim conversations on sexual ethics, would allow a feminist foot in the door.

It's too late, though. The logical contortions in this statement are necessary precisely because of the conversation-changing work that Muslim feminists and other scholars and reformers have done. Scrambling to reclaim their lost authority and assert their monopoly over what *Islam says*, the authors of "Navigating Differences" unwillingly grant the basic premise of the progressive approach they deplore. By distinguishing between what is established "by a decree from God" and what is decided by human beings living in historically varied circumstances ("prohibited in Islam"), they tacitly acknowledge that people make rules and that those rules change as society changes. However grudgingly, they admit that Islam is capacious enough to allow Muslims' interpretation and implementation of divine guidance to shift.

Navigating gingerly around a plain fact of the tradition they claim to uphold, the signatories to this tiresome statement cannot bring themselves to discuss difficult parts of Muslim texts and histories with honesty and transparency. They avoid the substantial writing and thinking that others have done to engage the tradition as a resource for addressing complex contemporary realities. In this, they are like the academic men who center gender and sexuality while assiduously ignoring the substantive work that those not of their persuasion have already done. Their responses are shaped around unspoken, unspeakable omissions. Like an empty can, their proclamations ring hollow.

3

Representing Islamic Studies

In the first section of this chapter, I reproduce verbatim a few vile words directed at me and discuss other ugly and threatening messages. The content may be upsetting or jarring, hence this cautionary note, but I suspect it will be sadly familiar to too many of my colleagues.

IN 2015, INVESTIGATIVE JOURNALIST Rukmini Callimachi published a major story in *The New York Times* on Islamic State enslavement of Yazidi women and girls, in which she argued that IS promulgated a "theology of rape."[1] I was one of her sources. During our conversation, I spoke at length about the presence of slavery in Islamic scripture and law as well as its varied manifestations in Muslim-majority societies of the past, making clear that slavery has an undeniable presence in Muslim texts and history. I acknowledged the Islamic State's grounding in a particular reading of the tradition. (Using both English-language propaganda and Arabic legal texts produced by the Islamic State, I had argued in

1. Rukmini Callimachi, "ISIS Enshrines a Theology of Rape," August 14, 2015, https://www.nytimes.com/2015/08/14/world/middleeast/isis-enshrines-a -theology-of-rape.html. A later project of Callimachi's was found lacking in reportorial safeguards. See David Folkenflik, "'New York Times' Retracts Core of Hit Podcast Series 'Caliphate' on ISIS," December 18, 2020, https://www.npr.org/2020/12 /18/944594193/new-york-times-retracts-hit-podcast-series-caliphate-on-isis -executioner.

talks and an article in progress that they were attempting to justify enslavement and concubinage as "religiously legitimate—not just permissible but actively good—a triumphalist reflection of the Islamic State's authority, its enactment of a continuous Muslim legal tradition, and a proving ground for the moral improvement of its adherents."[2]) I also pointed out the range of ways contemporary Muslims engage slavery, objecting to the widespread tendency to treat Muslim thought on slavery as monolithic and unchanging. I followed up the conversation by sending her some of my related publications.[3]

When it appeared, Callimachi's story left out my references to slavery in scripture, prophetic conduct, and Muslim history, citing only my observation, by which I stand, that there wasn't anything particularly religious about early Muslims' practice of slavery, which was consonant with widespread norms of the era and region. Also absent was my criticism of the double standard applied to Islam and Muslims. Even though slavery is present in the Bible and in the past of many Christian-majority societies, including the United States, few would assert that slavery is inextricable from Christianity. Should anyone do so, *The New York Times* would quite sensibly refuse to take their claim at face value.

Without ever misquoting me, the published story misled as to the tenor of my remarks. It cast me in the role of a credulous defender of Islam and featured a rebuttal to my seemingly naïve

2. Ali, "Redeeming Slavery," 41. The final published version's discussion of media tropes of Muslim women's oppression and Muslim men's oppressiveness analyzes Callimachi's treatment of the topic (44).

3. I sent Callimachi my Feminism and Religion blog post "ISIS and Authority" from earlier that year (http://feminismandreligion.com/2015/02/24/isis-and -authority-by-kecia-ali/) and "'What your right hands possess': Slave Concubinage in Muslim Texts and Discourses," in *Sexual Ethics and Islam*, 39–55, with the then-forthcoming updated coda on contemporary Muslim discourses, including that of the Islamic State, on slavery and concubinage. See Kecia Ali, "Coda 3," in *Sexual Ethics and Islam: Feminist Reflections on Qur'an, Hadith, and Jurisprudence*, 2nd edition (London: Oneworld, 2016), 67–71.

stance from a white, male, non-Muslim doctoral student at Princeton University, introduced as "a scholar of Islamic theology." I was at the time a tenured professor who had published four single-authored books about Islam, in which I had made the very points that Callimachi attributed to him, including that the Qur'an repeatedly mentions enslaved women (a subject of my first book) and that Islamic jurisprudence accepts and regulates slavery (the topic of my second book).

Hoping to set the record straight, I agreed to write a follow-up story for *The Huffington Post*.[4] My essay, despite a sensationalized title added by the editor, was blandly factual about the diverse practices of enslavement, slaveholding, and manumission in Muslim societies of the distant and recent past. My objective was not, and never has been, to minimize the presence of slavery in Muslim scripture and history—to the contrary, in fact. But I refused to essentialize Islam, reducing a vast array of ideas and practices to a supposedly universal and unchanging norm, or to treat the tradition and its adherents differently from other religions and their practitioners. Because I wanted readers to think comparatively and comprehensively about interconnected forms of violence, I concluded by situating the Islamic State rape of Yazidi women and girls in a region badly destabilized by U.S. intervention and occupation.[5]

I didn't read the comments. They found me anyway. Over the years, my work has periodically generated a handful of ugly emails and letters, a smattering of vicious tweets, and the occasional vituperative voice mail. A steady drip of noxious messages had begun after the *New York Times* story. I thought my historically

4. Kecia Ali, "The Truth about Islam and Sex Slavery History Is More Complicated Than You Think," *The Huffington Post*, August 19, 2015, https://www .huffingtonpost.com/kecia-ali/islam-sex-slavery_b_8004824.html.

5. As Wendy Hesford and Amy Shuman note, depictions of Islamic State rape of Yazidis do "cultural and political work." "Precarious Narratives: Media Accounts of Islamic State Sexual Violence," in Wendy S. Hesford, Adela C. Licona, and Christa Teston, eds., *Precarious Rhetorics* (Columbus: The Ohio State University Press, 2017), 41–61 at 44.

grounded, evidence-based *Huffington Post* piece would provide nuance and calm things down. Was I wrong! On blogs and in social media posts, prominent anti-Muslim polemicists accused me of blaming America for the Islamic State's practice of sex slavery. They and their followers deemed me an apologist for rape and enslavement. The reaction ramped up. I was a "liberal piece of shit," said one message. An email referred to my "vermin-riddled cunt." In her study of online abuse and harassment, Sarah Sobieraj notes that crudely calling attention to women's bodies in digital spaces occurs precisely because our bodies are otherwise not present. These essentialized biological references "force gender into the conversation" and are "flailing attempts to reassert the centrality of gender difference—and the gender inequality that comes with it."[6] My inboxes and Twitter feed were saturated with virulent misogyny. At least half the commenters and callers suggested I deserved, or perhaps secretly desired, to become a sex slave or be raped by jihadists. One man proposed that I become his own sex slave.

For weeks, I waded through messages suggesting that the government should hand me over to the Islamic State, or that I should resign from my job, or that Boston University should fire me. I forwarded voice mails to a stalwart colleague who passed along the gist of anything important and deleted the vitriol. I had my institution's support, which is sadly not a given in the face of coordinated outrage campaigns. The volume of ugliness was comparatively low. Unlike San Francisco State University professor Rabab Ibrahim Abdulhadi, whose advocacy for justice for Palestine has garnered repeated accusations of antisemitism, no one sued my institution seeking to get rid of me.[7] Unlike political scientist Larycia Hawkins,

6. Sarah Sobieraj, *Credible Threat: Attacks Against Women Online and the Future of Democracy* (New York: Oxford University Press, 2020), 18.

7. For the broad context of harassment, see Rabab Ibrahim Abdulhadi, "Foreword," to David Landy, Ronit Lentin, and Conor McCarthy, *Enforcing Silence: Academic Freedom, Palestine and the Criticism of Israel* (London: Zed Books, 2020), reproduced at https://mondoweiss.net/2020/06/enforcing-silence-in-the-academy/. On the lawsuit, see Rabab Ibrahim Abdulhadi, "The spirit of '68 lives on! Palestine advocacy

who was suspended by Wheaton College for a social media post in which she wore a hijab and expressed ecumenical solidarity with Muslims, I faced no professional repercussions for my views.[8] Unlike Rutgers University professor Audrey Truschke, who has been repeatedly targeted by Hindutva trolls for her historical scholarship on religion in South Asia, I got no explicit rape or death threats.[9] It was still miserable.[10]

and the indivisibility of justice," *Mondoweiss*, July 14, 2017, https://mondoweiss.net/2017/07/palestine-advocacy-indivisibility/.

8. There was considerable media coverage of the case. An interview with Hawkins provides her view of the situation, then still unresolved. Sandi Villarreal, "Dr. Larycia Hawkins on the 'Inquisition' at Wheaton and why she still wants to stay," *Sojourners*, January 26, 2016, https://sojo.net/articles/dr-larycia-hawkins-inquisition-wheaton-and-why-she-wants-stay.

9. Audrey Truschke, "Hate Male," *The Revealer*, July 14, 2020. https://therevealer.org/hate-male/. It doesn't count as a rape threat if they merely say you deserve to be raped. On downplaying violence, see Mary Beard, *Women and Power: A Manifesto* (New York: Liveright, 2018), 35 and Sobieraj, *Credible Threat*, 57–60. We say it's not that bad when it's actually terrible. Still, in relative terms, this wasn't *that* bad. See also Laurie Patton's discussion of having to classify in bureaucratic terms the severity of various types of correspondence concerning a faculty member at the center of a larger controversy. Laurie L. Patton, *Who Owns Religion? Scholars and Their Publics in the Late Twentieth Century* (Chicago, IL: University of Chicago Press, 2019), 1–2.

10. On the disparate costs of being visible, see Tressie McMillan Cottom, "Everything but the Burden: Publics, Public Scholarship, and Institutions," May 2015, https://tressiemc.com/uncategorized/everything-but-the-burden-publics-public-scholarship-and-institutions/. See also Baker, "Men Who Email Me," in *Sexism Ed*, 172–176, and Arlene Stein and Jessie Daniels, "The Perils of Going Public," in *Going Public: A Guide for Social Scientists* (Chicago, IL: University of Chicago Press, 2017), 139–161. For examples of more sustained and ugly campaigns, see Sobieraj, *Credible Threat*, on Gamergate. For a horrifying glimpse of Cambridge University professor Priyamvada Gopal's hate mail, see her "Dossier of White Hot Hatred," https://medium.com/@priyamvadagopal/the-dossier-of-white-hot-hatred-8d5cf0b64e9a. See also Beard, *Women and Power*, and Patricia A. Matthew, "Conclusion: Tweeting Diversity: Race and Tenure in the Age of Social Media," in Matthew, ed., *Written/Unwritten: Diversity and the Hidden Truths of Tenure* (Chapel Hill, NC: University of North Carolina Press, 2016), 241–260.

So, when the subject of public engagement came up on my Islamic studies listserv a few months later, I chimed in about the backlash to my attempt to engage a controversial topic, offered snippets of messages I had received, and noted that the whole experience made me less likely to talk to reporters on the record or write for broad popular audiences. The silence on the list about my message was itself revealing. Though I received a handful of supportive private replies from colleagues who were shocked (men) or dismayed (women and nonbinary people), not one of the hundreds of scholars on the list publicly acknowledged or engaged with my message. Later, when a tenured white male Muslim colleague came under fire for remarks about sexual slavery, listserv discussion raged for days. Certainly, Trump being in office altered the climate. But I suspect that the different reactions also owed to something else. By making public the sexualized misogyny directed at me—I'd repeated the bit about my cunt—I had violated an unspoken compact.[11] In her account of how misogyny works, Kate Manne points out that "shaming . . . results in a desire to sever the sightlines between the self and the other." "Victims of misogyny" are meant to feel ashamed. When we don't "try to hide or flee from exposure," others avert their eyes.[12]

Misogyny exists on a continuum and across multiple axes: the Islamic State's brutalities against women and girls, American media reliance on tropes of women's subjugation by Muslim men, disgusting gendered Islamophobic trolling and threats, and comparatively mild professional slights, including an unwillingness from colleagues to publicly acknowledge the toll of sexualized "digital toxicity."[13] Patriarchy is not undifferentiated. It is obviously

11. On whiteness and sexualized hate, see Truschke, "Hate Male"; Gopal, "Dossier of White Hot Hatred"; and Tressie McMillan Cottom, "'Who Do You Think You Are?': When Marginality Meets Academic Microcelebrity," *Ada: A Journal of Gender, New Media, and Technology*, No. 7, 2015. DOI: 10.7264/N3319T5T.

12. Manne, *Down Girl*, 121.

13. Sobieraj, *Credible Threat*, 97, 112.

not the same to be captured and repeatedly raped as to be told one deserves to be taken captive and repeatedly raped. Nonetheless, the latter has a chilling effect.

Islamic studies scholars who write, teach, or speak publicly about sex and violence must address real injustices perpetrated in the name of Islam, such as the rape of Yazidi women and girls, while refusing the racist stereotype of Muslim men as backward brutes and rejecting depictions of Islam as a uniquely oppressive tradition. At the same time, we must also reject the wishful insistence that Islamic State soldiers are simply not real Muslims. It is a tricky line to tread. Condemning bad behavior becomes proof of Muslim depravity, while offering interpretive context, as I attempted to do with the Islamic State's violence, becomes blameworthy apologetics. One can condemn the horrors IS adherents perpetrate *and* analyze how IS rapists and propagandists justify themselves with scriptural texts *and* situate those interpretations historically *and* contextualize them within a range of contemporary Muslim perspectives *and* consider how widespread journalistic depictions of Muslim barbarity play a role in dehumanizing stereotypes that justify military intervention and inhumane sanctions that have killed thousands upon thousands of Middle Eastern Muslims *and* consider how academics' personal identities and institutional locations shape how their expertise is presented by journalists and received by audiences. But no one can do all those things simultaneously.

This chapter explores shifts over the past few decades in how scholars of Islam are expected to engage lay audiences; the central roles gendered myths and misinformation play in widespread stereotypes and anti-Muslim discourses; and the different opportunities for and stakes of popular engagement for scholars depending on their religion, race, and gender.[14] It accepts that engagement

14. Resources on anti-Muslim sentiment include Deepa Kumar, *Islamophobia and the Politics of Empire* (Chicago, IL: Haymarket Books, 2012); Juliane Hammer, "Center Stage: Gendered Islamophobia," in Carl Ernst, ed., *Islamophobia in America* (New

with broad publics is incredibly important yet argues that for scholars who are women and/or Muslim, the means for doing so are deeply dysfunctional, in ways that are shaped by and in turn shape other forms of professional bias and discrimination.

Feeding the media

Public scholarship and media engagement are increasingly expected as a complement to specialized scholarly publications in an array of disciplines and fields.[15] As the humanities are increasingly threatened, projects to demonstrate relevance, impact, and marketability have flowered. Religious studies is no exception. The Public Understanding of Religion project has become central to the activities of the American Academy of Religion. Sacred Writes, in which I participated in 2021, is a grant-funded program to teach media skills to religion scholars. As the pyramid scheme that is doctoral training has become increasingly unstable, the idea of applied religious studies has gained ground as a way of imagining practical career paths outside the academic humanities.

These are not the only shifts, however. Laurie Patton describes new patterns of engagement and readership for religion scholarship from the late 1980s to the mid-1990s. These changes, welcome in some respects, have also brought new difficulties. Sometimes, academic approaches to religious traditions offend members of communities under study, who object to things published in specialized books for which they were not the intended audience.[16] Community members, sometimes backed by religious authorities or organizations, have taken issue with scholars' seemingly scandalous or

---

York: Palgrave, 2013), 107–144; and, on the rapid and coordinated spread of hate-filled discourses in the decade after 9/11, Christopher Bail, *Terrified: How Anti-Muslim Fringe Organizations Became Mainstream* (Princeton, NJ: Princeton University Press, 2014).

15. See, e.g., Nzinga, *Lean Semesters*, 43–45.

16. Patton, *Who Owns Religion?*.

theologically challenging presentations of their traditions. Tazim Kassam found herself mired in unexpected controversy for her portrayal of Ismaili sacred texts and their relationship to that community's—*her* community's—history and doctrine. A Muslim scholar getting pushback from other Muslims about her work carried out under the aegis of the secular academy illustrated the complex necessary "balancing acts" (Kassam's words) for scholars who belong to the communities they study.[17]

These dynamics are even trickier when the community in question is under heavy scrutiny, as Muslims have been after 9/11. At a time when an increasingly significant proportion of Islamic studies faculty was Muslim, September 11 intensified the expectation that scholars of Islam would engage various publics.[18] In the immediate aftermath of the attacks, scholars from all backgrounds fielded endless requests for interviews, sound bites, op eds, community forums, church presentations, and classroom visits. The very boring topic was, usually, "Why do they hate us?" The equally boring follow-up was, often implicitly and sometimes explicitly, "Why do they hate women?"[19] Teacher trainings were more meta: "How do we respond when our students ask, 'Why do they hate us? Why do they hate women?'"

Western public fascination with Muslim women's supposed oppression has a long history.[20] Since at least the 1979 Iranian

17. Tazim R. Kassam, "Balancing Acts: Negotiating the Ethics of Scholarship and Identity," in José Cabezon and Sheila Davaney, eds., *Identity and the Politics of Scholarship in the Study of Religion* (New York: Routledge, 2004), 133–162.

18. Morgenstein Fuerst, "Writing, Doing, and Performing Islamic Studies," 242, drawing on Ilyse R. Morgenstein Fuerst and Zahra M. S. Ayubi, "Shifting Boundaries: The Study of Islam in the Humanities," *The Muslim World*, 106:4, 2016, 643–654.

19. Although it ostensibly treats religion(s) broadly, Ophelia Benson and Jeremy Stangroom's *Does God Hate Women?* (London: Continuum, 2009) makes Islam and Muslims a central focus. Plenty of people think this is the right approach. The top review on Amazon as of July 4, 2023 gives the book five stars and observes: "the focus is primarily on Islam, and rightfully so." BooksJJC, "It's About Time," December 3, 2009.

20. Deeb and Winegar make a similar point about Islamophobic commentary in general. *Anthropology's Politics*, 19.

revolution, when the American public's eye turned toward Muslim women as a category, the fascination has been with sensationalized accounts of oppression.[21] These stereotypes gained new vitality after 9/11. Laura Bush's appeal to Afghan women's suffering to justify American invasion was only the tip of a very large missile.

Muslim women's hypervisibility, the discursive centrality of gender to popular discourses about Islam, and the presumed centrality of Islam to Muslim women's experience created a perfect storm. With Muslims, media tend to play up the religious dimensions of political and social questions. Every question becomes an Islam question, and many Islam questions become woman questions. I've been asked to explain South Asian American women's hesitancy around using daycare and Egyptian women's participation in the Cairo protests of early 2011 with reference to women's status in Islam. In the face of presumptions to the contrary, a key part of my job has been to explain that Islam does not explain everything.

Although aware of the need to counter widespread animus toward Muslims, many scholars of Islam trained in religious studies have understandably found it difficult to parrot formulas like "Islam means peace" or "the real jihad is the inner spiritual struggle" that politicians and some community figures offered after 9/11.[22] As with the more recent talking point that Islamic State soldiers are not real Muslims, the reality is obviously more complicated. Moreover, some Muslim academics, ranging from then-junior scholars like me to mid-career and senior colleagues, recognized

21. While the book would not appear until 1987, Betty Mahmoody's *Not Without My Daughter* is the classic example of what Abu-Lughod (*Do Muslim Women Need Saving?*) calls "pulp nonfiction." See also Megan Goodwin, "Abusing Religion: Race, Islam, and Not Without My Daughter," *The Revealer*, May 29, 2019.

22. A brief bump in sympathy for Muslims, prompted in part by coordinated anodyne messaging in mainstream media outlets, didn't last. Things soon got bad and have kept getting worse. See Brigette L. Nacos and Oscar Torres-Reyna, *Fueling Our Fears: Stereotyping, Media Coverage, and Public Opinion of Muslim Americans* (Lanham, MD: Rowman and Littlefield, 2007) and Bail, *Terrified*.

poisonous elements in our own community even as we objected to deadly and misdirected military campaigns overseas. Progressive Muslims, for lack of a better term, aimed to resist imperialist violence against Muslims while confronting and transforming ugliness within their (our) own texts and communities.[23]

Critiquing elements of one's community and tradition is loaded when audiences are so primed to believe the worst about Islam and Muslims. How can one condemn specific injustices without reinforcing negative ideas about Muslims, often hinging on women, gender, and sexuality? Leila Ahmed pointed out the problem in the early 1980s. Initially baffled by the apologetic presentations by Muslim women at the National Women's Studies Association panel on "Islam and Feminism," she came to understand their words as refusals of complicity with racist and colonialist depictions of Islamic oppression.[24] At the same time, she insisted on the urgent imperative for Arab/Middle Eastern/Muslim feminists to be able to grapple with patriarchy in their own cultures and societies.

Similar dynamics still shape public engagement on Muslims and Islam, as I found in my attempts to discuss slavery. Acknowledging that, as in Christianity, Islamic religious texts and the interpretive tradition and Muslim practice historically accepted slavery is both a requirement of intellectual honesty and a prerequisite of reckoning theologically with its implications for Muslim belief and politically with its resurgence among actors such as the Islamic State, the Taliban, and Boko Haram. Such statements, though, can be weaponized by anti-Muslim polemicists. Given how often, and in what ways, Islam and Muslims are in the news,

23. See Omid Safi, ed., *Progressive Muslims: On Justice, Gender, and Pluralism* (Oxford: Oneworld, 2003).

24. Leila Ahmed, "Encounter with American Feminism: A Muslim Woman's View of Two Conferences," *Women's Studies Newsletter* 8:3, 1980: 7–9 and Leila Ahmed, "Western Ethnocentrism and Perceptions of the Harem," *Feminist Studies* 8:3, 1982: 521–534.

a good portion of what we do as scholars is shaped by the imperative to respond.[25]

We have not escaped the predicament Ahmed signaled decades ago. In critiquing patriarchal elements of Muslim texts, history, and life, we chance reinforcing ugly anti-Muslim stereotypes about Muslim women's oppression. But the anti-imperialist project of pushing back against harmful stereotypes cannot be allowed to subsume or squash indigenous Muslim struggles against patriarchal violence or to prevent transnational solidarity among feminists. As Rochelle Terman has argued, we must refuse to "naturaliz[e] the double bind between Islamophobia and gender injustice."[26]

Locating speech

Just as it matters where critique comes from, it matters who gets to address audiences on topics related to Islam in general and Islam and gender in particular. Who we are and where we are located institutionally shapes both which invitations we get and how what we say is received. Annemarie Schimmel eventually became fed up with people asking her how she, as a woman, could study Muslims, with implicit assumptions about how "they" treat women.[27] For Muslims, the questions can be even more pointed, especially as carefully orchestrated anti-Muslim propaganda with gender at the center has become ever more prominent.[28] Five years after 9/11, amina wadud wrote: "Discourses about the multifaceted aspects of gender in Islam . . . are fraught with personal

25. Morgenstein Fuerst, "Writing, Doing, and Performing the Future of Islamic Studies," 251.

26. Rochelle Terman, "Islamophobia, Feminism and the Politics of Critique," *Theory, Culture & Society*, 33:2, 2016: 77–102 at 77.

27. Schimmel, "A Life of Learning," 13.

28. See Hammer, "Center Stage," and Megan Goodwin, "Gender, Race, and American Islamophobia," in Justine Howe, ed., *The Routledge Handbook of Islam and Gender*, 463–474.

consequences for Muslim scholars, activists, and the real lives of all Muslim women."[29] University settings, community events, and public forums each carry distinctive norms and bring specific risks for Muslim scholars, especially Muslim women of color. Having a diverse array of participants in discussions of Islam, women, and gender is vital—but the high, and highly unequal, costs of participation result in some scholars' regrettable but understandable withdrawal from many conversations.[30] As Truschke writes, "layered sexism is something experienced to varying degrees by most female academics. Gendered hate harms not only the women targeted but the academy as a whole. If historians, religious studies scholars, and other humanities professors are going to share their expertise with the public in the social media age—and I think we should—then we need to talk about the hate that this earns some women and how it echoes through the sexism that continues to pervade the academy."[31]

Sexism, however, is not the only form of discrimination Muslim women confront. Muslim women must contend with demonization of Muslims or gross overgeneralizations and oversimplifications, even from sympathetic outsiders.[32] Purveyors of condescension

29. Wadud, *Inside the Gender Jihad*, 56.

30. Sobieraj finds that "women assess whether they are 'up to' the toxic backlash that might result from their participation" (*Credible Threat*, 71; similarly, 116). Social media and other online venues are vital yet both "unpredictable" and "threatening" (80). Dealing with the preemptive and post-facto labor required to navigate them is "a draining response to an already exhausting problem" (81). Women minimize potential harassment in part by being very selective about public speaking (119–130). Some of the opportunities I have declined because of potential blowback are speaking on the record to a *New York Times* reporter, appearing on a nationally syndicated television talk show, appearing on a nationally syndicated radio show, and being the subject of a *Chronicle of Higher Education* profile. Like one of Sobieraj's informants, I aim "to be visible enough to influence the conversation but private enough to avoid becoming a target" (121).

31. Truschke, "Hate Male."

32. Namira Islam, "Soft Islamophobia," *Religions*, 9:9, 2018, https://doi.org/10.3390/rel9090280.

include prominent white feminist thinkers. Take Rebecca Solnit's now-classic essay "Men Explain Things to Me." It begins comically, with a man at a party cluelessly lecturing Solnit on her own book. Solnit explains compellingly how "what starts out as minor social misery can expand into violent silencing and even violent death."[33] Yet Solnit's derisive offhand reference to "those Middle Eastern countries where women's testimony has no legal standing" as "more extreme versions of our situation" should occasion a pause.[34] She does not specifically single out Muslims. That would be bad form. Not naming countries, though, suggests that the character-ization applies widely. The culturally powerful conflation of the Middle East with Islam means that her generalization feeds into pernicious stereotypes. For those of us who study Islam and Mus-lims, describing, analyzing, and condemning patriarchal laws and practices in the communities we study and to which some of us belong risks further entrenching the widespread perception that Islam is, if not uniquely oppressive to women, then at least worse than "our situation."

These ideas are widespread. Mary Beard prefaces her critique of durable Western misogyny in *Women and Power* with an implicit contrast with Others: "Women in the West have a lot to celebrate; let's not forget."[35] Lest one miss the point, she later writes, "strik-ingly, the Saudi Arabian National Council has a higher proportion of women than the US Congress."[36] Beard presumes, and assumes

33. Rebecca Solnit, "Men Still Explain Things to Me," *The Nation*, August 20, 2012, https://www.thenation.com/article/archive/men-still-explain-things-me/. On ig-noring women's words, see also Leigh Gilmore, *Tainted Witness: Why We Doubt What Women Say about Their Lives* (New York: Columbia University Press, 2017).

34. Rebecca Solnit, *Men Explain Things to Me* (Chicago, IL: Haymarket Books, 2015), 6. In "Men Still Explain Things to Me," published four years after the book's titular essay, Solnit foregrounds the terrible toll of domestic violence and murder on American women before noting the attacks on women in Tahrir Square during Egypt's uprising.

35. Beard, *Women and Power*, ix.

36. Ibid., 84–85.

her audience will share her presumption, that Saudi (again: Arab/ Middle Eastern/Muslim) women are oppressed relative to American women. One must take this hierarchy for granted to see its reversal as striking.

Scholars of Islam and gender have long rejected facile dichotomies of liberation versus oppression, but refusing the established terms of debate is easier said than done outside of specialist contexts.[37] When it comes to conversations for lay publics or even for colleagues in adjacent fields, things remain fairly dire. It is less a matter of bad communication and more a matter of entrenched, continually bolstered oversimplifications. The audience member at my talk who muddled the authorship of Sachiko Murata's *The Tao of Islam* was advocating the flip side of the binary West = good, Islam = bad. But that opposition must be rejected, along with the casual anti-Muslim hierarchies that white feminists reflexively offer.

Muslim academics who address tricky topics must maneuver carefully, especially when they deliberately address varied audiences. For those who write and speak about the tradition as insiders, as I sometimes do, the complications multiply. Significant attention has been paid to the way racialized groups who "look" Muslim have been caught up in the anti-Muslim hostility that followed 9/11.[38] Muslim women who cover their heads routinely must navigate a variety of responses to their appearance, often ignorant or hostile or both. As a white woman who rarely wears a headscarf, I am not visibly Muslim. But my name, the primary way that readers encounter me, advertises a religious identity insofar as it "sounds" Muslim.[39] Over and apart from the question of how

37. Judith Tucker, "Pensée 2: We've Come a Long Way, Baby—But We've Got a Long Way to Go," *International Journal of Middle East Studies*, 40:1, 2008: 19–21.

38. Aparajita De, ed., *South Asian Racialization and Belonging after 9/11: Masks of Threat* (Lanham, MD: Lexington Books, 2016).

39. The Aziz Foundation, "The Racialization of Muslim Sounding Names," January 2021, https://www.azizfoundation.org.uk/wp-content/uploads/2021/01/Bridge -Report-Muslim-sounding-names.pdf. The matter is muddier since my first name "sounds" Black to some and is mistaken for Turkish by others. Marcia Hermansen

I express my commitments in my writing or acknowledge them in the classroom, my name indicates something about me. My surname authenticates me as a Muslim, allowing people to presume to know my identity and to respond accordingly, in ways shaped by their own location.

Certainly, some Muslim academics, especially feminists, garner criticism from conservative co-religionists for our purportedly wayward, incorrect, or dangerous ideas. I have received scolding emails after public university lectures on Muhammad's biographies and other topics. In my social media years, I maintained active mute and block lists on Twitter, where Muslim men have occasionally suggested that I should face punishment for blasphemy.[40] In a similar vein, women colleagues who publicly criticized the "Navigating Differences" statement received a deluge of hateful messages from followers of the celebrity shaykhs who supported and signed the statement.[41] (I was off Twitter by then.) But many if not most of the hateful responses to scholars of Islam come from white right-wingers, mostly men. Sometimes they decide that I am an illegitimate representative of the tradition and so discount my descriptive and historical presentation of Muslim slavery or prophetic biography or Islamic marriage law. Sometimes these outsiders to the Muslim tradition proclaim, loudly, that insiders will attack me for having progressive views or will not recognize me as one of them. Sometimes they gleefully announce

---

engages these issues from a slightly different perspective. She writes, "as a liberal Muslim, I don't look Muslim enough to fulfill the requirements of certain dialogue partners, who expect their female interlocutor to cover her head and to have an Arabic-sounding name, or be visibly 'Other' or different in some striking way." "Muslims in the Performative Mode: A Reflection on Muslim-Christian Dialogue," *The Muslim World*, 94:3, 2004: 387–396 at 387.

40. The punishment for blasphemy is typically understood to be execution. For a more nuanced account and varied perspectives, see Muhammad Khalid Masud, Kari Vogt, Lena Larsen, and Christian Moe, eds., *Freedom of Expression in Islam: Challenging Apostasy and Blasphemy Laws* (London: I.B. Tauris, 2021).

41. On the statement, see "Navigating Omissions," preceding this chapter.

that I will get what is coming to me, outsourcing to their supposed enemies, my barbaric coreligionists, the violence, including sexual violence, they adjudge appropriate.

Authorizing representatives

Such obnoxious responses have the merit of making clear the presumption that only some people are considered qualified to give an account of Islamic tradition and Muslim belief. Presenting anyone as an authority on Islam and Muslims means deciding what establishes authority. For some, that qualification is study with religious scholars and impeccable personal conduct (including, for women, appropriate apparel).[42] For others, it is the status of objective outsider with a university credential. All of these criteria are typically drawn and interpreted in ways that privilege men.

Who speaks about Islam and Muslims is a question partly about who gets invited to speak and partly about who gets heard. Non-Muslims with academic degrees often serve as sources *about* Islam and Muslims in mainstream media. Their lack of Muslim-ness supposedly grants objectivity. Where the presumption is that the person being interviewed or invited to speak will do so *on behalf of* Islam or Muslims, the qualification for speaking is less often scholarly credentials than perceived religious authority or authenticity. Those asked to represent Muslims are typically male, usually Middle Eastern or South Asian, and nearly always Sunni. Muslims who are Black, whether African American or African, are rarely included, likewise Southeast Asian or East Asian Muslims. Women of any race or ethnicity are seldom asked to speak on behalf of Muslim communities, but when they are, they are usually Middle Eastern or South Asian.[43] What Kayla Wheeler notes

42. Both Muslims and non-Muslims may also make unflattering and inaccurate assumptions about the intellectual and political views of women who cover their heads. See Siddiqui, "Good Scholarship/Bad Scholarship," 155.

43. As noted earlier, however, when Muslim women are involved in anthologies or conferences, white converts are disproportionately likely to be included.

about depictions holds also for invitations: "Struggles over who gets to represent Islam to the non-Muslim public are often rooted in anti-Blackness, with Black Muslim women bearing the brunt" of negative judgements.[44] The tendency to invite white "experts" or brown Sunni men echoes curricular emphases in Islamic studies that center the Arab-Sunni Middle East, stretching into South Asia (and also erasing long-standing Afro-Arab and Afro-Persian populations in those places), and puts men's voices, whether insiders or outsiders, front and center.

When religious authenticity or authority is a qualification for presenter, gender and race also play a role. In 2016, I was invited to chair and moderate a discussion at a California university on "Women, Equality, and Violence." It was one of a series of projected interreligious dialogues under the rubric of "Race, Faith, and Violence." The series was to be co-sponsored by the school's Humanities and Ethics center and its Catholic Institute, where the proposed panelists for the series were visiting scholars: a (male) Catholic priest, a (male) rabbi, and a (male) Muslim academic. I declined, noting my policy of not participating in a supplementary or cosmetic role in otherwise all-male panels. I added that it seemed particularly egregious to have no women as full partners in a discussion of women's equality. (Since none of the visiting scholars were Black, I also suggested that they reconsider the wisdom of holding their planned conversation on race with the same participants.) They replied that they *were* going to be including a woman: me. (They planned to ask an African American man to chair and moderate the race manel.) I would ask "hard hitting and uncomfortable" questions and, as the organizer told me when we spoke, "hold their feet to the fire." I persisted in my refusal. The proposed setup would reinforce the notion that men are experts while women are at best petitioners and suppliants, at worst

44. Kayla Wheeler, "On Centering Black Muslim Women in Critical Race Theory," https://themaydan.com/2020/02/on-centering-black-muslim-women-in-critical-race-theory/.

scolds and nags. All-male panels plague academia generally, as well as industry and government events. But here, the interfaith framing added a particular twist. The panelists would speak authoritatively about their traditions. I would lend the session credibility by virtue of my identity as much as any scholarly expertise: a person of gender for the gender panel.

A woman could have been among the clergy or clergy equivalents included in those trialogues. Although the mainstream Catholic Church's refusal to ordain women means any Catholic priest would be male, many women in religious orders have theology degrees and academic appointments. There are plenty of women rabbis and rabbi-equivalents. Muslims famously do not ordain, although some communities have more formalized structures of authority. Although some of my Muslim colleagues have formal or informal religious learning, the one involved in this ultimately abandoned endeavor did not. Numerous women colleagues have traditional training far outstripping his.[45] For a professor without traditional learning or religious credentials or pastoral experience to take the Muslim spot in the series on a university campus alongside a priest and a rabbi says that maleness, brownness, and Muslim identity suffice.

Similar qualifications often obtain for the Muslim commentarial class, unless the topic is women and gender, in which case certain women with distinctly negative perspectives on Islam gain the spotlight.[46] Sa'diyya Shaikh has addressed how some women

45. Within Muslim communities that welcome non-male scholars, gendered diminution of women's authority persists. While my men Muslim professor colleagues are typically "Dr. Lastname" in American Muslim community settings, Muslim women with advanced degrees and/or faculty positions are usually "Sister Firstname." (I do not object to Dr. or Prof. Firstname when used regardless of gender.) For some particularly blatant examples of gendered disparities in how speakers are presented, see Kecia Ali, "All Male Nonsense," *Feminism and Religion*, May 26, 2015, https://feminismandreligion.com/2015/05/26/all-male-nonsense-by-kecia-ali/.

46. Tarek El-Ariss explores the question of who gets to be an expert and set the media narrative in "The Making of an Expert: The Case of Irshad Manji," *The Muslim*

from Muslim backgrounds present themselves as authorities on Islam by virtue of personal experience. Mediagenic figures such as Irshad Manji and Ayaan Hirsi Ali offer "testimonials" that present "sweeping, generalized, and essentialist statements about Islam and Muslim societies." Shaikh agrees with Terman that concern over Islamophobia cannot be allowed to silence Muslim, or formerly Muslim, women's complaints and critiques, including those that depend on their individual experiences. "To be clear," Shaikh writes, "all women have the incontrovertible right to be critical of sexist practices within their societies and importantly to bring their experiences to bear on such critique." Neither the production nor the reception of these women's claims is innocent, though. For Shaikh, "invocations of experiences by native informers dubiously serving the interests of empire in the current political context demands more careful scrutiny."[47]

Troubling genres

For numerous reasons, including the prominence of these popular figures, the circulation and consumption of material on women, gender, sexuality, and Islam is a lot more complicated than it used to be. Of course, teaching undergraduates has always been different than addressing specialist colleagues at a conference. Speaking to or writing for laypeople has always required yet another register. How I teach differs from how I speak in an op-ed, from how I talk to the congregation at my mosque, from how I write for an audience of Islamic law specialists—or feminist colleagues in Jewish

---

World, 97:1, 2007: 93–110. See also Moustafa Bayoumi, "The God That Failed: The Neo-Orientalism of Today's Muslim Commentators," in *This Muslim American Life: Dispatches from the War on Terror* (New York: New York University Press, 2015), 99–117. We still lack a study of the thought and reception of figures such as Ayaan Hirsi Ali that takes gender seriously as an analytic lens alongside race and religion.

47. Sa'diyya Shaikh, "Feminism, Epistemology, and Experience," *Journal for Islamic Studies*, 33, 2013: 14–47 at 22.

studies. In religious studies classes, it makes sense to focus at length on the definition of religion and its modern history. For a religious audience with a loyalty to a particular version of the tradition, it makes sense to explore how today's popular notions about what is authoritative represent only a narrow slice of premodern perspectives. The same scholar can and must use different approaches. That is not new.

Now, though, less separates our university classes, our social media feeds, our email inboxes, our voice mails, and our community work. The pandemic only exacerbated existing fuzziness between work and home, and between the internet and IRL. Lines between and among public, semipublic, and private online spaces are blurrier than they used to be. Because things travel quickly and far, it is easier for them to be taken out of context. I'm not suggesting that we should try to establish impermeable demarcations between personal and professional spaces but rather insisting that we must address what it means that boundaries are so fluid, acknowledging that scholars are affected in different ways. We communicate with colleagues and students on social media; we consume and comment on and create media that bridge online and in-person venues. Digital technologies that make scholars' work accessible are a boon, especially given the increased institutional expectations for public communication and individual desires for participation in transformative community projects. But broader audiences can mean flattened discourses and, simultaneously, ramped-up responses.

One way to understand these dynamics is as "context collapse."[48] Previously, one might say one thing in a book for specialists and a different thing in a public lecture and yet a third thing in a tweet, recognizing genre differences and expecting different audiences. Now, one must contend, especially in the case of social media, with

---

48. On context collapse, mostly in the context of social media, see danah boyd, "how 'context collapse' was coined: my recollection," https://www.zephoria.org/thoughts/archives/2013/12/08/coining-context-collapse.html.

"concurrent multiple audiences."[49] An example from one's carefully contextualized scholarly writing on a difficult topic such as
slavery or sexual violence can be deployed by a bad-faith debater
as a gotcha to prove Muslim depravity (ask me how I know). Conversely, an outreach talk that avoids grim specifics may lead to the
accusation that one is glossing over ugly details to engage in apologetics (again, ask me how I know). Ilyse Morgenstein Fuerst and
Zahra Ayubi argue that given the "multitude of audiences that
Islamic studies scholars are responsible for addressing" there are
"a corresponding multitude of argumentative registers, timbres,
and trajectories for scholarly contribution."[50] Trouble arises when
work intended for one audience is judged, in good faith or otherwise, by standards appropriate to another.[51] At the same time,
although navigating different audiences requires differences in
emphasis, and varied venues shape the level of granularity with
which a topic is addressed, distortions and lies have no place. Propaganda is not public scholarship. Yet there are real consequences
to insisting on complexity, especially for those whom audiences
already view as less authoritative.[52]

49. Alice Marwick and danah boyd, "I tweet honestly, I tweet passionately: Twitter users, context collapse, and the imagined audience," *New Media & Society*, 13:1,
2010: 114–133 at 130.

50. Morgenstein Fuerst and Ayubi, "Shifting Boundaries" 648.

51. What Michelle Moravec observes in another context about citational practices
applies to all facets of Islamic studies scholars' public-facing work: "the claim that a
fixed and unwavering set of research practices unites academics is inaccurate. Vari-
ability exists; we simply accord some authors more latitude than others." Michelle
Moravec, "Embracing Amateurs: Four Practices to Subvert Academic Gatekeeping,"
Australian Feminist Studies, 36, 2021: 222–235 at 230.

52. Scholars, including some who foreground gender justice, have argued that
acknowledging the strength, power, wide reach, and persistence of misogynist interpretations, especially pointing to scriptural acceptance of gendered hierarchy, or
pointing out reductionist logics in some arguments for women's rights, weakens the
case for egalitarianism. One peer reviewer of an early manuscript for my *Marriage
and Slavery in Early Islam* thought my book "would appeal to those who continue to
see Islam, Islamic law, and women in Islam in Orientalist terms." It would allow

Gendered and racialized lenses determine to what extent our words and works are perceived as credible, let alone expert, and what kind of reaction they garner. In American culture broadly, women are often disregarded and disbelieved.[53] The likelihood women's accounts will result in opposition, whether by denial or harsh reprisals, rises when we are feminists, are gender-nonconforming in other ways, are from marginalized groups, and/or are working in spheres dominated by men.[54] Although online attacks can still be awful and disruptive, in academia as elsewhere, racial privilege and job security buffer sexism's effects.[55] As Sobieraj writes, "women who are marginalized not only receive more and qualitatively different digital pushback, but the content often feels (and *is*) more deeply threatening to them."[56] Because the same people who are disproportionately victimized are least likely to have the resources to pay the professional costs, "the most

---

"misogynist elements" among Muslims to interpret my primary sources "to demand women's obedience to husbands, their seclusion in the homes, and . . . see the existence of slave women as a positive Islamic step." Though this was "clearly not" my intent, my focus on jurists' normative discourse obscured how Muslim law as practiced often upheld women's rights and protected their interests; my source selection, the reviewer wrote, reinforced transactional and hierarchical norms of marriage while ignoring elements of Muslim tradition that stressed companionship and good relations. Others have argued that some Muslim feminist work on the Qur'an is counterproductive and even "anti-women" (see, e.g., Asma Barlas, "Secular and Feminist Critiques of the Qur'an: Anti-Hermeneutics as Liberation?," in "Round-table: Feminism and Islam: Exploring the Boundaries of Critique," *Journal of Feminist Studies in Religion*, 32:2, 2016: 111–121 at 113).

53. Miranda Fricker's concept of "testimonial injustice," which "occurs when prejudice causes a hearer to give a deflated level of credibility to a speaker's word," is helpful here. Fricker, *Epistemic Injustice: Power and the Ethics of Knowing* (Oxford: Oxford University Press, 2007), 1. Yung In Chae applies this concept to her field in "White People Explain Classics to Us," *Eidolon*, February 5, 2018, https://eidolon.pub/white-people-explain-classics-to-us-50ecaef5511. See also Gilmore, *Tainted Witness*.

54. Sobieraj, *Credible Threat*, 131.

55. Cottom, "Everything but the Burden."

56. Sobieraj, *Credible Threat*, 97. See also Matthew, "Conclusion," 251–5.

underrepresented voices and perspectives are likely to be the first pushed out."[57] The burden of hate falls unequally but we all pay the "epistemological costs of patterned exclusion."[58]

Although the risks and benefits of public-facing work are unequally distributed, our polarized, Islamophobic, and expertise-wary cultural climate affects Islamic studies scholars regardless of background.[59] Positionality is not just a matter of personal situation or identity. Far more than anyone's specialized scholarship, writing like my *Huffington Post* piece that attempts to respond to and participate in mainstream conversations confronts crucial challenges. My own failed attempts to work with a journalist to engage and provide nuance, and then to sidestep ubiquitous oppositional framing in a blog post, illustrate systemic constraints. How can one be responsible to the historical record while remaining attentive to the presumptions of an intended nonspecialist audience, especially when the engagement is likely to be brief? As I argue in the next chapter, although the classroom is challenging in other ways, it provides the setting for an extended encounter, and thus more grounds for transformative engagement.

57. Sobieraj, *Credible Threat*, 130.

58. Ibid., 135.

59. Morgenstein Fuerst, "Writing, Doing, and Performing," 243. Though the same expectations "affect Islamic studies faculty of color more than white colleagues in the same position," she argues that "*doing Islamic studies* already assumes labor that includes scholarship, service, administrative, and advisory work and that attends to geopolitical realities as they play out internationally, nationally, regionally, and on one's specific campus regardless of a faculty member's particular expertise."

ROE REVERSAL

AFTER TEXAS ENACTED DRACONIAN abortion restrictions in
2021, numerous left-leaning pundits and white feminists criticized
the ruling by likening its proponents to fanatical Muslims, with
epithets like Texas Taliban and Y'all Qaeda.[1] At the time, Sajida
Jalalzai—herself a Texan—wrote that "using Islam to critique the
abortion ban" obscures "the very religious, very Christian, and very
white roots of anti-choice movements in the United States."[2] Fear-
ing the same outcome, when the Dobbs v. Jackson opinion undo-
ing abortion rights at the national level was leaked weeks before the
final ruling, Ariana Afshar published an article in the progressive
online outlet *Truthout*. Its title pleads, "Stop Comparing Leaked
'Roe' Reversal to Sharia Law and Taliban's Rules."[3] No dice. After
the United States Supreme Court overturned Roe v. Wade in
June 2022, Barbra Streisand tweeted, "this Court is the American
Taliban," a comparison made by many others.[4] An image I saw

1. See, e.g., E. J. Montini, "Texas goes Taliban on abortion rights. Is Arizona next?,"
AZ Central, September 1, 2021, https://www.azcentral.com/story/opinion/op-ed/ej
-montini/2021/09/01/texas-abortion-law-supreme-court-arizona-next/5683457
001/ and https://www.reddit.com/r/yall_qaeda/.

2. Sajida Jalalzai, "Please Stop Using Islam to Critique the Abortion Ban: It Only
Excuses the Very Christian, Very White Roots of Anti-Choice Movements," *Religion
Dispatches*, September 3, 2021, https://religiondispatches.org/please-stop-using
-islam-to-critique-the-abortion-ban-it-simply-excuses-the-very-christian-very-white
-roots-of-anti-choice-movements/.

3. Ariana Afshar, "Stop Comparing Leaked 'Roe' Reversal to Sharia Law and Taliban's Rules," *Truthout*, May 14, 2022, https://truthout.org/articles/stop-comparing
-leaked-roe-reversal-to-sharia-law-and-talibans-rules/.

4. I make an exception here to my policy of only citing social media with permission, given that this tweet was widely reported in the media and remains up more
than a year after its initial posting. Barbra Streisand (@Barbra Streisand), Twitter,

making the rounds online shortly after the decision used the veil as synecdoche for Islamic gender oppression: a picture of the court edited to show the women justices clad in chador and niqab.

As Jalalzai, Afshar, and others have pointed out, the lazy short-hand shariah = misogyny undersells historically Christian, typically white, and specifically American patriarchy. It reflects an urge to minimize and externalize domestic problems and is conceptually related to the long-standing equation of terrorism to foreign actors consistently imagined as Muslims, notwithstanding the fact that even under the government's definition, a considerable majority of violent extremist acts in the U.S. for decades have been perpetrated by right-wing and white nationalist groups. The emphasis on Muslims as perpetrators prevents effective countermeasures against white supremacist terror at home while serving as specious justification for disproportionate surveillance and policing of Muslims within the U.S. and overt and covert violence against Muslims abroad.

Beyond the damage it does by reinforcing dehumanizing images of Muslims as barbaric and backward, the smug presumption that shariah is the pinnacle of gender oppression ignores the complicated intellectual history and variegated contemporary politics surrounding abortion (like everything else) among Muslims. One of the few bright spots in the aftermath of the Dobbs verdict was seeing American Muslim women experts in bioethics and

---

June 24, 2022, https://twitter.com/BarbraStreisand/status/1540412913076297729 ?s=20. Also see, e.g., Ruth Cutler, "The American Taliban rules on Roe," *CT Mirror*, June 27, 2022, https://ctmirror.org/2022/06/27/roe-v-wade-and-the-american -taliban/. Interestingly, Egyptian-born human rights advocate and longtime Iowa resident Shams Ghoneim, presumably aware of the theological and geopolitical distinctions involved, mentions both Afghanistan and Iran and offers "Ayatollah Supreme Court." Shams Ghoneim, "Opinion: Supreme Court justices, with lifetime terms, are oppressing women," *Iowa City Press-Citizen*, July 15, 2022, https://www .press-citizen.com/story/opinion/2022/07/15/opinion-u-s-supreme-court -going-way-taliban/7812480001/. Note that the URL includes a reference to the Taliban.

constitutional law weigh in publicly and authoritatively.[5] Judging by commentary on social media and blogs, here, too, it was complicated to thread the needle: summarizing a millennium of technical juristic debates on gestational stages, fetal personhood, and women's autonomy, as well as addressing issues of religious freedom in the United States, while acknowledging the anti-abortion stances of numerous contemporary Muslim thinkers. Too much emphasis on the legal tradition's clear prioritizing of a pregnant woman's health and welfare over that of the fetus, and you're ignoring regressive laws in Muslim-majority countries. Too much criticism of male Muslim authorities who frame pregnant women's abortion decisions as necessarily familial and communal, and you're a brainwashed Westernized liberal.

The case of abortion illustrates how scholarship cannot be anything but political. Ethical and political commitments to individual bodily autonomy, like commitments to anti-racist work and ending domestic violence, cannot be necessarily linked, and certainly cannot be reduced, to confessional loyalties. But it is foolhardy to suggest that by considering the real-world implications of our research we somehow violate eternal precepts of scholarship.

5. Examples include Zahra Ayubi, "There Is No One Islamic Interpretation on Ethics of Abortion," *The Conversation*, July 8, 2022, https://theconversation.com /there-is-no-one-islamic-interpretation-on-ethics-of-abortion-but-the-belief-in -gods-mercy-and-compassion-is-a-crucial-part-of-any-consideration-184534; Ayubi on NPR's All Things Considered, January 11, 2023, https://www.npr.org/2023/01/11 /1148488925/amid-abortion-bans-muslim-americans-turn-back-to-their-faiths -ruling-on-abortion; and Asifa Quraishi-Landes, "Abortion Bans Trample on the Religious Freedom of Muslims Too," *San Francisco Chronicle*, June 24, 2022, https:// www.sfchronicle.com/opinion/openforum/article/abortion-bans-religion -17259119.php. Quraishi-Landes was among the interviewees on PBS News Hour segment hosted by Amna Nawaz, "Faith Leaders Discuss How Their Religions Approach the Divisive Issue of Abortion," August 11, 2022, https://www.pbs.org /newshour/show/faith-leaders-discuss-how-their-religions-approach-the-divisive -issue-of-abortion.

I cannot accept that Shahab Ahmed's "analysis" of reformist scriptural interpretation is delivered from error because he avers that he is "taking no position on either the abolition or maintenance of slavery, nor on the affirmation or denial of equal legal and social rights to women."[6] Rather, the opposite. Only someone who cannot imagine their own freedom and rights jeopardized could remain aloof on these matters. Someone who cannot fathom, or does not care, that for others these are more than interesting intellectual questions seems unsuited to pronounce on the issues involved.

6. Ahmed, *What Is Islam?*, 513. On the constructive dimensions of Ahmed's book, see Zaman, "An Islam of One's Own," and Michael E. Pregill, "I Hear Islam Singing: Shahab Ahmed's *What Is Islam? The Importance of Being Islamic*," *Harvard Theological Review*, 110:1, 2017: 149–165 at 163.

4

Professing Islamic Studies

I DID MY DOCTORAL COURSEWORK at Duke University in the 1990s, first in the History department then in the Graduate Program in Religion. Our year-long Islamic Civilization survey was structured around Marshall Hodgson's posthumous three-volume *The Venture of Islam* (1974–1977).[1] My final paper argued for revising the syllabus to include newly published work on women and gender. Rather than advocate a wholesale reorganization of the course, as some women's historians were doing in their fields, my reimagined survey kept the existing structure and emphases but chose new texts to supplement Hodgson's. For example, I suggested Denise Spellberg's *Politics, Gender, and the Islamic Past* (1995),

---

1. On Hodgson, see Lydia Kiesling, "Letter of Recommendation: The Life of Marshall Hodgson," October 9, 2016, *The New York Times Magazine*, https://www.nytimes.com/2016/10/09/magazine/letter-of-recommendation-the-life-of-marshall-hodgson.html. Hodgson died before *The Venture of Islam: Conscience and History in a World Civilization* (Chicago, IL: University of Chicago Press, 1974–1977) was complete. The eventual publication of its third and final volume owes considerably to the labors of his widow and various colleagues. A certain Mrs. Armour, who worked as an administrative secretary for the University of Chicago Committee on Social Thought, helped Phyllis Hodgson find a place for his archives. Both women are briefly mentioned in the endnotes to Michael Geyer, "The Invention of World History from the Spirit of Non-Violent Resistance," in Edmund Burke III and Robert J. Mankin, eds., *Islam and World History: The Ventures of Marshall Hodgson* (Chicago, IL: University of Chicago Press, 2018), 55–81 at 75, n. 6.

which uses "the legacy of 'A'isha bint Abi Bakr" to show how early internecine conflicts were deeply shaped by competing accounts of ideal womanhood and ideal women.[2] For the Ottoman era, I swapped out a ponderous biography of Mehmet the Conqueror for Leslie Peirce's *The Imperial Harem* (1993), which closely analyzes the gendered familial power dynamics that Hodgson superciliously dismissed as "harem politics."[3] I got an A on the paper, which later circulated in photocopy among my student colleagues. When I began teaching, its bibliography formed the core of my seminar on women, gender, and Islam.

Despite my awareness that curricula tend to exclude women and gender, other classes I developed were structured around men's books, to which I added primary texts or secondary sources to address absences and lectured to fill gaps. Structural obstacles to balance persist even for people committed to inclusion. The omissions and barriers described in previous chapters reverberate in the classroom. Women and gender as topics, and women's scholarly work, are still often ignored or relegated to sidebars. Even courses taught by those of us who know better often neglect work by and about people who aren't men.[4]

Questions about curricula and syllabi return us to the foundational questions raised in Chapter 1 about what is central and peripheral to the study of Islam and Muslims. Decisions about what topics to cover, and which texts to assign to students, are intellectual, political, and logistical. They are shaped by *where* we teach, *which classes* we teach, and *who* we are while teaching. Our institutions, departments, curricula, and students shape expectations for topical coverage, what amounts and types of materials we

2. D. A. Spellberg, *Politics, Gender, and the Islamic Past: The Legacy of 'A'isha bint Abi Bakr* (New York: Columbia University Press, 1995).

3. Leslie P. Peirce, *The Imperial Harem: Women and Sovereignty in the Ottoman Empire* (Princeton, NJ: Princeton University Press, 1993).

4. For an egregious example, see my Islamic law syllabus described in Kecia Ali, "Muslims Are People, Islam Is Complicated," in Dorroll, ed., *Teaching Islamic Studies*, 161–172.

assign, and what sorts of surveillance and challenges we may face from administrators, colleagues, students, and hostile outsiders— as well as what resources and support we have available. Drawing on surveys of syllabi and overviews of introductory texts, I show some common patterns below.

Gendering the survey

Decades after my proposed revisions to Duke's Islamic Civ course, women and gender remain marginalized in classroom surveys of Islam. Though the self-selected pool is too small to derive statistically meaningful conclusions, the nine introductory Islam syllabi spanning 1997–2007 hosted at the Wabash Center for Teaching and Learning repository show that instructors routinely shunt women and gender to the margins.[5] All include between one and four classes on themes such as "Women and Gender in Islam," "Muslim Women," or "Women in Islamic History."[6] In a study undertaken for the International Institute of Islamic Thought, Faisal Islam and Zahid Bukhari surveyed 105 introductory Islam syllabi collected in 2004 and 2005 and found that fewer than four of every ten courses included "gender and human rights" as a topic. In comparison, seven out of ten discussed "Islamic theology and intellectual currents."[7] To correct what they perceive as key omissions and

5. As of May 1, 2020, sixty-one syllabi at the Wabash Center for Teaching and Learning syllabus repository contain the keyword *Islam*, the latest dating to 2014. The nine courses I discuss here, taught between 1997 and 2007, are basic overviews for undergraduates, with titles such as Islam, Introduction to Islam, Islamic Tradition, Introduction to Islamic Religion, and Experiencing Islam. Most of the other fifty-two are survey courses on world religions, Abrahamic traditions, or women and religion that include material on Islam and Muslims. Some are more specialized courses on gender, hermeneutics, or Muslim modernity.

6. Eight syllabi list topics for individual sessions.

7. Faisal Islam and Zahid H. Bukhari, "Islam 101: A Survey of 'Introduction to Islam' Courses in American Colleges and Universities," in Ahmad, Bukhari, and Nyang, eds., *Observing the Observer*, 178–218 at 185.

distortions in the typical Intro syllabus, Islam and Bukhari propose a sample syllabus of their own. It allots a week for gender and human rights. Only the penultimate course session focuses on gender.

In 2018, Ermin Sinanović, then director of research and academic programs at IIIT, began compiling materials to update Islam and Bukhari's survey. The project was never completed. My analysis of the three dozen relevant syllabi collected, most of which are from 2015–2018, suggests improvement in the topical coverage of women and gender compared to what Islam and Bukhari reported.[8] The proportion of courses that cover women and gender is twice what they found, and more akin to what the Wabash syllabi show: four of every five courses that list specific topics include at least one session on women or gender, if one includes sessions on "family," "life-cycle," and "feminism."

These more recent courses vary considerably in how much such content they include. Fifteen courses, just over four out of every ten, devote between one and three sessions to women/gender, with no other associated content.[9] Slightly fewer, about one in three courses, allocate one or two sessions and integrate some bonus women elsewhere *or* have a session or two addressing related topics without specifically designating them as women/gender. For

8. In June and July 2018, student researchers Sibbir Ahmad, Amatunoor Frederickson, MdAbdur Rahim, Sefa Secen, and Brian Wright collected about four dozen syllabi under the supervision of Ermin Sinanović. Initial findings were presented at the 2018 Summer Institute of Scholars but were never published. As with the original sample, these syllabi came from a variety of institutions, including liberal arts colleges, large public institutions, and private research universities. My analysis here excludes courses that are explicitly comparative (e.g., "Judaism, Christianity, and Islam"); courses designed for upper-level or seminary students; and those dated 2006 or 2007, a period covered by the Wabash syllabi. (All dated syllabi are from 2010 and after; most of the undated syllabi can be reliably dated to after that point based on their assigned texts.) A few files turned out to contain only publicity flyers. The remaining three dozen comprise a sample a third the size of the original.

9. Five (14%) have one session on women/gender/associated topics and ten (28%) have two or three.

example, a module on ethics focuses on abortion and a session on
the Qur'an reads the chapter "Women." (This type of integration
isn't entirely new; among the Wabash syllabi, one course had a
session on temporary marriage during its Shiʿism unit and another
hosted a guest lecture on women at shrines during the Sufism
unit.) Just one syllabus implicitly touches on masculinity, by
means of a reading assignment. None lists it as a topic. Only two
of these syllabi, less than one in twenty, consistently integrate
women and gender as topics throughout the term. Three times as
many, one course out of six, pay no attention to women and gender at all. It is fair to say that these courses on average devote a
week to women and gender, mostly segregating coverage to designated sessions near the end of the term. These syllabi demonstrate
what a recent analysis of modules in three British universities
found: the persistent "'sequestration' of teaching about gender to
the peripheries of Islamic studies."[10]

In addition to focusing on men's actions and ideas, introductory Islam courses in all three groups of syllabi also mainly assign
men's books. Among the Wabash syllabi, some include no books
by women, while the others mostly assign women's books for
sessions on women. One course requires Sachiko Murata and
William Chittick's *The Vision of Islam*, but lists it throughout the
syllabus as Chittick, *Vision of Islam* as if he alone had written it.[11]
Books by men are disproportionately assigned in the introductory syllabi Islam and Bukhari surveyed. All seven authors whose
books are assigned most frequently are men, and most are white
and non-Muslim. *The Vision of Islam* is the only text with a
woman author among the top five most frequently assigned

10. Scott-Bauman et al., *Islam on Campus*, 181. Scott-Bauman and her collaborators
did their research during 2016 and 2017 (116).

11. Sachiko Murata and William C. Chittick, *The Vision of Islam* (New York: Para-
gon House, 1994). It has since been republished repeatedly, including by I.B. Tauris
(London, 2006). As far as I can tell, Murata's name has always appeared first on the
cover.

books.[12] (Although they do not falsely attribute the book solely to
him, Islam and Bukhari list Chittick first even though Murata's
name appears before his on the cover and in the publication data.[13])
Islam and Bukhari's proposed syllabus requires eight books. All are
by men except Leila Ahmed's *Women and Gender in Islam*.

The newer syllabi collected by IIIT researchers show that faculty still mostly use men's books. Nearly two thirds of courses
taught no books by women. In courses that required a book written, co-written, or edited by a woman, it usually accompanied
multiple books by men. Faculty assigned an average of three books
per course.[14] Across three dozen syllabi, seventy books appeared
at least once as required texts.[15] Just a dozen, about one in six of
these texts, were written, co-written, or edited by women. The
Norton Anthology volume on Islam edited by Jane Dammen
McAuliffe and Ahmed's *Women and Gender in Islam* appeared
on three syllabi apiece; Murata and Chittick's *The Vision of Islam*
on two, one of which erroneously listed Chittick first.[16] Every
other book assigned more than once was by a man, including textbooks by David Waines, William Shepard, and Andrew Rippin.
Only John Esposito's *Islam: The Straight Path* (on five syllabi) and
Frederick Denny's *An Introduction to Islam* (on six) appeared on
more than three syllabi. The materials used to teach introductory
courses on Islam are many and varied. Eight of every ten books
showed up only once in three dozen syllabi. It is even more striking, therefore, how overwhelmingly faculty turn to men's books.

12. Some authors have more than one book often used, which accounts for the
discrepancy between most frequently assigned authors and most frequently assigned
books.

13. Islam and Bukhari, "Islam 101," 192.

14. The number of required books ranged from zero to seven.

15. As with Islam and Bukhari's original survey, I analyze only required texts,
leaving aside recommended books and supplementary materials in readers and on
course management sites.

16. Jane Dammen McAuliffe, ed., *The Norton Anthology of World Religions: Islam*
(New York: W. W. Norton, 2015).

The disproportionate reliance on men's books owes partly to the conservative nature of syllabi. A syllabus for an Ivy League course taught by a full professor in 2011 assigned books published in 1983, 1988, 1992, 1992, and 2011—the last an updated edition of Esposito's textbook initially published in 1988. In this instance, two of his five required books were by women, but the tendency to preserve one's curriculum from year to year tends to favor men's books. Another course from a different Ivy League school, taught by another full professor in 2017, required four books by men. Its syllabus additionally recommended three supplementary books for each of the course's twelve units, thirty-five by men and just one by a woman. But the emphasis on men's books cannot be blamed merely on backward-looking senior faculty. Numerous courses taught by recently graduated scholars assigned no books by women, and the professor who included only one book by a woman out of forty titles on his syllabus required a man's book from 2015.

In designing courses around men's books, faculty reproduce the absences in those books. Most of the frequently assigned texts devote little space to women as historical actors or gender as a social phenomenon, also usually failing to engage women's scholarship on these and other topics. They also tend to reenact the double standard according to which Muslim men's thought and texts get space while the few women cited are usually (white) outsiders.

To be sure, today's textbooks have improved on their predecessors. Esposito and Denny's surveys, still the most frequently required in Intro to Islam classes, provide useful illustrations. The first edition of Frederick Denny's *An Introduction to Islam*, published in 1985, included fifteen pages of "Suggestions for Further Reading," comprising hundreds of items of which only sixteen—about one item per page—were written, edited, co-written, or co-edited by women.[17] Although Denny recommended numerous publications by Muslim men, including men outside the academy, only *What*

---

17. Frederick Mathewson Denny, *An Introduction to Islam* (New York: Macmillan, 1985).

Everyone Needs to Know about Islam and Muslims by Suzanne Ha-
neef, an American convert, was a confessional publication by a
Muslim woman. Similar patterns obtained in Esposito's *Islam: The
Straight Path*, published a few years later.[18] More material by and
about women appears in subsequent editions of these ubiquitous
textbooks.[19] The fourth and most recent edition of Denny's text
(2011) contains seventy items written or edited by, or co-written
or co-edited by, women, in a substantially expanded list of suggested readings.[20] These works are distributed very unevenly.
None of the works listed in sections on creed or legal thought are
by women, but women wrote the majority of the books in a new
subsection on "Women and Islam" and the section on "Islam and
Muslims in North America."[21]

18. John L. Esposito, *Islam: The Straight Path*, Oxford, 1988. Of the 136 items in
Esposito's *Select Bibliography*, thirteen are by women and four are co-authored or
co-edited by mixed-gender pairs or groups (12.5%). Four of these seventeen items
are by Annemarie Schimmel. The men's works that Denny and Esposito cite tend to
further reinforce those absences. Moojan Momen's *An Introduction to Shi'i Islam*
(New Haven, CT: Yale University Press, 1985), for instance, lists just eleven women
in its thirty-five-page index. Of these women, only Rabia al-Adawiyya is not a wife,
daughter, or mother of a prophet or imam.

19. By the time the third edition of Esposito's book was published (New York:
Oxford University Press, 1998), several vital books on women and gender had been
out for years, including Fatima Mernissi's *The Veil and the Male Elite* (1991), Leila
Ahmed's *Women and Gender in Islam* (1992), and amina wadud's *Qur'an and Woman*
(1992), as well as edited volumes and studies of, for instance, Egyptian modernism.
None made it onto Esposito's list, although the total proportion of works by or co-
authored/co-edited by women was a bit higher, at 14% (26 / 184 items) in this edition. This ratio parallels that in Denny's condensed introduction to *Islam and the
Muslim Community* (San Francisco: Harper and Row, 1987), in which among twenty-
nine total items listed, three are by women, one is jointly by a woman and a man, and
the remaining twenty-five are by men.

20. Frederick Denny, *An Introduction to Islam*, 4th edition (New York: Routledge,
2016 [2011]).

21. Though the "Women in Islam" section is new, quite a few of the texts were
published before the first edition of his book. Jane I. Smith and Yvonne Haddad's
Islamic Understanding of Death and Resurrection (Oxford: Oxford University Press,

Newer editions of Esposito's book, which also include a higher proportion of work by women, show less pronounced topical segregation. In the fifth and most recent edition (2016), scholars who aren't men wrote/edited/co-wrote/co-edited more than fifty items, nearly one in four. This is close to double the proportion in the first edition, where that figure was one in eight.[22] There is no separate section on women and gender, so Natana DeLong-Bas's *Oxford Encyclopedia of Islam and Women* appears under "Reference Works," for example, and "Qur'anic Studies" includes Barbara Stowasser's monograph on women in the Qur'an and its commentary and amina wadud's *Qur'an and Woman*.[23] Some gendered patterns remain. Few works by women appear in sections such as "Sufism" or "Muslim Politics," while half of the books in "Islam in the West" have at least one woman author or editor. Despite these imbalances, both Denny's and Esposito's surveys integrate women's scholarship better than Aaron Hughes's *Muslim Identities: An Introduction to Islam* (2013), which suggests as many readings by women for its last chapter, "Constructing Muslim Women," as for the previous ten chapters combined.[24]

Despite the improvement in the proportion of publications by women in their suggested supplementary texts, women remain

---

2002) seems oddly placed among the ethnographies of daily life rather than among the texts on creed and theology, suggesting gendered considerations in its classification.

22. John Esposito, *Islam: The Straight Path*, 5th edition (New York: Oxford University Press, 2016). Fifty-three had at least one woman involved.

23. Natana DeLong-Bas, ed., *Oxford Encyclopedia of Islam and Women* (New York: Oxford University Press, 2013) and Barbara Stowasser, *Women in the Qur'an, Traditions, and Interpretation* (New York: Oxford University Press, 1994).

24. Hughes, *Muslim Identities*. Of the sixteen items listed for Chapter 11, fifteen are by women and one is co-authored by a woman and a man. Of 164 "Further Reading" items listed for other chapters, sixteen have at least one woman author or editor. Two chapters have no suggested works by women (0 / 13 and 0 / 17 respectively), while most of the rest have one or two. One chapter has 3 / 24 and another has 4 / 20—one book by a woman and three by mixed-gender authorial/editorial teams.

largely absent as historical actors in these standard introductions. The fourth edition of Denny's textbook refers to a handful of contemporary academics. The fourth edition of Esposito's *Islam: The Straight Path* (2011) includes a sprinkling of women from the contemporary Middle East and South Asia: Pakistani preacher Farhat Hashmi, Egyptian internet entrepreneur Heba Raouf, and Jordan's Queen Raina.[25] Not all make it into the fifth edition, which adds a couple of white American anti-Muslim polemicists. Still, after women from the Prophet's family and household and the famous eighth-century mystic Rabia al-Adawiyya, neither Denny nor Esposito includes any Muslim women for more than a thousand years, until the late twentieth century.[26]

Popular textbooks by men recommend other men's textbooks near-exclusively. All the "Introductions to Islam" in the fourth edition of Esposito's textbook are by men, with the fifth adding the co-authored introductory book by Jonathan Bloom and Sheila Blair (2002) to round out the dozen listed works.[27] The lone item by a woman among Denny's seventeen "General Introductions to Islam" is Annemarie Schimmel's *Islam: An Introduction* (1992).[28] Schimmel's book appears on just one of the three dozen syllabi recently collected by IIIT. Though it remains in print, it is hard to find in the wild. I don't recall ever seeing it at a conference book display. Unlike with Denny's or Esposito's textbooks, I've never gotten an advertisement for an exam copy of Schimmel's book or

25. John Esposito, *Islam: The Straight Path*, 4th edition (New York: Oxford University Press, 2011).

26. This holds for both the fourth and fifth editions of *Islam: The Straight Path*. Chase F. Robinson's *Islamic Civilization in Thirty Lives: The First 1,000 Years* (Berkeley: University of California Press, 2016) does a bit better, including, in addition to Aisha and the ubiquitous Rabia, 'Arib ("courtesan of caliphs") and the "hadith scholar" Karima al-Marwaziyya.

27. Jonathan M. Bloom and Sheila S. Blair, *Islam: A Thousand Years of Faith and Power* (New Haven, CT: Yale University Press, 2002). In earlier editions, only reference works and Qur'an translations are broken out from the list of secondary sources.

28. Annemarie Schimmel, *Islam: An Introduction* (Albany: SUNY Press, 1992).

had its newest edition show up unsolicited in my department mailbox. Numerous factors are at play here, including the specific presses involved. Oxford, which publishes Esposito, operates on a very different scale than SUNY, which publishes Schimmel.

Just as what has been cited continues to be cited, what has been assigned continues to be assigned and therefore revised and updated. Faculty mostly do not, and should not, assign overviews that take no account of the Gulf War or 9/11 or the so-called War on Terror. Still, no newer textbooks by women seem to have made inroads into the Islam 101 market. Carole Hillenbrand's *Introduction to Islam: Beliefs and Practices in Historical Perspective* (2015), tailored for "the undergraduate student and general reader," mentions substantially more women than its male-authored competitors.[29] It appears just once among the seventy books found in the updated set of IIIT syllabi. Catharina Raudvere's *Islam: An Introduction* (2015) is absent entirely, as is the survey by Bloom and Blair.[30]

Centering decisions

Designing courses requires both selecting materials to assign and making decisions about coverage. One reason textbooks matter so much is that a nonspecialist teaching an intro course, or someone teaching at an institution where the norm is that only one book will be assigned, may structure their syllabus to align with their chosen textbook. That means that the textbook author's answers to questions like the following can shape faculty priorities: What is this course about? What information do we want students to know? What key ideas do we want to impart? What skills and competencies are we aiming to teach? More pragmatically: what topics, people, and approaches are at the center of our courses? Who must

---

29. Carole Hillenbrand, *Introduction to Islam: Beliefs and Practices in Historical Perspective* (New York: Thames & Hudson, 2015), 9. Many but by no means all of these women appear in a chapter devoted to women.

30. Catharina Raudvere, *Islam: An Introduction* (London: Bloomsbury, 2015).

be included and, a necessary corollary, who can be safely left out? The answer is, often, women. Yet because of the popular interest in matters such as veiling, women and gender are less likely to be omitted entirely from introductory courses on Islam than to be pushed to the side, cordoned off as their own special topic, or addressed haphazardly in response to student queries without engaging the robust scholarly resources available.

Limiting classroom discussions of women and gender issues to one week in a semester-long course positions men as the ungendered norm, the rightful focus and center of attention, just as having a designated unit on Shi'ism, as I've done in the past, implicitly positions Sunni Islam as the standard from which others deviate. Religious studies classes on Islam and Muslims often emphasize (male-authored) Arabic texts and (male-dominated) Middle Eastern histories. This is true even though the demographic weight of Islam lies firmly in Asia and Islam has been for more than a millennium an African religion, and despite the long-standing existence of Muslim diasporas from Northern Europe to South America. Women have been deeply involved with vital political, historical, intellectual, and social developments across Muslim societies, and men's engagement with all these things has been shaped by their gender. These facts should be considered in designing introductory courses on Islam.

Obviously no course can delve deeply into every topic. Some things will get cursory attention and others must be left out entirely. Muhammad's life could be the lens for a semester-long exploration of topics such as Islamic origins, medieval hagiography, early modern polemics, and twentieth-century apologetics, including the gendered dimensions of these phenomena. Alternatively, the life of Muhammad could be covered in a fifty-minute lecture that gives the conventional narrative undergirding later developments in Islamic law or scriptural interpretation. Including one thing means excluding something else. Complicating one standard story means forgoing many other questions. All instructors make trade-offs.

Explaining to students our choices about what to include and what to omit can be pedagogically useful. A sophomore enrolled in Islam 101 neither needs nor benefits from a detailed history of academic Islamic studies or a full recounting of its latest controversies. But introducing the basic question of how professors decide what to emphasize in the study of Islam and Muslims can help students engage the tradition and situate what they are learning in a wider frame.

Rather than either take for granted the centrality of Arab-Middle Eastern locations, texts, and histories, or pretend no such presumptive center exists, I ask my students to think about why and how certain topics become central, and what the implications of that centering are for understanding Islam. My approach is informed by how colleagues treat these issues in their research and writing. For example, in her study of Persianate historiography, Mimi Hanaoka places geographic and linguistic "peripheries" in complicated, ongoing, fluid conversations with the "center." Hanaoka shows how Islam becomes a language through which centrality and marginality are asserted, assumed, and affirmed. She recognizes, but does not take for granted, the centrality of the Arab world and the Arabic language as a locus of Muslim identity—not naturally or obviously, but because of dynamics both internal and external to the Muslim tradition. In a complementary vein, Kayla Wheeler problematizes the form of "hegemonic Islam" that "naturalize[s]" certain regional norms and customs, including in matters of dress, as truly Islamic, and delegitimizes other practices, growing out of other histories—in particular, "practices and beliefs created within African-American Islam." Using Black Muslim women's fashion, Wheeler analyzes how women's sartorial decisions are embedded in community contexts while drawing from transnational aesthetic, material, and political currents.[31] Wheeler shows the falsity of notions of stagnant Muslims mired in a timeless

31. Kayla Renée Wheeler, untitled essay at *The Black American Muslim*, https://www.theblackamericanmuslim.com/kayla-rene-wheeler.

past in contrast to a modern, forward-looking, ever-changing West, and explores how Arabocentric norms are implied and invoked in conventional narratives. Though Hanaoka specializes in the medieval, Asian, and textual, and Wheeler the contemporary, Atlantic, and material, both acknowledge existing presumptions while working to expand our understanding of how people claim Islam.

One key pedagogical challenge is how to treat the assumptions students, both Muslim and non-Muslim, arrive with. Faculty teaching about Islam and Muslims typically confront more misinformation and misconceptions than those teaching other traditions, where plain ignorance may prevail. This is doubly the case when it comes to women and gender. Classrooms often mix students who know little about Islam and Muslims (and are aware of their ignorance), Muslim students who combine some basic knowledge with significant lacunae (and are unaware of the limitations of their knowledge), and others who cleave to deeply held, if shallowly rooted, beliefs about Muslim violence and degeneracy (and vigorously contest any suggestion that they might be wrong). Instructors must simultaneously address lack of information, unconscious assumptions and biases, and strong convictions about *what Islam says* on women and gender from those who make broad-brushstroke condemnations of patriarchal texts and practices as well as from those engaged in apologetic defenses of Islam as a religion, sometimes in contrast to degenerate Muslim cultural norms.

Ignoring stereotypes is a doomed endeavor but engaging them directly can also backfire. Huda Fakhreddine notes that students often perceive efforts by racialized Muslim faculty to either side-step or counterbalance ugly misrepresentations of Islam in the classroom as avoidance, inadvertently confirming the erroneous ideas.[32] Courses must be structured in such a way that faulty

---

32. Huda Fakhreddine, "Teaching against Stereotype," *Almanac* (University of Pennsylvania), April 17, 2018, 8. There is little analysis of student or colleague perceptions of Muslim faculty, but scholars have attended to Muslim students.

assumptions can be debunked and replaced with nuanced alternative perspectives and knowledge. Hussein Rashid acknowledges that teaching through stereotypes risks validating them: "starting with their preconceived notions of what Islam is reinforces that what they think is correct, and makes it more difficult for me to introduce a more expansive vision of Islam."[33] He instead advocates showing contestation and argument between and among Muslims as a way of disrupting presumptions of a static, unified tradition. And broadening the range of Muslims whose histories, texts, ideas, and practices are engaged is crucial. Wheeler's "Black Islam Syllabus," a continually expanding online resource, curates sources by and about a group often excluded from depictions and analysis of the Muslim tradition, helping faculty educate themselves, diversify their courses, and shift how students conceptualize Islam and Muslims.[34]

A focus on specifics rather than generalizations is vital for any teaching about Islam and Muslims. It is both particularly necessary and especially powerful when gender is in the mix. Presenting locally grounded, changing, and contradictory examples serves to rebut the presumption that Islam, and especially its scriptural-legal tradition, explains women's lives. Instead, students can analyze how and when Islam is invoked, by whom, and to what ends. Shenila Khoja-Moolji uses discussion of high-profile topics and events

Scott-Baumann et al. ("Islam and Gender on Campus," in *Islam on Campus*, 96–118) find "systemic gendered discrimination against Muslims on university campuses" in the UK. Shabana Mir's ethnographic *Muslim American Women on Campus: Undergraduate Social Life and Identity* (Chapel Hill: University of North Carolina Press, 2014) is grounded in student experiences.

33. Hussein Rashid, "Diverse Muslim Narratives: Rethinking Islam 101," *The Wabash Center Journal on Teaching*, 2:1, 2021: 143–158 at 143.

34. Layla Abdullah-Poulos, "How #BlackIslamSyllabus is Enhancing Islamic Studies—Talking with Dr. Kayla Wheeler," June 15, 2020, https://blog.hautehijab .com/post/how-blackmuslimsyllabus-for-college-students-was-created-a-conversation-with-dr-kayla-wheeler. A link to the syllabus can be found at https://kaylarenee wheeler.com/blackislamsyllabus/.

"to disrupt my own as well as my students' desires to come to universal truths about gender, islam, and muslims."[35] She points to the way the attack on Malala Yousafzai in Pakistan and the kidnapping of Nigerian girls by Boko Haram "have been abstracted from their local contexts and specificities and rearticulated as examples of oppression of Muslim women by muslim/brown/black men and as illustrations of Islam as an extremist ideology."[36] Along similar lines, Lila Abu-Lughod illustrates the inadequacy of the category of honor crimes, frequently used to explain many diverse instances of gendered interpersonal violence against Muslim women and girls.[37] But unless we give students more of a handhold, more actual content, the effect may be to reinforce the association between Muslim women and victimization.[38] We have to take care not to leave students too eager to generalize, even about the power of stereotypes. Abu-Lughod insists on "historicizing" as part of responsible pedagogy: "Rather than generalizing about timeless forms of gendered orientalism or imperial feminism, I think we should track such shifts and relate them to geopolitical developments."[39]

Veiling is a subject I sometimes steer away from in the classroom because it involves assumptions that are hard to dislodge. To do it justice, one must linger long enough to approach the topic from multiple perspectives. Yet explored attentively, veiling shows how complex any account of Muslim tradition and practice must

35. Shenila Khoja-Moolji, "Poststructuralist Approaches to Teaching about Gender, Islam, and Muslim Societies," *Feminist Teacher*, 24:3, 2014: 169–183 at 169. Capitalization follows the original.

36. Ibid., 172.

37. Abu-Lughod, "Seductions of the 'Honor Crime,'" in *Do Muslim Women Need Saving?*, 113–142. See also Mahmood, "Feminism, Democracy, and Empire: Islam and the War of Terror," in Scott, ed., *Women's Studies on the Edge*, 81–114 at 96–99.

38. Scott-Bauman et. al., *Islam on Campus*, 182–4.

39. Lila Abu Lughod, "On Teaching Gender and Islam in the Middle East: An Interview with Lila Abu Lughod (Conducted by Jacob Bessen)," originally published in *JADMAG* 7.2, 2019 (Pedagogy) and available at jadaliyya.com.

be. One can explore relevant scriptural passages and their inter-pretation, as well as those texts' deployments by various actors in different contexts. One can also note the myriad times and places when people have felt no need to provide scriptural justi-fications for their clothing. Additionally, exploring the varied occasions when veiling has become *a thing* offers meaningful op-portunities to radically particularize the stories we tell. The when and where and who and why of bans on women's head and/or face coverings in Iran under the Shah, modern Turkey, and con-temporary France reveal common themes and equally salient dif-ferences. Sustained consideration of divergent cases of *must cover or else* and *must not cover or else* illustrates how useless it is to attempt to derive a single truth about veiling. Supplementing these inquiries with meaningful engagement of not whether but *how* women cover, as in Su'ad Abdul-Khabeer's careful delineation of how the "hood-jab" helps create "Muslim cool," reorients the study of Islam and Muslims in ways that invite students to consider how certain people, texts, ideas, and practices have come to be understood as central.[40] Analyzing what Liz Bucar has termed "pious fashions," a phrase some might understand as oxymoronic, provides another perspec-tive on veiling as a socially embodied practice.[41]

Ultimately, it takes complementary and intertwined strategies to diminish the power of stereotypes. Including material about people, places, and practices that are underacknowledged and un-derexplored disrupts tidy and inaccurate stories. Showing internal diversity and change over time among Muslims helps students resist the lure of pat answers. Pushing back against the attempts to know "what Islam says" is key for understanding how Islam is con-tinually, collectively formed and reformed, and how it is no differ-ent in this way than other traditions. Done effectively, this work allows our students to critique the Christian-centric foundations

40. Su'ad Abdul-Khabeer, *Muslim Cool: Race, Religion, and Hip Hop in the United States* (New York: New York University Press, 2016).

41. Elizabeth Bucar, *Pious Fashion: How Muslim Women Dress* (Cambridge, MA: Harvard University Press, 2017).

of religious studies and think about how people conceptualize religious traditions—and equips them to navigate a world in which ideas about what Islam is and who Muslims are have real-life consequences for geopolitics, humanitarian issues, and political realities in the West and beyond.[42]

Jasmin Zine has argued that anti-Islamophobia education must "hel[p] students develop a critical literacy of the politics of media and image-making" so they understand "how power operates through the politics of representation." Only with that awareness is it possible to both analyze and dismantle "individual, ideological, and systemic forms of discrimination and oppression," which are based partly in pernicious stereotypes.[43] Those stereotypes are often rooted in questions of women and gender—which is why teaching that only brings women and gender in when it must address stereotypes is so badly flawed. If we fail to engage the complexities of scriptural texts, legal interpretations, historical norms, class and status differences among women, and Muslim women's diverse approaches to all the questions prompted by living in modern societies, we remain locked in an unhelpful dance in which the oppressed/liberated poles are the only viable answer. Our job is partly to show lifeworlds in which those are not meaningful categories.[44]

Learning outcomes

Even if teaching about Islam and Muslims is especially fraught, our teaching must convey that Islam and Muslims are not exceptional. We may imagine ourselves teaching Islamic studies, but nearly all our undergraduates and many of the graduate students, too, will

42. Rashid, "Diverse Muslim Narratives," 144.

43. Jasmin Zine, "Anti-Islamophobia Education as Transformative Pedagogy: Reflections from the Educational Front Lines," *American Journal of Islamic Social Sciences*, 21:3, 2004: 110–119 at 115, 113.

44. Anthropologists are among those who have written most meaningfully on this topic. See, e.g., Abu Lughod, "On Teaching Gender and Islam in the Middle East," and Saba Mahmood, *Politics of Piety: The Islamic Revival and the Feminist Subject* (Princeton, NJ: Princeton University Press, 2005).

instead consider their time in our classroom as "religious studies" or "anthropology" or "international relations" coursework. Such understandings shape what we, and they, consider indispensable. Here, I speak from my own context within religious studies.

A religious studies course has a variety of possible intended outcomes. One is to impart *religious literacy*, including "a basic understanding of the history, central texts (where applicable), beliefs, practices, and contemporary manifestations of several of the world's religious traditions as they arose out of and continue to be shaped by particular social, historical, and cultural contexts."[45] In the case of Islam, this means basic information such as: Who was Muhammad? What is the Qur'an? When did Islam originate? Where do Muslims live today? But *literacy in religious studies* teaches us to distrust conventional wisdom on matters such as these as sometimes useful fictions. Any scholar worth their salt will inculcate a suspicion of easy answers to questions like *Who was Muhammad?* One should know the generally agreed upon answer but also understand why people have been arguing over that question for a millennium and a half and how the stakes as well as the answers have changed over the centuries.

The study of Islam and Muslims within a religious studies program typically also aims to help students understand how *religion* as a category is formed and deployed and shifts. How did we come distinguish religion from other categories of human endeavor? Within a religious studies class on Islam, there are still other decisions to make in shaping curricula. Do we want students to comprehend how processes of interpretation are contests over power? Do we seek to convey how religion—with Islam as our example—regulates sexual behavior and gender performance

---

45. Diane L. Moore's two-part definition of religious literacy has been taken up by the American Academy of Religion for some of its public-facing activities and by other programs that seek to increase such literacy. See, for example, Harvard Divinity School's Religion and Public Life program, "What is Religious Literacy?," https://rpl .hds.harvard.edu/what-we-do/our-approach/what-religious-literacy.

among its adherents? Is one of our goals to help them recognize creativity and beauty in the world's religious traditions?[46] Are we to encourage them to understand interlocking practices of marginalization and exploitation, motivating them to act and helping them learn how to do so effectively? All the above?

Some of those who teach about Islam are not primarily Islamicists. They might be involved in religious studies but not usually focused on Muslims, or teaching about people who happen to be Muslim in a field that does not usually pay significant attention to religion. Those who come to the subfield or the topic as outsiders may feel at sea. This discomfort can be counterbalanced by ease with the kinds of generalizations that frustrate specialists. It's good to study Islam and Muslims as they intersect other topics, traditions, and areas of teaching. It's a problem to compartmentalize Muslims and to assume, wrongly, that if it's about Muslims, it's always religious; if it's about Islam, it's not like anything else.

Students will inevitably ask basic questions about Islam tangential to the lesson plan. Those that aren't about jihad will probably be about women and gender, mostly veiling. As a U.K. study found, "heightened public interest renders encounters with Islam in the different campus settings evocative of questions on women and gender" even where gender is not deemed sufficiently important to warrant formal acknowledgment as part of a module.[47] Trustworthy introductory books and reference publications, such as the *Encyclopedia of Women and Islamic Cultures*, address the veil and other flashpoint topics. The crucial word here is *trustworthy*. Faculty, whatever their specialization, possess the requisite skill for sorting reliable from unreliable sources. These are skills our

46. Kathleen Foody, "Pedagogical Projects: Teaching Liberal Religion After 9/11," *The Muslim World*, 106:4, 2016: 719–739. Boston University's general education model for undergraduates includes a unit in "Philosophical Inquiry and Life's Meaning," listed first among a dozen items, https://www.bu.edu/hub/advising-and-the-hub/hub -requirements-for-students/hub-requirements-for-entering-first-year-students/. As of the Fall 2023 semester, our introductory Islam class satisfies this requirement.

47. Scott-Bauman et. al., *Islam on Campus*, 181.

students are still developing. What these resources reveal about Islamic religious doctrines or Muslim beliefs or practices is that the answers to our students' questions are nearly always complicated. Explaining how and why things are complicated, and how to assess the reliability of sources on charged topics, can often be a good use of class time, especially if it advances other course goals.

Other strategies for responding in the moment include *distinguishing* among kinds of texts and phenomena: scripture, interpretation, practice of various kinds at various levels; *assessing* whether a given comparison is helpful or harmful (for instance, contrasting Muslim realities with Christian ideals, or vice versa); *illustrating* diversity and change across time, across space, and within societies; and *tracing* themes (e.g., anti-Muslim hostility or the persistence of patriarchal norms) without losing historical specificity. Ultimately, what anyone needs to teach about Islam and Muslims are the skills for evaluating evidence, contextualizing information, and making connections between and among various levels of analysis that humanities and social science faculty already possess.

Effective instruction depends on these and other skills, in complex relationship with institutional context, student receptivity, and faculty identity. Who we are necessarily shapes how we approach our topics—and how colleagues and students perceive us and our courses. Just as stereotypes shape our students' perceptions of Islam and Muslims, widespread biases, including those based on gender, sexuality, age, and race, shape students' perceptions of their instructors. The fact that student evaluations, widely relied upon in U.S. institutions, are deeply biased is generally acknowledged.[48] That these ratings can thwart women's professional advancement is seldom taken seriously. Even less frequently is it recognized that concerns about evaluations may shape instructors' pedagogical decisions. For instance, women who teach about

48. Troy Heffernan, "Sexism, Racism, Prejudice, and Bias: A Literature Review and Synthesis of Research Surrounding Student Evaluations of Courses and Teaching," *Assessment & Evaluation in Higher Education*, 2021, DOI: 10.1080/02602938.2021 .1888075.

gender, like people of color who teach about race, are more likely to be perceived as doing so excessively as compared to male or white colleagues even when they teach the same topics using the same materials.[49] And students are more likely to complain about challenging material or a focus that they dislike when the professor is one who is "presumed incompetent."[50] As Meera Deo puts it in her study of legal academia: "Despite deep investment in students, women are more likely to be presumed incompetent in the classroom, enduring challenges to their authority and direct confrontations."[51] Like the fear of blowback from public speaking that leads to caution about accepting invitations, wariness about student responses may constrain women's curricular choices.

For these and other reasons, we must not romanticize classroom instruction. Even setting aside the "systemic ills of the university," students can behave in racist and sexist ways, from disrupting class repeatedly to attempting to intimidate faculty or colluding with outside harassers such as Campus Watch.[52] (I personally know colleagues who have experienced all these things.) More often,

49. In one instance, a law professor of color who taught about racism and civil rights was perceived as too fixated on that topic compared to a white colleague who taught the exact same syllabus during the same term. Both were women. Meera E. Deo, *Unequal Profession: Race and Gender in Legal Academia* (Stanford, CA: Stanford University Press, 2019), 77–78.

50. Deo alludes to the classic study Gabriella Gutiérrez y Muhs, Yolanda Flores Niemann, Carmen G. González, and Angela P. Harris, eds., *Presumed Incompetent: The Intersections of Race and Class for Women in Academia* (Boulder: University Press of Colorado, 2012).

51. Deo, *Unequal Profession*, 6; see also Pittman, "Race and Gender Oppression in the Classroom." Deo focuses on women of color law faculty but finds that "white women have similar gender-based interactions with students" (57), including "complicated classroom dynamics" and "gender-based slights in evaluations" (72), although "the intersectional raceXgender bias plaguing women of color is even more pronounced" (77).

52. Emily Brier, "Pandemic Pedagogy: Practical and Empathetic Teaching Practices," *SPECTRA*, 8:2, 2021: 31–37 at 36. Brier concludes that "working toward a classroom that interrupts the violent realities in which it resides is, in fact, the work of teaching."

students operate in good faith but under unreasonable pressures: underprepared and inadequately supported, especially as faculty address difficult topics, including colonialism, patriarchy, and white supremacy. The burdens of classroom teaching, like most academic labor, are unevenly distributed. Professors carrying heavy teaching loads, whether in terms of number of courses or number of students, may not have the luxury of making micro-adjustments to their pedagogy. Classes with a high proportion of students from traditionally underserved and historically excluded groups are likely to present faculty with more challenges simply because the institution meets fewer and fewer of their needs, even as faculty have less and less bandwidth to manage those needs.

And still, the opportunity for sustained, deep, complex learning and thinking about Islam and Muslims is precious. Meeting once or twice or three times weekly for months allows faculty to introduce concepts, undermine tacit assumptions, offer scaffolding for new knowledge, and support students as they consider, engage, modify, and reject theories, approaches, and ideas. Something magical can happen when learners consistently engage religion as a concept, Islam as a contested term, and Muslim histories and traditions as complex, dynamic, and varied. Courses that seriously consider people who aren't men as historical actors and significant thinkers, including through their writings and other work, build stronger knowledge about Islam and Muslims, and prepare students to live in a world in which Islam and Muslims are a vibrant, diverse, and meaningful presence.

Conclusion

A BEGINNER'S GUIDE TO ERADICATING SEXISM IN ISLAMIC STUDIES

THIS BOOK HAS FOCUSED ON SEXIST and misogynist patterns within academic Islamic studies. It confirms the suspicions and convictions those with experience of bias have long held about the ways feminized scholars and work are treated. It presents a set of tools for all of us in the field, whatever our own backgrounds and histories, to use in scrutinizing our professional world. Intellectual historians, scholarly biographers, and ethnographers of religion all recognize the crucial role of context and networks in our subjects' lives and careers. We understand that what they read shapes what they write. We notice the crucial role of patrons who promote writers and their work. We consider the role of peers, interlocutors, and publicity—as well as persecution, or the fear of it. We seldom turn the same critical lens on our own working conditions, considering the texts produced within our disciplines, or the dynamics of our conferences, advisor meetings, seminars, or keynote lectures. We must, though, because bias and discrimination harm both individual scholars and the field as a whole.

It's tempting to think of sexism as a legacy problem. But it's not just a matter of waiting for the old guard to become emeriti. Despite some improvements over the decades, recent publications, including by junior scholars, continue to marginalize women's scholarship. Men in some subfields, including those early in their careers, still edit manthologies. Updated and new textbooks say little about women between the Prophet and the present. Professors fresh out of grad school design courses that skip or skim over women and gender and fail to assign books by anyone who isn't a man. Some things have changed but a lot of things haven't. They won't change unless we act deliberately to change them.

In wanting to reshape our professional contexts, Islamic studies scholars are not alone. Judicious assessments of the patriarchal status quo have appeared for fields as disparate as architecture and economics.[1] Although there are disciplinary particularities on display, much resonates with Islamic studies. For instance, in *Where Are the Women Architects?*, Despina Stratigakos finds a husband recognized alone for work done jointly with his wife as well as women architects being nearly excluded from prestigious prizes, being seldom invited as speakers at academic forums, being channeled into less glamorous subfields, having their work omitted consistently from syllabi, and being underrepresented in Wikipedia entries.[2] In classics and medieval studies, scholars actively contest sexist and racist norms and patterns, highlighting the interconnections between and among them.[3] Some initiatives cross

1. #EconomistsToo, "A Dispiriting Survey of Women's Lot in University Economics," *The Economist*, May 23, 2019, https://www.economist.com/finance-and-economics/2019/03/23/a-dispiriting-survey-of-womens-lot-in-university-economics. The findings of Alice H. Wu's "Gender Stereotyping in Academica: Evidence from Economics Job Market Rumors Forum" are summarized in Justin Wolfers, "Exposing a Toxic Milieu for Women in Economics," *The New York Times*, August 20, 2017, Y BU 3.

2. Despina Stratigakos, *Where Are the Women Architects?* (Princeton, NJ: Princeton University Press, 2016), on recognizing a husband alone (3), on prizes (80), on syllabi (23, 68), on subfields (13–15), on invitations (25), and on Wikipedia (4, 69–76).

3. Dorothy Kim, "Teaching Medieval Studies in a Time of White Supremacy," https://www.inthemedievalmiddle.com/2017/08/teaching-medieval-studies-in-time-of.html; Dan-el Padilla Peralta, "Classics Beyond the Pale," *Eidolon*, February 20, 2017, https://eidolon.pub/classics-beyond-the-pale-534bdbb3601b; and,

fields (#CiteBlackWomen). Others are grounded in specific disciplines (#WomenAlsoKnowHistory). Scholars in Jewish studies, early Christianity, and Asian religions have worked to note the characteristic exclusions in their fields and to remedy them, in ways that can be instructive for scholars in Islamic studies.[4] Some scholars turning critical eyes on their fields have concluded that projects of inclusion must contend with the methods of exclusion that constitute the discipline itself.[5]

In Islamic studies, as elsewhere, improving things requires understanding the specific damaging dynamics at play. But change is not just a matter of admitting that problems exist. Change requires shifting how we perform our work. Although it makes no pretense of offering a fully fleshed-out plan for fixing problems that are long-standing, widespread, and deeply rooted, the remainder of this chapter offers practical advice for reviewing peers' work, inviting project participation, citing scholarship appropriately, and designing inclusive courses. Effective interventions will necessarily depend on the specific circumstances and the broader context, including where you and any others involved are situated socially and institutionally.

Throughout, the onus of change should be primarily on those who are most professionally and personally secure. Although

---

more generally, the *Eidolon* archive. *Eidolon* founder and chief editor Donna Zuckerberg's *Not All Dead White Men: Classics and Misogyny in the Digital Age* (Cambridge, MA: Harvard University Press, 2018) is primarily concerned with the misogyny-saturated use of classics in the manosphere, but the implications stretch beyond the field.

4. There is a particularly good literature in Jewish studies. The "The Patriarchy Issue" of *AJS Perspectives* (Spring 2019), a publication of the Association for Jewish Studies, reveals through contributions from thirty students and scholars the way the operations of patriarchy, sexism, and misogyny in Jewish studies (and Jewish texts, thought, and history) are necessarily specific. See also Thompson, "The Birdcage," and Sarah Imhoff, "Jews, Jewish Studies, and the Study of Islam," in Sheedy, *Identity, Politics and the Study of Islam*, 121–137.

5. Tyson, *Where Are the Women?*

those initiating projects can take important measures at the outset to promote inclusion and balance, all the work cannot fall on editors and organizers and authors. Participants have roles to play as well. For instance, white faculty, especially those who are tenured, should at the very least ask about the racial composition of conferences they are asked to join. Men, especially those who are tenured, should ask about how many women *have committed to* contributing to an edited volume they are participating in. ("We've invited" is, for reasons explored below, not a reliable indicator of results.) Some changes are incredibly easy to implement for those with secure standing, like asking about other presenters or contributors. A personal policy of not participating in all-white or all-male panels carries little professional risk for those with tenure, who don't have to weigh the ethics of participating against a needed line on their CV. Others are a bit more challenging for anyone, like overhauling a syllabus or reframing projects to engage a slightly different body of literature. In no case does trying guarantee success.[6] However, we all must start someplace. Doing something is better than not trying at all.

Reviewing

Although the increased presence of women in the academy generally and Islamic studies specifically can be seen in the greater proportion of individual publications by women and their greater likelihood of inclusion in collective publications, there are still wildly exclusionary projects. For instance, as I was working on this book, the *Wiley Blackwell Concise Companion to the Hadith* (2020) was published.[7] It contains seventeen chapters written by fifteen

6. Alison Joseph writes about ending up with a male-dominated volume despite her best efforts: "It's Not That Easy: On the Challenges Facing an Editor," May 29, 2019, Feminist Studies in Religion @TheTable "Manthologies," https://www.fsrinc .org/its-not-that-easy-on-the-challenges-facing-an-editor/.

7. Daniel W. Brown, ed., *The Wiley Blackwell Concise Companion to the Hadith* (Somerset, NJ: John Wiley & Sons, 2020).

men. Within moments of looking at its table of contents, I had thought of three women and nonbinary scholars who could have been included. A colleague on Twitter immediately found half a dozen women listed in the online program for an upcoming symposium on hadith. There was no overlap in our lists. Since it was so easy for nonspecialists to quickly identify numerous potential contributors, to achieve the complete exclusion of women and nonbinary scholars from a large volume based on invited contributions with a long lead time shows both the obstacles to balance in a male-dominated subfield as well as the problem with using peer review alone as a remedy: it comes late in the process. Although a peer reviewer had pointed out the gendered exclusions in his pre-publication report on the manuscript, no corrective measures were taken.[8]

Peer review is the supposed gold-standard for academic publications. When it works well, it is a gift. Dedicated attention to one's work from knowledgeable readers aware of and attuned to pertinent scholarly conversations should be prized. A constructive and well-informed peer review, whether sympathetic or critical, is worth its weight in gold. Unfortunately, peer review often functions poorly. It becomes one more set of hurdles to clear, in ways that prop up academic patriarchy and frustrate everyone involved.

Beyond the fact that it often comes late in the game, ways the peer review process undercuts scholarship on women and gender as well as work by scholars who are not men include:

- editors assigning reviewers unsympathetic to gender analysis to assess work on gender;
- editors choosing reviewers without appropriate expertise because they work on women or gender in a distant area;
- reviewers failing to notice when important and relevant publications by women and nonbinary scholars are omitted from articles, chapters, and books;

8. Personal communication with reviewer, December 2019.

- reviewers noting such exclusions but not insisting on changes;
- editors asking for changes but allowing perfunctory references that reflect no actual engagement with the work in question;
- reviewers insisting on citations to or framing around the work of men who are irrelevant to the project at hand; or
- in anticipation of reviewers' judgments, scholars opting to frame their work in relation to such men's ideas.

Fortunately, there are strategies to mitigate bias and improve the process whether you are receiving a review, reviewing others' work, or commissioning reviews as an editor.

Strategies for recipients of peer reviews

It is human nature to find criticism hard to take. Try not to get defensive. Give the benefit of the doubt to reviewers. They might be doing their level best. Probably nobody ever taught them how to review a manuscript.[9] You can often learn even from poorly framed or obnoxious reports. If the reviewer doesn't think gender analysis is useful for your project or simply dislikes feminist scholarship, you can and should push back against that dismissal. But if the objection is less all-encompassing, maybe you need to tweak your introduction to explain why you are not doing the thing the reviewer thinks you should be doing. Or you might need to explain to the editor in your author response to a revise-and-resubmit why you left out and will continue to leave out Fancy Big Name Man Scholar, relying instead on engagement with Less Well Known but More Germane Woman Thinker.

If a review seems very condescending or unhelpful, especially but not only if it comes with a rejection, consider sharing it with a peer or, if you are junior, someone senior whose judgment you

---

9. A good starting point is Jo Van Every, *Peer Review: A Short Guide* (2019).

trust. Bonus points if they are on the journal's editorial board. They may well be willing to bend the editor's ear about the inappropriate and unprofessional tone of the review they passed along.

Strategies for reviewers

If you are invited to do a pre-publication review of an article or book manuscript, you can say no if it is outside your area of expertise and explain your reasoning to the editor. Those who don't work on women and gender often assume that just because you work on a gender-related topic or, sometimes, simply because you're a woman, you're an expert on all things related to women. In two decades, I've been asked only a handful of times to review manuscripts about Islamic law that aren't also about gender, but I'm regularly invited to assess research about marriage or veiling or women's education in contemporary Turkey, or Pakistan, or Indonesia. I decline these requests, noting that it would be a disservice to authors to be reviewed by someone who doesn't know the particulars of the case. Such requests presume that women and gender are the entirety of the story, when a fair review requires deep knowledge of historical, cultural, and textual materials *in addition to* gender studies theories and methods.[10]

If you are turning down a review assignment for this or any other reason, feel free to suggest names of others potential reviewers, along with a sentence about why you think their expertise is applicable.[11] Editors are people too. Their networks are limited. They may not know people better situated than you are to review a given manuscript. On the other hand, everybody else might already have said no. Our peer review system is badly frayed. Review times can be ridiculous. Unsurprisingly, the effects of the pandemic

10. See Salaymeh, "Imperialist Feminism and Islamic Law."
11. Nyasha Junior, "Speak Three Names," https://nyashajunior.com/noextracredit /130820-speak-three-names.

on the peer review system are gendered.[12] You are not personally responsible for fixing this situation by reviewing more than your share of manuscripts or by finding an alternate reviewer, though editors will appreciate a quick no, so they can move on to the next name on their list. However, you might consider making it a point to accept certain kinds of articles or, in the case of book manuscripts, which are usually not anonymized, projects by junior scholars whose professional advancement hinges on timely evaluations.[13]

In doing your review, you may find that a scholar has left out essential work. Whether it is an obvious omission or simply something helpful that they might not know about, suggest that work. Perhaps also include a more pointed note to the editor in the case of the former, suggesting that barring a reasonable justification for the omission from the author, publication should be contingent not just on a perfunctory citation but actual engagement with that specific work's substantive ideas.

12. A study showed that "during the first wave of the pandemic, women submitted proportionally fewer manuscripts than men. This deficit was especially pronounced among more junior cohorts of women academics." Although the pattern was "less pronounced," women also accepted proportionately more peer review invitations in most fields. These "findings suggest that the first wave of the pandemic has created potentially cumulative advantages for men." Flaminio Squazzoni, Giangiacomo Bravo, Francisco Grimaldo, Daniel García-Costa, Mike Farjam, and Bahar Mehmani, "Gender Gap in Journal Submissions and Peer Review during the First Wave of the COVID-19 Pandemic. A study on 2329 Elsevier journals," *PLOS ONE*, 16:10, 2021, https://doi.org/10.1371/journal.pone.0257919.

13. I have found it very helpful to have a personal policy about peer reviews to serve as a default. Your policy could be a certain number per year, how many you are willing to have pending at any given time, or, as some have proposed, a figure that reflects the burden you place on the peer reviewing system. If you submit two articles per year, requiring two reviewers apiece, then you should review four articles. A book manuscript might count as much as three articles. It doesn't matter precisely what your policy is so long as it is appropriate to your situation. Obviously, you can make exceptions, but try to do so only for excellent reasons. Feeling guilty is not an excellent reason. See, for a parallel discussion of (non-academic) endorsements, Catherine Lacey, "Blurbs: Some Complaints and a Proposal," September 21, 2023, https://catherinelacey.substack.com/p/blurbs-some-complaints-and-a-proposal.

Strategies for editors

Probably the single most important thing you can do as an editor for a journal or a book series is build a strong network of demographically, institutionally, and intellectually diverse potential authors and reviewers. Assessing where you are, setting goals for what you'd like to see, and then moving incrementally in that direction is a long-term project. Interim measures to improve your review process will help you insofar as they blunt the harmful impact of sexist reviews and create a welcoming, vibrant climate for productive scholarly exchange.

In working as an editor, you may find yourself needing to either mitigate or enforce reviewers' judgments. If you get an unnecessarily harsh or offensive review, do not pass it directly on to the author. Either send it back to the reviewer for sober reconsideration or revise it yourself to signal key questions and necessary revisions in a respectful way. On the other hand, if reviewers point out lack of inclusion in an edited volume or note an author's failure to cite work by marginalized scholars or point out that, for example, all the work on Islamic feminism is at least a decade out of date, consider carefully before leaving it to the author's discretion to fix. Most likely, they won't. Not only does this result in dated work getting into print, reviewers whose considered and careful guidance seems to make no difference are unlikely to continue providing it—especially if they are already comparatively overburdened with institutional and professional service.

Along with journal and series editors, who are typically faculty volunteers, professional editors who solicit proposals, review manuscripts, and shepherd books to publication at university and other scholarly presses have key roles to play in achieving parity. Promoting gender equity includes, obviously, publishing and promoting books by authors of all genders in due proportion. It means scrutinizing tables of contents for edited volumes and requiring justification for those that include no or few contributions by women (or, for instance, by scholars who aren't white). It might mean working with authors to seek balance while a publication is in process, or with the press to update submission and review guidelines. It might mean desk rejecting work that short-shrifts extant scholarship by women and insisting that authors cite relevant women's scholarship and talk about women in the body of their work where appropriate. And it should mean thinking about who counts as sufficiently prestigious to be asked for endorsements for books so that women aren't only being asked to blurb books on women and gender.

Inviting

Some months back, a colleague emailed me. He wanted to be sure I'd seen the call for proposals for a conference on a key concept in Muslim thought. His note was welcome. Actively soliciting participation from appropriate scholars is a key strategy for having a balanced event and, where a goal is an eventual publication, an inclusive table of contents. I was interested, as one of three focus areas emphasized the relevance of the concept to gender dynamics and family law. Unfortunately, the framing document for the project cited no women at all while referencing tangentially related work from white male philosophers outside of Islamic studies. An edited volume of contributions from Muslim women that specifically tackled the core concept from the perspective of gender and family law? Missing. Kant and Rawls? Present and accounted for.

After sighing gustily, I wrote back declining the invitation, noting that I had put a moratorium on new endeavors so I could finish pending projects. Then, mustering all the tact and delicacy I could, I expressed my frustration with the omissions of women's contributions from the project overview and call for papers. I received a very civil reply admonishing me not to read too much into the total absence of women's names, ideas, and publications from the document. But the silence speaks volumes. Ignoring vital work that women scholars have already done sends a very clear signal about whose work will be taken seriously. When we are all overcommitted and scrambling to find time for the work that matters, a project where at the outset the organizer cannot be bothered to make even a token attempt to incorporate existing publications directly on the conference topic does not bode well. Some of us have had enough of beating our heads against unyielding walls.

Initial planning

Good faith efforts can go a long way toward ensuring inclusive results in a conference or edited volume. Achieving balance requires a carefully thought-through process, groundwork, substantial planning, and perseverance. Graduate programs generally do not teach you how to put together a conference, so scholars are often ill prepared to organize things, let alone consider gender and other forms of demographic balance in doing so. Good intentions are no substitute for deliberate strategies to foster inclusion at every stage of the process.

At the start of any project, consider whether the way you've framed the topic forecloses or encourages balance. A call for contributions on prominent modern intellectuals will generate proposals about men. A call for work on reformers makes space for women and the scholars more likely to write about them. Certain subfields, like American Islam, have a more balanced cadre of specialists, which makes organizing a symposium or proposing an online roundtable easier. But as the Giorgio Levi Della Vida Award volumes discussed in Chapter 1 show, it's possible to achieve parity on nearly any topic. Still, if you are determined to focus your project so narrowly that your pool of potential contributors is overwhelmingly comprised of men, you might consider a comparative angle to bring fruitful new perspectives. When I was writing *Marriage and Slavery in Early Islam*, very few women had published on early Islamic law. However, drawing on work on Roman and Jewish parallels and modern Muslim family law allowed me to be in dialogue with women's scholarship and to have a richer conversation than I otherwise would have had.

Networks and participation

Having a diverse set of collaborators not only brings new perspectives into a conference or a publication, but also expands your network for future scholarly endeavors. Inclusion starts with your own co-organizers. If you are a white dude, seek out white women and scholars of color for your conference organizing committee, being mindful not to make the work burdensome for already overburdened faculty.[14] If you are tenured or tenure-track faculty, be in conversation with contingent scholars as you conceptualize your edited volume, but do not expect them to take on grunt labor uncompensated. If you're from the Ivies, make a real effort not to merely reproduce your own networks. If you've been noticing patterns, you will be aware of what obstacles are keeping which people from participating in whose projects. Proceed accordingly.

Inclusion doesn't mean relaxing standards to guarantee representation. Rather, it means designing one's process to compensate for structural inequities. Taking gender parity and other forms of inclusion seriously means rejecting the pernicious idea that diversity threatens to compromise scholarly standards, rather than being a path to and a characteristic of excellence. It also means noticing where our ideas of what constitutes excellence are already gendered and racialized, and being willing to consider why we value what we value. Diverse perspectives make for more robust institutions, structures, and scholarship.[15]

Diverse perspectives don't just show up, though. You have to seek them out. Fixing a lack of diversity in one's reading or one's

14. If they're from your institution, arrange to have someone else step in with their other duties while the work is ongoing. Write a graduate student into the grant if you do not have administrative support, so that you can limit service-burdened colleagues' role to networking/inviting/helping with the list of participants rather than the tedious work of booking flights, organizing itineraries, or uploading abstracts.

15. For one exploration of the benefits of teams that are demographically as well as professionally varied, see Scott E. Page, *The Diversity Bonus: How Great Teams Pay Off in the Knowledge Economy* (Princeton, NJ: Princeton University Press, 2017).

network requires corrective strategies from the outset when one is seeking contributions or inviting participants. (Ideally, it begins years earlier. Networks take time to root and flourish.) Fantasy writer Nalo Hopkinson describes her process for ensuring good representation of Black writers in an anthology she edited. Rather than simply evaluating submissions with an eye toward authors' identities, she actively encouraged submissions from Black authors as well as "non-black writers" she "felt were creatively up to the task." With a sufficiently diverse pool of contributions received, she then chose which to include without attending to authors' backgrounds. She handily met her goal percentage of Black authors.[16]

In organizing an event or a publication, good communication between and among co-organizers, funders, and potential participants is essential. For one thing, having to explain your process makes you think it through. It's less likely you'll miss an obvious step. Outlining your process in advance also means you can solicit feedback, ideally from a diverse network of interlocutors.

Selection criteria

Clarifying and seeking advice about your process for recruiting and selecting participants means you'll need to specify your criteria for inviting people. What are the individual desiderata? If applicable, what do you want for the whole group? If you can't explain how you're choosing, you probably haven't thought enough about it. If someone suggests that your approach will exclude whole categories of scholars, rethink it. If you're trying to reach broader scholarly and public audiences by inviting scholars with name recognition and popular appeal, you may confront the problem that those who'll draw big audiences are men. The criterion of reputation reinforces existing inequalities. As Sarah Imhoff and Susannah Heschel note, "When scholars use language of

16. Nalo Hopkinson, *Report from Planet Midnight Plus . . .* (Oakland, CA: PM Press, 2012), 84–86.

'good fit,' 'stature' or 'prestige,' these can often signal implicit bias. If you are part of an organizing committee, push for explicit criteria: Is 'stature' about the number of publications, the current academic position or something else? Is 'good fit' about matching research interests, or is it a cover for inviting the good old boys?"[17]

Being clear about selection criteria helps keep unarticulated, unconscious biases at bay. Creating a rubric, or a point system, or a set of guidelines, takes more time initially but can lead to a better result. Measures like these are now used in college admissions as well as in faculty hiring. Anonymous evaluations can also help eliminate implicit bias. Even people who pride themselves on their lack of prejudice can presume white men's greater competence. Perhaps the most famous example of effective intervention to reduce bias is in orchestra auditions. A few decades ago, selection committees began to have performers audition behind a screen, walking to the stage on carpet or barefooted so that the clacking of high heels rather than the clomp of men's dress shoes wasn't a giveaway. When committees judged candidates solely on their playing, the proportion of women hired soared.[18]

Greater reliance on anonymized selection, however, won't fix academic discrimination. A violinist's performance of a preselected concerto movement allows anonymity in a way that specialized scholarship doesn't. Someone qualified to judge an article in early Islamic legal history may be able to tell from its subject matter and sources who wrote a manuscript stripped of obvious identifiers. Beyond journal publications, moreover, academics seldom select anonymously, whether for jobs or symposia. Certainly, conference organizers and volume editors could choose participants more

17. Susannah Heschel and Sarah Imhoff, "Where Are All the Women in Jewish Studies?," *The Forward*, July 3, 2018. https://forward.com/culture/404416/where-are-all-the-women-in-jewish-studies/.

18. Claudia Goldin and Cecelia Rouse, "Orchestrating Impartiality: The Impact of 'Blind' Auditions on Female Musicians," *The American Economic Review*, 90:4, 2000: 715–41.

often via anonymized submissions. Still, some feminized topics and approaches are less well regarded, even if those making selections don't know the identity of the potential contributor. And even an inclusively framed call for papers could lead to a homogenous participant group, especially in male-dominated subfields, depending on which networks the call circulates through. Anonymized evaluations must be coupled with strategies to broaden the pool from which selections are made and the topics and approaches deemed desirable. Building inclusive networks will also be important for those events and initiatives for which anonymized evaluation is inappropriate or impossible.

If your event or publication is by direct invitation and you're aiming for adequate representation of women and nonbinary scholars, starting with a list that's 10%, 20%, or even 30% scholars who aren't men won't do. Although one frequently hears anecdotally that women turn down invitations more frequently, a comprehensive study of colloquium invitations in six academic disciplines found no gender differences in acceptance rates.[19] Perhaps it's that, for reasons explored in earlier chapters, relatively few women have attained prominence, and those who have are disproportionately white. A handful of luminaries get more than their share of speaking invitations, while junior and mid-career women, to say nothing of the contingent scholars among whom women are overrepresented, are often overlooked and under-invited. A cable show featuring authors had to start with a list of potential guests that was 80–90% women to achieve gender parity among guests, largely because it was harder to get well-known women to participate than

19. Christine L. Nittrouer, Michelle R. Hebl, Leslie Ashburn-Nardo, Rachel C. E. Trump-Steele, David M. Lane, and Virginia Valian, "Gender Disparities in Colloquium Speakers at Top Universities." *PNAS*, 115:1, 2018: 104–108, https://doi.org/10.1073/pnas.1708414115. Ed Yong summarizes its key findings: "Women Are Invited to Give Fewer Talks than Men at Top U.S. Universities," *The Atlantic*, December 2017, https://www.theatlantic.com/science/archive/2017/12/women-are-invited-to-give-fewer-talks-than-men-at-top-us-universities/548657/.

well-known men. Among midlist authors there was no appreciable difference.[20]

Because this is a systemic problem, achieving gender balance requires digging a little deeper than the first few names that come to mind.[21] With conferences, edited volumes, and other projects, the earlier someone pays attention to parity, the better, including thinking about *which* women should show up on the lists. The fewer the women in a given subfield, the more overburdened they're likely to be. If you're aiming for 10–30% women, you're going to have to invite at least 50% women. You should probably be doing this anyway. It also covers you if a couple of women in your project ultimately bow out, as scholars of all genders sometimes do. If you only had one or two women, you now have a manel or a manthology on your hands. If you're aiming for half the participants being women, your initial invitee list should be mostly women. If you end up with 90% women, congratulations. Bet you don't, though.

A word about tokenism: if you're a panel or conference organizer faced with the choice of no (or too few) women, or an all-white line-up, or a panel on race that includes no Black people, versus an offensively last-minute invitation, I suggest the latter. The closer to showtime you are, the more you'll have to do to mitigate the damage and make the invitation attractive. You'll probably need several choices of invitees. You may need to grovel. Start by owning up to your mistake: "It was brought to our attention that our conference on gender and law has three men and no women as keynote speakers. We're mortified that we missed that and promise we'll never let anything like that happen again." Say something about how you'll fix the problem in the future. That

20. Steven I. Weiss, "Closing the TV-Guest Gender Gap," *The Atlantic*, March 3, 2015, https://www.theatlantic.com/entertainment/archive/2015/03/how-to-get -more-women-on-tv/386378/.

21. Kristian Petersen's Women of Islamic Studies crowdsourced database (https://drkristianpetersen.com/women-of-islamic-studies/) is one resource. When I go on research leave, during which I do not accept new invitations to contribute, speak, consult, review, and so forth, I link to it in my autoreply.

may mean specifics: "Going forward, our initial list of invitees will be at least half women and nonbinary people." Or, if you don't have the specifics yet: "Once this event is over, we're going audit our processes to figure out where we went wrong to ensure we don't repeat our mistakes." Then circle back to the invitation: "In the meantime, we've still got this event going on: are you willing and able to present your important research on X while helping us balance our event?" At that point, the ball is in the invitee's court. You may want to make the invitation by phone—email and ask for a phone call, note that it's time-sensitive—if you need a speedy reply. If you do send the invitation by email, note that you're under a tight deadline, and that if you don't hear by a specific date/time, you'll proceed to the next name on your list. If you leave the invitation open-ended and move to the next name on your list, you might end up in the awkward situation of having to withdraw the first invitation. Or, of course, you could add both speakers.

Once a project winds up, evaluate your process and results. If things went well, congratulations. What were the most useful strategies? Where can you improve in future iterations? If things went poorly, that's useful information, too. Consider: Whom did you approach initially? How did you generate that list? What did their suggestions look like? How did you follow up? What did *that* list of suggestions look like? The point is not self-flagellation but learning how to do better next time. Understanding what went wrong involves noticing where you could have chosen differently and where you can try something else.

A brief note on email

Email is exhausting for everyone, but it is worse for some scholars. Many women get what we might euphemistically term problematic correspondence. This includes messages that are in themselves perfectly civil but by steady accretion of requests or demands for labor pose a burden. Strangers, often men, frequently presume on women in ways that sap us. Casual sexism and racism manifest in writing just as they do in person. If we sometimes snap at something that seems little, be assured that it isn't.[22]

In a salutation, the safest course is to use earned titles unless invited to do otherwise. The more likely a person is to have their title omitted in everyday interactions, the more important it is to adhere punctiliously to protocol. As someone now senior, I usually take the liberty of addressing correspondence to colleagues with whom I am not personally acquainted with Professor Lastname (or Firstname, if I may) if they are a faculty member or Dr. Lastname (etc.) if not. I sign such emails with my first name only, leaving my full name and professorial title to the signature/address lines of my email, thereby inviting them to first name terms.

A simple question that gets at appropriate respect is: would you send a similar email to a man with a prestigious position and title? This applies both to your chosen greeting and to the substance of the email. Are you asking them for onerous labor based on slight or no acquaintance? Obviously, a query about potential doctoral supervision is different than a request for feedback on an independently researched study hundreds of manuscript pages long. If you are asking for a favor, is your tone polite or entitled? Even if the request is appropriate and respectful, be mindful that women faculty, especially women of color, are comparatively overburdened with service and are the least likely to have any extra time to do work outside the scope of their regular ongoing duties.

Citing

As I worked on this book, I heard at least a dozen accounts of citation-related shenanigans. Although scholars of all genders can and do misstep, the cases people told me about all involved men

---

22. See, e.g., Baker, "Men Who Email Me," in *Sexism Ed*, 172–76. On microaggressions perpetrated by white colleagues, see Stacey Patton's "Dear White Academics" (*Chronicle of Higher Education*, October 24, 2014, but as of this writing no longer available at the *Chronicle*'s Vitae site).

overstepping. Nearly all those whose work was used inappropriately were women. One author wrote a co-panelist's conference
paper argument into his book without crediting her. The editor of
a book moved several substantial paragraphs from a woman contributor's chapter to that of a man, noting her authorship only in
an endnote. A doctoral candidate's prospectus carefully cited work
by numerous men outside his area, then proceeded to reproduce
without acknowledgment the directly relevant results of a woman's
fieldwork and analysis. Another scholar published essentially a
gender-swapped version of an award-winning book and never
once mentions the author or her work. Here's one more, in a colleague's own words: "A male scholar in our field duplicated my
dissertation work without citing me, and at a fancier institution.
He published articles as though I did not exist and got his book
out first. Important senior men in the field defended him and I was
set back several years, resulting in lasting damage to my career. He
has just landed a very fancy endowed chair position." Some but
not all of these offenses are plagiarism. But they all reveal pervasive gendered disparities, which overlap and intersect those in-
volving seniority, race, and institutional prestige, in how women's
intellectual contributions are treated.[23]

Failures of citation are always collective failures. Doctoral training failed to provide a balanced introduction to the literature, or
even to address the issue of imbalance. Colleagues failed to flag
omissions in early iterations of the project. Peer reviewers didn't
catch the exclusions or didn't think they mattered enough to insist
on revisions. Editors green-lit the project anyway. Good-guy colleagues offered enthusiastic blurbs and positive reviews. When
instructors add the book to their syllabi, or journalists or popular-
izers rely on it for their writing, the cycle begins anew.

Failures of citation do damage. There's a real but difficult to
quantify effect that not engaging women's and feminist work has

23. These examples are all drawn from the U.S. and the U.K., but plagiarism of
work by global South-based researchers of all genders is an equally pressing issue.

on the field. There's a professional cost to individual scholars, especially those who are early in their careers, which grows as institutions increasingly rely on impact metrics for tenure and promotion. Then there's the affective dimension of others' crappy citational politics. Unlike the professional damage, this impact doesn't disappear when you reach full professor status. Having someone ignore your obviously relevant work takes an emotional toll, and sustained anger exacts a physical price. And finally, it takes time to address such failures by pointing them out privately and publicly, on your own behalf or that of your colleagues, students, and mentees. This time, which is already scarcer for women because of domestic and service overloads, could be spent doing other valuable work.[24]

Preventing citational disasters requires cultivating an awareness of how biases manifest in things you read, review, blurb, endorse, or assign, as well as those you write. You, like everyone, can and should do better in your own citational practice. You must also keep in mind that mistakes are inevitable. I've defined projects poorly. I've cited men in my text and women in my notes. I've left out things I should have included and included things that I could've safely left out. A widely quoted if dubiously sourced sentiment from Maya Angelou via Oprah expresses it best: when you know better, you do better. So here are some questions to ask, roughly in order of how they present themselves when you embark on a project or engage another's work.

Are you knowledgeable enough to responsibly evaluate this manuscript, review this published book, or accept this invitation to co-author or give a keynote lecture? White women are socialized to have a less expansive sense of our own capacities than

24. To give just one example, one day instead of revising Chapter 2—ironically, the chapter on citation—I spent several hours engaged in phone conversations, Twitter DMs, and rapid-fire emails when a man on the tenure track tweeted about the work of a woman doctoral candidate in my department's graduate program in a way that effectively took credit for it. By the time he deleted his thread, I'd lost a day's work.

(white) men, so while humility is necessary for everyone, it's also useful to have some sort of external check. If you don't know people working in the field and aren't aware of decades of work that has been done, then your choice is either to opt out or to do the work to get up to speed. But that doesn't necessarily mean becoming a full-fledged expert. It means recognizing that there *are* experts and knowing how to engage with and direct others to their work. There's a widespread tendency to assume that thinking and writing about women and gender doesn't require expertise. I advocate instead reading, learning from, and of course citing the existing literature.

If you're writing in your area of specialization, do you engage the work of women and nonbinary scholars who've written on the topic? What about scholars of all genders publishing in languages other than English? From the global South? Who are precariously employed or independent scholars? If you're not finding any, is it a matter of not knowing folks beyond your established networks?[25] Or, if appropriate searches and queries don't turn up anyone, consider how are you defining your topic. If you are looking for famously influential thinkers, you will not find many women thusly categorized. If you cast your net a bit more broadly, you're likely to turn up others whose work is, indeed, connected to the topics you're interested in.

How are you deciding what's relevant? Determinations of relevance are always subjective. There are some publications that, given a particular topic, you'd have to have an excellent reason not to cite. But it's impossible to include everything. Whether it's a because of publisher's word limit for a manuscript, the constraints of a fourteen-week syllabus, or simply our own finite capacity to read and assimilate existing and new scholarship, choices are

---

25. Kane, *Beyond Timbuktu*, 161, gives a compelling illustration of "the compartmentalization of knowledge production" for the study of Islam in Africa just among Francophone and Arabophone scholars deeply enmeshed in the region. The problems are, again, structural.

unavoidable. But, too often, scholars chose to exclude published work that's directly on point while citing the thing that everyone always cites, which is usually by a man. A series of individually defensible choices may end up indefensibly excluding a universe of work.

Choices about whose work to cite are fraught for other reasons as well. Increasingly, we talk publicly about sexual harassment and assault by religious and scholarly figures. Some of these figures are considered foundational to our fields and/or subfields. How and when do we read their works? Should we ever cite them or write about them? Should we assign their works in courses? As I've become aware of credible public accusations against scholars I've cited approvingly and taught and engaged extensively, I've been forced to confront these issues. Likewise on learning of credible but not public accusations. Withholding citation, especially when it's something that readers expect to be cited, may suggest that the work is shoddy or insinuate that the author is morally suspect.[26] As feminists and progressives wrestle with this issue, I worry about increasingly public weaponization of perceived moral failings as an argument against citing Muslim feminists. But the reality is that this already happens. People who disapprove of us don't cite our work and seldom get called to account for it. As always, power is at play. Those whose work goes uncited must be outside the circles of power and prestige that make excluding their work unthinkable.

Back to your own citational patterns: when you cite works by scholars who aren't men, are you simply using them as repositories of facts or are you engaging their analyses? Are you naming women thinkers and writers in the body of your text if you're also naming men? If you are discussing activists or bloggers or tweeters, are you crediting their ideas appropriately? Are you inadvertently

26. See Sarah Scullins, "Making a Monster," March 24, 2016, https://eidolon.pub /making-a-monster-3cd90135ef3f and Eric Vanden Eykel, "On Citing Monsters. Or Not," https://evandeneykel.medium.com/on-citing-monsters-or-not-827b91398208.

diminishing some people's authority by how you frame their contributions?

Although plagiarism, as I know from experience, is a problem, citational ethics involve more than the deliberate theft of intellectual property. Things can get fuzzy. Ideas circulate and mutate in amorphous extended exchanges. Similar concepts arise independently in people's works. People sometimes unintentionally claim others' ideas as their own because they've forgotten that they heard them in a conference paper or read them somewhere. Sometimes scholars take sloppy notes. Sometimes things get garbled in drafting. That's where a scholarly community comes in, and peer review should serve as a check. Whose work do we allow to pass as conventional wisdom and who do we insist on crediting? It matters whose ideas are recognized as *ideas*, worthy of attribution, rather than simply a kind of common property subject to assimilation.

Counting citations in one's own work is a good way to get a preliminary gauge for parity. People notoriously overestimate women's presence and participation in mixed groups. I suspect the same is the case for inclusion in references and bibliographies. Despite its limitations, taking a deep breath and doing some quick math will tell you things that you are otherwise unlikely to learn. Of course, counting citations has its limits. Tally marks will not tell you whose work is really being engaged. If the goal is what Jenn Jackson of the #CiteBlackWomen initiative terms "structural inclusion," meaning the citations are integral rather than merely an afterthought, ratios won't suffice.[27] But if you are looking at your own work, or work that you are reviewing, you can add this qualitative dimension as well. I suggest trying this at a relatively early stage in the process. If, as is likely, you discover significant imbalances, you'll have time to correct them.

27. Jenn Jackson, "Why citing black women is necessary," December 21, 2018, https://www.citeblackwomencollective.org/our-blog/why-citing-black-women-is-necessary-jenn-m-jackson.

Assigning

Assigning works by women scholars and talking about women and gender aren't the same thing, but they are linked. My imaginary Islamic Civ curriculum, discussed in Chapter 4, added content about women and analysis of gender; the inclusion of women's books was a byproduct. Making course content inclusive usually leads to more author diversity and including more books by scholars who aren't men often means more attention to gender. But when I've been the one adding gender in, with my own framing around primary sources, my required texts have often been sorely lacking. Following established patterns, using widely available course materials, I was following the path of least resistance and the path of least resistance is paved by patriarchy.

As with other phenomena discussed in this book, bad patterns are mutually reinforcing, and positive changes can likewise proliferate. Just as reading is the foundation for our writing as scholars, learning is the foundation for teaching. Our teaching builds on what we were taught. Adjustments to our teaching matter for the undergraduates in our classes, most of whom will never become part of the professoriate, but also for our graduate students, some of whom will. Most faculty care deeply about pedagogical effectiveness and about student success in and out of the classroom. Many of us are also overwhelmed by unrealistic administrative demands, too many classes and preps at teaching-heavy institutions, publication expectations, and, well, life. I'm not suggesting an immediate and total overhaul of each of your classes to achieve The Perfect Syllabus™. Instead, I offer strategies for assessing and increasing the proportion of course materials that are neither by nor about men. These strategies can also be modified to assess and improve along other axes of inclusion. The point isn't to meet an arbitrary metric of Enough Women So That Harridan Will Stop Nagging Me but to help your course content better reflect the richness and complexity of Islam and Muslims, and the scholarship on both.

These are not just Islamic studies problems. Scholars in other fields have written extensively about how to go about integrating women and gender into existing courses as well as about designing courses from scratch. Their strategies can be adopted and adapted for courses about Islam and Muslims.[28] But you can make improvements to your courses without doing extensive background reading by choosing one of your existing courses to modify.

Pick a syllabus to start with. Get ready to mark it up and make notes.

What's on the syllabus? What is essential, centered, investigated at length? What is passed over quickly, referred to along the way? Who are the main examples? Who are the colorful outliers? Are women and/or gender addressed at all? How? In a segregated week? As a sidebar to various sections? If you're using a textbook, does the textbook routinely talk about women? If not, are you supplementing it with other sources? Have you considered what this practice conveys about which topics really matter?

Who's on the syllabus? Which texts are assigned? Are some required and others supplementary? Obviously, *which topics* you teach informs *whose work* you assign. If you are assigning work by women, which women? Are all the women white? Are all the Muslims men? Are any of your required readings by Black people? If you are teaching a class about Islam centered outside of the U.S., how many (if any) of the books you are assigning were initially written in a language other than English? In a non-European language? The Qur'an doesn't count.

Do some quick categorizing. Of the total items assigned, how many are by men? Is there a difference in the length and types of materials you assign by men and by others? Do you assign books by men and journalistic pieces by women? Video explainers, magazine articles, and podcasts are great. But if students buy men's books while women only get clicks, it reinforces publishers' habit of promoting men's books for course adoption and recruiting men as textbook authors.

Are you pleased by what this review turned up? If so, terrific. Likely, however, at least some of your readings or course organization could do with an overhaul (good luck!) or, more realistically, a refresh.

Most course modification happens incrementally. In the case of a book-a-week seminar, vanishingly rare in undergraduate contexts outside of upper-level humanities courses in elite institutions, replacing one book with another is relatively straightforward. You can ask colleagues for recommendations, request exam copies, and read reviews. Still, even looking for new publications requires deliberate attention to inclusivity. Otherwise, especially if you ask men for suggestions about what new books to read, you'll get a disproportionate number of works by men. Men's books may also be more likely to get reviewed, meaning you're less likely to learn about women's books through journal and online reviews. Between 2006 and 2020, for example, nearly seven out of ten Islam books reviewed in the *Journal of the American Academy of Religion* were by men.[29] And citational disparities mean works by scholars who aren't men are less likely to come to your attention in things you read.

In classes where you rely on one book, or a few books supplemented by shorter pieces, it's less like laying paving stones and more like playing Jenga. Everything rests on and supports everything else. Messing with your course architecture is a hassle. But small experiments can allow you to broaden and diversify your course by changing a case study; using a novel or memoir by a woman in place of a text you've been using; or, if you assign

29. Ali and Serrano, "The Person of the Author," 564. There is a gap, albeit a narrowing one, between the proportion of women members of the American Academy of Religion and the proportion of books by women reviewed in the society's journal (562–64).

biographical presentations or Wikipedia-editing projects, offering lists of individuals that are more than half women.

Caveat scholar

Syllabi, both symptom and vector of academic patriarchy, bring this conversation full circle. There is much we can and should do to diversify our syllabi and make our teaching more inclusive, but adjustments by individual professors are insufficient to the task at hand. For inclusion to take root sustainably in the Islamic studies classroom, other policies and practices must shift as well. For instance, something as seemingly simple as textbook choice is profoundly shaped by the interlocking structures of academic sexism. Even a cursory survey of syllabi, bookstore shelves, and publisher catalogs shows that surveys and trade books about Islam, the Qur'an, Islamic Law, Sufism, or Muhammad tend to be written by men. Any answers as to why must be part speculation, but reasonable extrapolation from experience suggests some answers.

It's likely that women are asked less often than men to write introductory or popular works. (There is no data on this.)[30] Unlike scholarly monographs, which scholars usually write and then shop around to university presses, textbooks and trade books are typically written at publishers' behest. At the mid-career and senior levels, when scholars are likely to take on such projects, invitations go to those whose reputations—built in part from reviews and citations of earlier publications as well as media appearances—have brought them to publishers' notice. Women remain overrepresented among contingent faculty and underrepresented among the tenured faculty to whom such invitations are typically extended.

---

30. See Johanna Hanink, "More Women Classicists Need to Write Big," *Eidolon*, March 2, 2017, https://eidolon.pub/more-women-classicists-need-to-write-big -cc1994ad1747.

If women are approached to write introductory or trade books, it's possible that they decline more often. (There is no data on this.) Maybe—again, this is informed speculation—women, unfairly burdened with heavier professional service and unequal domestic loads, turn down invitations for lack of time.[31] Perhaps some say no because they feel inadequate to the task. Insecurity can be an artifact of sexism. But the decision to devote scarce, precious writing time to specialized monographs, and avoid books that seek a student or a general audience, is a rational response to the lesser professional rewards and greater risks of undertaking such work for women. Decisions about which opportunities to pursue or accept are conditioned by both women's disproportionate likelihood of facing unpleasant pushback for public-facing work and the understanding that media engagement and popular writing, including in trade books, tends to be viewed as less serious and rewarded less well when women do it.

Risks of being perceived as doing insufficiently authoritative work include delayed or denied tenure or promotion. Tenure and promotion are notoriously opaque. The processes clearly have discriminatory outcomes when looked at systemically, but proving malfeasance in any given case is nigh impossible.[32] We know that women, especially Black women and women of color, are judged more stringently for professional advancement than men. Introductory or general audience work by women is often deemed unserious while accessible books by men garner kudos for demonstrating impressive mastery and enviable intellectual scope.[33] A

---

31. Park's analysis in "Research, Teaching, and Service," remains relevant, although there is copious newer research substantiating gendered and racialized service inequalities. See also Nazli Kibria, "The Feminization of the Department Chair" for an account of how expectations for those occupying roles have shifted. *Inside Higher Ed,* January 31, 2023, https://www.insidehighered.com/advice/2023/01/31/women-chairs-face-mushrooming-demands-inadequate-support-opinion.

32. See Matthew, *Written/Unwritten,* García Peña, *Community as Rebellion,* and Deo, "Tenure and Promotion Challenges," in *Unequal Profession,* 79–98.

33. Ali and Serrano, "The Person of the Author," 569.

trade book by a white man may be gauged sufficient for promotion from associate to full professor, while a woman of color may be penalized for it. So, if women are turning down invitations more often, it's hard to argue with their reasons.

Ultimately, even as individual faculty work to diversify their syllabi, there must be movement in other professional domains. Editors should acquire, publish, and promote women's books appropriately. Book reviewers should treat women's nonspecialized publications in the same way as those by men, and journal editors should ensure that treatment, in addition to promoting parity in whose books get reviews in the first place. Institutions should assign equal value to everyone's textbooks and general-audience or trade books in merit, tenure, and promotion evaluations. Departments should normalize teaching about gender and encourage balanced and inclusive assigned readings on everyone's syllabi. They must also recognize that faculty who are marginalized tend to be penalized in student evaluations, and they should adapt the weight given to those evaluations—and push for university administrations, including institutional tenure and promotion committees, to do the same. In other words, as this book has argued throughout, our professional activities are intimately interconnected and forms of discrimination are mutually reinforcing.

Paying attention to our often-unspoken norms and default practices, "we may see that this version of the world has been built or constituted through repeated acts that can be both analyzed and interrupted," as Judith Butler writes in another context.[34] Just as various forms of exclusion compound over time and across domains, so can ameliorative measures. Individual actions can create cracks in a seemingly seamless wall, generate momentum toward transformation, and perhaps result in seismic shifts. Trying to fix sexism one citation at a time is like bailing out a leaky yacht with a teacup. But small positive changes can have far-reaching implications. How we

34. Judith Butler, *What World Is This: A Pandemic Phenomenology* (New York: Columbia University Press, 2022), 72–73.

work shapes our work and continually shapes and reshapes our field. Our individual steps to cultivate inclusive research and teaching practices can contribute to a systemic shift toward humane systems of knowledge production and circulation, inside and outside the academy.

Although this book's focus has been on the gender inequality within Islamic studies as a specific instance of academic sexism, sexist discrimination cannot be divorced from other forms of injustice even within the academy. Beyond the intersectional dimensions of gender discrimination, there are fundamental economic and political stakes to the academy as it stands. Yes, it matters when people should cite women but don't; when women associate professors spend longer than men before coming up for promotion to full professor; when scholars who aren't men, especially scholars of color, are comparatively overburdened with university and professional service; and when women full professors are paid less than purportedly comparable men.[35] However, if tenured women merely fight to keep parity with tenured men, we miss the broader issues of unjust resource distribution and the larger threats to academic workers' well-being. The gap between haves and have-nots even within academe, even among those with tenure-track jobs, is growing. It behooves us all to operate differently.[36] Universities would be healthier if salaries were reallocated more fairly not only

35. Amanda Kulp, Lisa Wolf, and Daryl Smith, "The Possibility of Promotion: How Race and Gender Predict Promotion Clarity for Associate Professors," *Teachers College Record*, 121, 2019. See also Joya Misra, Jennifer Hickes Lundquist, Elissa Holmes, and Stephanie Agiomavritis, "The Ivory Ceiling of Service Work," January–February 2011, https://www.aaup.org/article/ivory-ceiling-service-work, and the University of Maine's report on the experiences of promotion to full professor on their campus. https://umaine.edu/risingtide/resource/report-on-the-experiences-in-the-process-of-promotion-to-full-professor-at-umaine-2011/. On measuring "comparability," see Ali and Serrano, "The Person of the Author," 575.

36. Even tenure-track positions are not necessarily good jobs with a livable wage. Karen Kelsky wrote about this for *The Chronicle of Higher Education*, in an article no longer found at https://chroniclevitae.com/news/934-disappointed-with-the-offer.

across tenure-line faculty, not only among all faculty including lecturers and per-course adjuncts, but across all categories of workers, including provosts, graduate students, department staff, and custodians. We're not going to immediately abolish the two-tier system for academic jobs, let alone radically redefine the university, but as we imagine and implement small changes to our personal and collective practices, we can align them with the broader transformations so badly needed.[37] After we manage to bring what Butler calls "these iterable structures . . . to a halt," together we can set the gears in motion in a different, more just, direction.

37. Worth a read: Cinzia Arruzza, Tithi Bhattacharya, and Nancy Fraser, *Feminism for the 99%.* (London: Verso Books, 2018), and Jessa Crispin, *Why I Am Not a Feminist: A Feminist Manifesto* (New York: Melville House, 2017).

ACKNOWLEDGMENTS

IN HER TRENCHANT "On Acknowledgments," Emily Callaci points to the work this customary feature of scholarly books does. "At their best," she writes, "acknowledgments dismantle the myth of the lone, self-contained genius-at-work, and instead expose the messy interplay of institutional support, finances, intellectual genealogies, and interpersonal chaos that shape how an idea is brought into the world. In aggregate, they offer a glimpse into the political economy of academic life, revealing truths that we intend to share, as well as many that we do not." I hope that this book itself does some of the work of dismantling, exposing, and revealing. It remains for me to acknowledge in "righteous, comradely" fashion the many people and institutions that have helped and supported me along the way.[1]

When I complained yet again about Princeton University Press's pattern of releasing books by men that utterly disregarded women's contributions to their topics, Fred Appel suggested that I write about it. Jenny Tan, then on the editorial staff at Princeton, offered incisive comments on an early draft. Peer review often functions as an elitist gatekeeping tool, but the anonymous reports for both proposal and manuscript were thoughtful, thorough, and constructive. Reader 2 was a gem. During production, James Collier and Nathan Carr were efficient and helpful.

1. Emily Callaci, "On Acknowledgments," *American Historical Review*, 125:1, 2020, 126–31 at 127.

Boston University students, staff, and faculty have assisted in various ways over what turned out to be a much longer-term project than I had initially hoped. Magda Mohamed assembled a reading list on insiders and outsiders. Henry Kruell gathered material from journals. Ateeb Gul double-checked all my numbers for Chapter 2 and performed other minor but significant editorial labors. Wendy Czik, capable administrator for the Department of Religion, coordinated various elements of academic life during my stint as chair in the time of corona. Library staff pulled off minor Interlibrary Loan miracles. Jane Parr, Archivist for Acquisitions at the Howard Gotlieb Archival Research Center, scanned pages from a Festschrift. The members of the Religion faculty writing group, Andrea Berlin, Margarita Guillory, Laura Harrington, April Hughes, Deeana Klepper, and Anthony Petro, have provided good advice, consistent support, and strong coffee for years. As Associate Dean for the Humanities, Karl Kirchwey supported our group's occasional writing retreats. BU's Center for the Humanities supported indexing for this book. During his time at BU, Michael Pregill was a valued conversation partner and reliable reinforcement when trouble came knocking.

Outside of BU, Hamada Altalib devoted hours to the ultimately fruitless task of helping organize a bibliometric investigation of citational practices, a project on which Amany Marey worked briefly. Sumayya Ahmed introduced me to Rachael Clemens, who spoke with me at some length about bibliometrics and the vagaries of citation measurement. Saulat Parvez of the International Institute of Islamic Thought arranged access to syllabi compiled by its researchers.

Many of the ideas in this book were tested out in lectures and panels and at conferences sponsored by the Institute of Islamic Thought, University of Exeter, Smith College, Uppsala University, the International Qur'anic Studies Association, Feminist Studies in Religion, Harvard University, and Yale University. In addition to participants in my home department's colloquium, colleagues and students at the University of Colorado in Boulder; at Boston

University's Center for the Humanities, where I was supported by a Jeffrey Henderson senior fellowship; at the Islam, Gender, Women program unit in the American Academy of Religion; and in Notre Dame's Madrasa Discourses project read drafts of Chapter 2 in whole or part. Participants in the Symposium on Gender and Authenticity in the Islamic Past at Yale University read a draft of Chapter 3.

Ilyse Morgenstein Fuerst read an embarrassingly rough early version of the whole manuscript and made immeasurably helpful suggestions, as did Najwa Mayer at a much later stage. Juliane Hammer, Aysha Hidayatullah, and Saadia Yacoob also read the whole thing in one form or another, and some parts two or three times. They provided sound advice as well as sustained encouragement through the long crisis of the pandemic. Others who read portions of the manuscript include Jonathan Brockopp, who also moderated the AAR forum; Lailatul Fitriyah and Mahan Mirza, who provided responses to my draft chapter at Notre Dame; Sarah Imhoff; Harvey Stark; and Hussein Rashid. Although the parts of the manuscript that she discussed with me mostly didn't make the cut, Kayla Wheeler's comments were formative.

Just as a book's references can never fully reflect its author's intellectual formation, any list of those who have informed one's thinking on a given project will be inevitably incomplete. That's no reason for failing to make the attempt. Among those whose valued insights and provocations over the years helped shape this book are Kelly Baker, Karen Bauer, Edward Curtis, Kerry Danner, Ash Geissinger, Megan Goodwin, Zareena Grewal, Ali Mian, Shabana Mir, Martin Nguyen, Sara Omar, Fatima Seedat, Laury Silvers, and amina wadud. I cannot say whether they will recognize themselves in the final product or feel I have done justice to our exchanges.

I was eight years on Twitter before abandoning ship in late 2022. Using the hashtag #WomanQuestion, I tallied women encountered in or, more often, missing from the work of colleagues. My tweets were often accompanied by a clip of a scowling, scolding figure I called purple hairbrush girl. I appreciate that anonymous

GIF maker as well as all the users who pointed me to useful resources and engaged with my posts. At a critical moment, Rachel Schine tweeted "stay mad and write down why." Those are words to live by.

I am grateful for the energy, generosity, and collective wisdom of the colleagues who comprise the listserv formerly known as Islam-AAR, in which I have participated for essentially my entire professional life. Traces of our occasionally fraught exchanges appear throughout this book. I owe to their collective wisdom the usage of "Islamic studies" rather than "Islamic Studies" for our shared field.

Finally, at the suggestion of Katherine Crocker, I offer a land acknowledgment here. I live and work on the land of Massachusett and Wampanoag peoples. I acknowledge historical wrongs done to these peoples as well my complicity in perpetuating them today. I intend to learn more and do better going forward.

APPENDIX

A Note on Method

ONE RECURRENT CONCERN raised about the claims of gender bias I have researched for *The Woman Question* has been that my sources are deliberately unrepresentative or simply happenstance. It has been suggested that choosing different texts would yield different results. Although I know that viewing quantitative work as more scientific and rigorous than qualitative work itself reflects gendered bias, I nonetheless hoped to test my findings against a representative sampling of Islamic studies books. That proved impractical, as I discovered in an initial attempt, which I describe in more detail below. Existing bibliometric and network analysis tools are geared toward data sets analyzable via automation, which mostly means articles in journals covered by indexes such as SCOPUS. These indexes, routinely used in the sciences and social sciences despite their widely acknowledged biases, are even less reliable for humanities articles and are essentially useless for books.

In the fields and disciplines that comprise Islamic studies, and especially in religious studies, books are esteemed as a primary vehicle of scholarly communication. Incentives to produce them are high. Humanities departments at research universities and elite liberal arts colleges typically require a book for tenure and another for promotion to full professor. Peer-reviewed journal articles are expected as well but will not suffice to clear these professional hurdles. And yet, despite books' importance, the references in them and citations to them cannot be digitally mapped in the ways those in articles can. Tracking citations of books and other publications in Google Scholar or Web of Science, with its "algorithmically generated" author records, is error-riddled and unreliable.

If one cannot use automated data for citation counts, one must then generate a sample oneself and manually enter all references. Generating a statistically robust sample of books on its own is possible, but the labor requirements for data entry, data cleaning, coding, and generating visualizations to track gendered citations proved impossibly onerous. What follows lays out the measuring and data collection necessary for undertaking quantitative analysis of citations, limns my abandoned bibliometric project, then discusses how I ultimately generated the numbers I used, including the assignment of gender to individual authors. I hope that others, equipped with newer tools or different competencies, will pursue these lines of inquiry further.

On measuring

Measuring gender gaps in citation—where women should be cited but are not—requires knowing probabilistically how many citations to women's works there should be compared to citations to men's works. This requires some census of women within subfields and ways of connecting those subfields to specific publications. Michelle Dion, Jane Lawrence Sumner, and Sarah McLaughlin Mitchell's study of the gendered citation gap in political science uses journal article citations, evaluated with a tool for predictive assessment of gender via author first names, measured against women as members of the discipline's professional organization and some of its specific subfields.[1] Parallel data do not exist for

---

[1]. Michelle Dion, Jane Lawrence Sumner, and Sara McLaughlin Mitchell, "Gendered Citation Patterns across Political Science and Social Science Methodology Fields," *Political Analysis*, 26:3, 2018: 312–27, and Jane Lawrence Sumner, "The Gender Balance Assessment Tool (GBAT): A Web-Based Tool for Estimating Gender

Islamic studies. The American Academy of Religion allows members to indicate interest in various fields but not in a way that would allow us to compare the proportion of women in the Contemporary Islam program unit, say, with the proportion in the Qur'an unit—or, for that matter, to benchmark Islamic studies against other fields or the AAR as a whole. There may be other methods of estimating these proportions and using them for measuring journal citation gaps, such as tracking proportions of paper presenters over a series of meetings. I encourage those so inclined to develop and apply appropriate methods to investigate gender gaps in citations within and beyond journal publications.

What I tried

In this book, my quantitative discussions of citation look primarily at two main types of literature: overviews and historiographies in introductions to the field (Chapter 1) and a small sample of nine books that attempt to speak broadly about the Islamic tradition (Chapter 2). These books, published between 2014 and 2018, all appeared after my first foray into looking at women's exclusion from certain scholarly texts in "The Omnipresent Male Scholar" (2013) up to the point at which I had completed the first draft of this book in early 2019.[2] I wanted to check whether these books were representative of the field more broadly.

Since automated tools were unsuited to the task, to evaluate whether the specific Islamic studies books discussed in *The Woman Question* were representative required a corpus of manageable size, since data entry would need to be done by hand. Given my interest in Islamic studies particularly as it intersects religious studies/theology, I chose the American Academy of Religion

Balance in Syllabi and Bibliographies," *PS: Political Science & Politics*, 51:2, 2018: 396–400.

2. Kecia Ali, "The Omnipresent Male Scholar," *Critical Muslim*, 8, 2013: 61–73.

annual meeting book exhibit as my base. The AAR meets jointly with the Society for Biblical Literature as well as the International Qur'anic Studies Association. Although idiosyncratic in various ways, AAR/SBL is a large scholarly meeting with a sizeable book exhibit. At the 2018 annual meeting, I collected book catalogs and/ or order sheets from every university press and for-profit academic publisher and exhibitor (e.g., ISD) at the book exhibit that might offer academic books on Islam and Muslims. I skipped confessional Christian publishers (e.g., Fortress Press, Wipf and Stock) and large trade publishers (e.g., HarperCollins). I chose print materials rather than attempting to compile a list of titles on display. It would have been impossible to know whether a book on Islam was not there because the publisher did not bother to bring it or because demand was so great that copies sold out.

Some publishers displayed more than one catalog, in which case I collected all that might potentially contain books on Islam (i.e., I did not pick up a smaller catalog if it was clearly for a different field, e.g., Jewish studies). Some larger publishers use an order sheet that lists books by author or sometimes-truncated title instead of a catalog. In those cases, I did another layer of research to determine the year of publication and ascertain the topic more precisely. Order sheets often include older books, while catalogs tend to feature newer publications. When a catalog had a section on Islam, I restricted myself to works mentioned there.

To keep the comparisons with my chosen sample as fair as possible, I limited the corpus by date, language, type of volume, and topic. I included only books with a publication date of 2017, 2018, or 2019. I excluded edited volumes as well as reference works (including a slew of "online companions") and basic textbooks, although I included more specialized books that might also be adopted for courses (*Shariah: What Everyone Needs to Know*, or *Islam and Analytic Philosophy*). I excluded autobiographies and memoirs. I also left out editions and/or translations unless the primary contribution was a scholarly study accompanied by a text or a translation. Some presses (e.g., DeGruyter) include books in German and other European languages in their catalogs; I excluded all works not in English. There were a handful of translations of contemporary scholarly works that I also excluded, since the immediate aim of my study was to understand the scholarly habits prevailing in anglophone Islamic studies.

To keep the focus as clear as possible, and to keep the universe of citations within these books (necessary for network analysis) as close to comparable as possible, I also excluded explicitly comparative studies (e.g., X in Islam and Christianity) and those primarily focused on interreligious encounter or dialogue. I also excluded books on art history, architecture, archaeology, and literature if they didn't mention religion, faith, Islam, or Muslims in the title or description.

The resulting corpus was 167 books.

Hamada Altalib from Yale University School of Medicine, whose work includes informatics and data science, devised a preliminary spreadsheet to enter bibliometric data, where I tagged each book with up to two categories: Islamic law, Qur'an, Muslim origins, lived religion, philosophy/theology/mysticism, Islam and politics, violence/extremism/jihad, Muslims in the West/Islamophobia, and gender/sexuality. I entered a gender for the author(s) (on assigning gender, see below) and would have done so for the authors of cited works.

By tracking gendered citation patterns, with reference to authors' gender, I intended to determine whether the nine books I analyze closely were representative or unusual in their citational practices. I also wanted to know whether overall women cite men more than men cite women, as I expected, and whether, as is common, women cite women more than men cite women. I was also curious about specific effects: within this pool of books, are there women who are citing men, suggesting they are writing on similar topics, while the men in turn do not cite them despite the topical overlap? Network analysis, which allows one to visualize clusters of citations as well as directionality, would have illustrated these things.

Gender is not the only relevant variable in tracking citational patterns in any field. Variables including career stage, race, and religious identity might have affected my conclusions. Had the project progressed, I would have had to decide which author characteristics to track in addition to gender. Did it matter if authors were tenured, on the tenure track, or independent/contingent at the time of publication? What about whether they were "professed Muslims," in the sense that they said something explicitly in their book about their religious identity? What about race, and if so, which categories would I use? How would I identify an author's race correctly? Would I also code for ethnicity? I ultimately abandoned the project before I had to confront these questions, but anyone pursuing related analyses might consider them.

Attempting to design and implement this study was time-consuming. Beyond the hours spent educating myself about bibliometrics and network analysis, I devoted approximately thirty hours to selecting and doing preliminary data entry for this initial sample of books. Altalib spent hours helping me refine categories and building the spreadsheet. Rachael Clemens of the School of Information and Library Science at the University of North Carolina—Chapel Hill spoke with me at length about possible approaches to pursue. Despite the considerable expertise of the people involved, and my ability to fund research assistance through my university, it proved difficult to find people both qualified and available to undertake the work. Amany Marey, a Yale postdoctoral researcher in another field, had begun working on the project but was prevented by university regulations from continuing to assist. I reluctantly conceded defeat. I am grateful to all of them for their time and goodwill.

On counting

Although I ultimately did not undertake any significant bibliometric analysis, I did so. much. counting. Here, I lay out the rules I applied in counting women as historical figures and thinkers as well as scholarly authorities in main texts, bibliographies, indexes, and notes. I also explain how I counted contributors and contributions to edited volumes. As Sumner points out, "counting is tedious and prone to human error."[3] While nothing can be done about the tedium, I tried to reduce errors by having Boston University doctoral student Ateeb Gul take a second pass at all the indexes, notes, and text for the books I discuss in Chapter 2. When our numbers differed, I sought to reconcile the discrepancies. Sometimes, a third count left a small margin of error. In such cases I rounded off what I report, erring on the side of understating rather than overstating male dominance.

Indexes

I counted only headwords, not individuals listed in subentries. I did not count entries that merely point to other entries. Occasionally, indexers split references to one person under two or more names, or index the same set of entries under variations of the same name. When I caught such errors, I corrected for them. It is likely I missed some instances.

I did not count deities (Al-Lat, Allah, Jehovah), being unwilling to assign gender to them, but did count angels, prophets, and historical figures. Of course, my choice to assign Jesus and Buddha, for example, to the latter group alongside Mary, Moses, and Muhammad itself reflects theological assumptions.

Notes and bibliographies

In discussing the proportion of notes that contain references to women's scholarship, I count notes that include at least one publication authored, co-authored, edited, or co-edited by a woman. If a note lists five books by men and one book by a woman, I count that note as including women's work. Thus, the often-pitiful

3. Sumner, "The Gender Balance Assessment Tool (GBAT)."

proportion of notes citing women usually overstates their presence. I did not count total citations of works or total number of unique works cited.

Books differ in how they organize bibliographies or lists of works cited, if they even include them. Some separate primary and secondary sources. Others segregate Arabic, or Arabic and Persian, texts from those in European languages, not distinguishing between classical texts and modern scholarship. When I break out categories in my analysis, I say so. In discussing the proportion of works written or edited by women in bibliographies, I've remained mindful that the near-totality of edited and published premodern works by Muslims are by men. I don't blame contemporary scholars for that historical legacy.

Edited volumes

My primary interest in edited volumes was determining the proportion of substantive contributions by people who aren't men. By substantive contributions, I basically mean full-length chapters. I used my own judgment as to whether introductions were substantive, with length a significant but not the sole criterion. I counted chapters co-authored by a mixed-gender team as .5 man-authored, even on those rare occasions that there were three rather than two co-authors. (I am unaware of chapters in my sample co-authored by a woman and a nonbinary scholar.) I treated a chapter written jointly by two women as woman-authored.

I also looked at the proportion of men among the contributors. Contributor lists typically include editors, regardless of whether they have also contributed chapters, as well as authors of supplementary materials such as forewords. If a book lacked a listing of contributors, I compiled my own from the table of contents.

Ratios of contributors and contributions sometimes differ. Co-authorship leads to more contributors than chapters and multiple contributions by the same person result in fewer contributors than chapters. Where applicable, I indicate whether I am discussing contributors or contributions.

On gendering

Since the point of counting was to determine whether men are overrepresented in scholarly publications, assigning gender was a necessary step. (My identifications of scholars as men or women do not differentiate between cis and trans people.) Where I know that an author identifies as nonbinary, I tried to count them as such even if they came to do so after the publications in question. When I know a group includes nonbinary people, I typically say something like "scholars who aren't men," a phrase I also sometimes use for a group comprised exclusively of women. Although I hope I haven't misgendered anyone, any harms should be mitigated by my presentation of such data in aggregate. As for the concern that inaccurate gender identifications might vitiate my findings, that would only be the case if I a) made a considerable number of mistakes and b) disproportionately assumed that more women or nonbinary authors were men than the reverse, leading me to overcount men and thus overstate my case for gender discrimination.

To assign gender, I used personal knowledge and paid attention to pronouns and context cues, but otherwise assumed the gender usually associated with a given name. That is, I assumed that someone named Saadia was a woman, and someone named Tariq was a man. For ambiguous names, or when someone was identified with initials only, I consulted author blurbs, university websites, and other sources. These labor-intensive searches did not always yield information. Where the gender of an individual listed in an index was unclear, I checked whether the author used a pronoun in the main text where the individual was discussed. If the author made a mistake, I probably reproduced it.

Hoping to assign gender more quickly and reliably, I converted a few PDF and Word files to plain text to run their bibliographies through Jane Sumner's Gender Balance Assessment Tool, which uses L. Mullen's algorithm for predicting gender.[4] It was reasonably accurate for my *Lives of Muhammad*, but left a 10% margin unknown. For Ahmad Atif Ahmad's *Pitfalls of Scholarship*, it deemed 4% unknown—all men, as far as I can determine, because the women were accounted for in the 8% assigned to them. I couldn't get the tool to read several other submitted files. Given that I had only paper copies of some books, and so would have been able to use this tool only after either scanning and converting files to readable text or retyping the bibliographies, I chose not to do more. For those looking for a quick estimate of gender proportions of authors in their own work in progress, or in work they can easily convert to plain text files, the GBAT is a very useful resource, although estimating gender in the references of English-language Islamic studies works is complicated by names transliterated from Arabic, Persian, Urdu, and other languages. The challenges in attempting to track the gender of cited authors in non-English sources would presumably be magnified. Nonetheless, I trust that given the ongoing development of digital tools, others will find ways to do this work.

4. GBAT, https://jlsumner.shinyapps.io/syllabustool/. Mullen, L. (2021), gender: Predict Gender from Names Using Historical Data. R package version 0.6.0, https://github.com/lmullen/gender. I performed these assessments in February 2023. As Sumner notes, "Gender prediction is based on given names. Citations without given names (or with only initials) will either produce no estimate or a wildly inaccurate one. The algorithm predicts the gender most commonly associated with the name. This may not be the true gender of the author."

FURTHER READING

THIS LIST, which could easily have been five times as long, highlights work worth engaging. Some is specific to Islamic studies, some provides useful perspectives from other fields and disciplines, and some ranges across academic areas. Many other important resources are cited in footnotes to the chapters. Although my notes do not differentiate between sources I present as background or support for my analysis and publications I critique, I trust that readers can determine for themselves which works will be helpful for the inquiries they wish to pursue.

State of the field

Aisha M. Beliso-De Jesús, "Confounded Identities: A Meditation on Race, Feminism, and Religious Studies in Times of White Supremacy," *Journal of the American Academy of Religion*, 86:2, 2018: 307–40.

Ayesha S. Chaudhry. "Islamic Legal Studies: A Critical Historiography." In Anver M. Emon and Rumee Ahmed, eds., *The Oxford Handbook of Islamic Law* (Oxford: Oxford University Press, 2018), 5–44.

Juliane Hammer and Micah R. Hughes, "Gender, Feminism and Critique in American Muslim Thought." In Roberto Tottoli, ed., *Routledge Handbook of Islam in the West*, 2nd edition (London: Routledge, 2022), 494–513.

Justine Howe, ed. *The Routledge Handbook of Islam and Gender* (London: Routledge, 2021).

Marion Katz, "The Textual Study of Gender." In Léon Buskens and Annemarie van Sandwijk, *Islamic Studies in the Twenty-first Century: Transformations and Continuities* (Amsterdam: Amsterdam University Press, 2016), 87–107. Open access: https://library.oapen.org/handle/20.500.12657/30676.

Ilyse R. Morgenstein Fuerst, "Job Ads Don't Add Up: Arabic + Middle East + Text ≠ Islam," *Journal of the American Academy of Religion*, 88:4, 2020: 915–946.

Ilyse R. Morgenstein Fuerst and Zahra M. S. Ayubi, "Shifting Boundaries: The Study of Islam in the Humanities," *The Muslim World*, 106:4, 2016: 643–654.

Laurie L. Patton, *Who Owns Religion? Scholars and Their Publics in the Late Twentieth Century* (Chicago, IL: University of Chicago Press, 2019).

Sohaira Siddiqui, "Good Scholarship/Bad Scholarship: Consequences of the Heuristic of Intersectional Islamic Studies," *Journal of the American Academy of Religion*, 88:1, 2020: 142–174.

Citation

Sara Ahmed, "Making Feminist Points," September 11, 2013, https://feministkilljoys .com/2013/09/11/making-feminist-points/.

Feminist Studies in Religion @TheTable "Manthologies." May 2019, https://www .fsrinc.org/thetable-manthologies/.

Meena Krishnamurthy and Jessica Wilson, "What's Wrong with Current Citation Practices in Philosophy?," December 14, 2015, https://whatswrongcvsp.com /2015/12/14/whats-wrong-with-current-citation-practices-in-philosophy/.

Carrie Mott and Daniel Cockayne, "Citation Matters: Mobilizing the Politics of Citation toward a Practice of 'Conscientious Engagement,'" *Gender, Place & Culture: A Journal of Feminist Geography*, 7, 2017: 954–973.

Christen A. Smith and Dominique Garrett-Scott, "'We are not named': Black women and the politics of citation in anthropology," *Feminist Anthropology*, 2:1, 2021: 18–37.

Victor Ray, "The Racial Exclusions in Scholarly Citations (Opinion)," *Inside Higher Ed*, April 27, 2018, https://www.insidehighered.com/advice/2018/04/27/racial -exclusions-scholarly-citations-opinion.

Public scholarship

Tressie McMillan Cottom, "Everything but the Burden: Publics, Public Scholarship, and Institutions," May 2015, https://tressiemc.com/uncategorized/everything -but-the-burden-publics-public-scholarship-and-institutions/.

Priyamvada Gopal, "Dossier of White Hot Hatred," July 16, 2020, https://medium .com/@priyamvadagopal/the-dossier-of-white-hot-hatred-8d5cf0b64e9a.

Johanna Hanink, "More Women Classicists Need to Write Big," *Eidolon*, March 2, 2017, https://eidolon.pub/more-women-classicists-need-to-write-big-cc1994ad1747.

Sarah Sobieraj, *Credible Threat: Attacks Against Women Online and the Future of Democracy* (New York: Oxford University Press, 2020).

Audrey Truschke, "Hate Male," *The Revealer*, July 14, 2020, https://therevealer.org /hate-male/.

Pedagogy

Layla Abdullah-Poulos, "How #BlackIslamSyllabus is Enhancing Islamic Studies—Talking with Dr. Kayla Wheeler," June 15, 2020, https://blog.hautehijab.com/post/how-blackmuslimsyllabus-for-college-students-was-created-a-conversation-with-dr-kayla-wheeler. A link to the syllabus can be found at Wheeler's website: https://kaylareneewheeler.com/blackislamsyllabus/.

Shenila Khoja-Moolji, "Poststructuralist Approaches to Teaching about Gender, Islam, and Muslim Societies," *Feminist Teacher*, 24:3, 2014: 169–183.

"On Teaching Gender and Islam in the Middle East: An Interview with Lila Abu Lughod (Conducted by Jacob Bessen)," originally published in *JADMAG*, 7.2: (Pedagogy), 2019 and available at jadaliyya.com.

Courtney M. Dorroll, ed., *Teaching Islamic Studies in the Age of ISIS, Islamophobia, and the Internet* (Indianapolis: University of Indiana Press, 2019).

Sexism and the academy

AJS Perspectives, "The Patriarchy Issue," Spring 2019.

Kecia Ali and Lolo Serrano, "The Person of the Author: Constructing Gendered Scholars in Religious Studies Book Reviews," *Journal of the American Academy of Religion*, 90:3, 2022, 554–578.

Kelly J. Baker, *Sexism Ed: Essays on Gender and Labor in Academia* (Chapel Hill, NC: Raven Publishing, 2018).

The Chronicle Review, "The Awakening: Women and Power in the Academy," April 6, 2018, B1–B24.

Lorgia García Peña, *Community as Rebellion: A Syllabus for Surviving Academia as a Woman of Color* (Chicago, IL: Haymarket Books, 2022).

Susannah Heschel and Sarah Imhoff, "Where Are All the Women in Jewish Studies?," *The Forward*, July 3, 2018.

Tricia A. Matthew, ed., *Written/Unwritten: Diversity and the Hidden Truths of Tenure* (Chapel Hill: University of North Carolina Press, 2016).

Danica Savonick and Cathy Davidson, "Gender Bias in Academe: An Annotated Bibliography," http://blogs.lse.ac.uk/impactofsocialsciences/2016/03/08/gender-bias-in-academe-an-annotated-bibliography/.

Despina Stratigakos, *Where Are the Women Architects?* (Princeton, NJ: Princeton University Press, 2016).

Jennifer Thompson, "The Birdcage: Gender Inequity in Academic Jewish Studies," *Contemporary Jewry*, 39, 2019: 427–446.

Sarah Tyson, *Where Are the Women? Why Expanding the Archive Makes Philosophy Better* (New York: Columbia University Press, 2018).

INDEX

As this book argues, indexes matter—which makes preparing one fraught. In working with David Luljak on this index, I have stuck closely to the policy and guidance of the Press, although there are inevitable gray areas. "A Note for Authors on Preparing the Index" has this to say about when people should be named:

> Authors' names in notes should be indexed only if the note includes some discussion of their work or viewpoint. Do not index authors/titles in the bibliography. Names in prefaces or forewords may be indexed, but only if they have something to do with the subject matter of the book, not just how the book came to be written.

It is unsaid but understood those who appear in the main text should normally appear in the index.

By my count, 174 women, 105 men, and three nonbinary scholars appear in this index.

Blair, Sheila, 106; *Islam: A Thousand Years of Faith and Power*, 151, 152

blasphemy, 129

Bloom, Jonathan, 106; *Islam: A Thousand Years of Faith and Power*, 151, 152

blurbs. *See* endorsements

Bohlander, Michael, *Visions of Shari'a*, 34n57

Boko Haram, 124, 157

book reviews, 14, 46–47, 48, 97, 104–5, 108, 190, 190n, 193. *See also* peer review

Boston University, 117, 161n46

Brill: *Studies in Islamic Law and Society*, 33–36; *Texts and Studies on the Qur'an*, 37

Brooten, Bernadette, 56

Brown, Jonathan A. C., *Misquoting Muhammad*, 79, 82, 84, 90–94, 97, 101–2

Bucar, Liz, 158

al-Bukhari, Muhammad, *Sahih al-Bukhari*, 91

Bukhari, Zahid, 144–47; *Observing the Observer*, 19, 21–22

Bulletin (journal of Middle East Studies Association), 41

Bulletin of the School of Oriental and African Studies, 48

Bush, Laura, 123

Buskens, Léon, *Islamic Studies in the Twenty-first Century*, 19, 23, 25–26, 26n29

Butler, Judith, 193, 195

Callimachi, Rukmini, 114–16

calls for proposals, 174

Cambridge Companions series, 28–31, 34

Campus Watch, 163

caretaking, 50–51

Çelik, Zeynep, 58

Center for Near Eastern Studies, University of California, Los Angeles, 58

Chaudhry, Ayesha, 12, 31, 94, 99

Chittick, William, 1, 105; *Vision of Islam*, 146–47

Christianity: and anti-choice movements, 138–39; religious studies based on conceptions of, 158–59; and slavery, 115, 124

citations, 70–109; counting, 187; cumulative effect (path dependency) of, 71–74, 76, 76n30, 183, 186; as curation, 70; ethical issues in, 186–87; gender bias affecting, 18, 52, 71–109, 182–87, 202–3; harms resulting from failures of, 73–74, 108, 183–84; methodological issues in studying, 201–10; peer review and, 70; professional implications of, 73–74, 108, 183–84; purposes of, 70–71; racialization of, 71, 74; recommendations for combating sexism in, 184–87; self-assessment of one's practices of, 184–87; of women's scholarship, 21–23, 26n29, 26n30, 74–109. *See also* bibliographies; endnotes/footnotes; indexes; women: main text mentions of

#CiteBlackWomen initiative, 167, 187

Classical Islamic Theology (Cambridge Companions series), 28

Clemens, Rachael, 206

Cockayne, Daniel, 75

Cold War, 8

colleges. *See* academia

colonialism/imperialism: Islamic studies shaped by, 6, 8–9; as Western status quo, 4

Committee on Public Understanding of Religion (American Academy of Religion), 121

comparative religion, 49–50

concubinage, 112–13, 115. *See also* sexual slavery

International Association for the
   History of Religions, 17
International Institute of Islamic
   Thought (IIIT), 21, 144–45, 147,
   151–52
*International Journal of Middle East
   Studies*, 46
International Qur'anic Studies Association, 204
invitations, for scholarly works and
   functions, 174–82
Iranian revolution (1979), 122–23
IS. *See* Islamic State
Islam: converts to, 4, 4n11, 25, 149;
   criteria of authority for commenting
   on, 130–33; defining, 42–44; diverse
   practices in, 63, 110–11, 133, 156–59,
   162, 164; feminism within, 53–54,
   97, 103; media representations of,
   123–25; Middle East conflated with,
   47–48, 127; public scholarship and,
   114–33; racialized conceptions of, 4,
   45; and slavery, 114–16; statement
   on sexual and gender ethics of,
   110–13. *See also* Muslims; Muslim
   women; Sunni Islam
Islam, Faisal, 144–47
Islamic Awareness (website), 41n78
Islamic Law and Society (journal),
   57n118
Islamic legal studies, 30–37, 56–57,
   79–80
Islamic State (IS), 114–17, 120, 124
Islamic studies: conceptions and definitions of, 19–20, 40–49, 84, 143;
   critical approaches to, 23–24 (*see
   also* critique); demographics of,
   7–8, 7n14, 18; feminists and, 84;
   gender bias in, 5, 17–60; gender
   politics of, 4, 5–6, 8–11, 110; political
   context for, 8–9; public scholarship
   as component of, 121–33, 137n59;
   racialized conceptions of, 45; regional focus of, 7n14, 44–49, 153–55;

scholarly disciplines contributing
   to, 3, 46–47; subfields of, 18, 26–40,
   45–46, 49–58; teaching of, 19n5, 22,
   142–64; text-centric approaches to,
   3, 24, 32, 38, 43–46, 49, 52
Islamic Studies (journal; Islamabad), 46
Islamic Studies (journal; Oxford), 46
Islamophobia, 5, 119, 125, 133, 137, 159

Jackson, Jenn, 187
Jackson, Sherman, 13n28
Jalalzai, Sajida, 138, 139
James, William, 101
Joseph, Suad, *Encyclopedia of Women
   and Islamic Cultures*, 22n15
Journal of Africana Religions, 46
Journal of Middle East Women's Studies,
   46
Journal of Near Eastern Studies, 41n76
Journal of Shi'i Studies, 47
*Journal of the American Academy of
   Religion*, 24, 46, 104, 148
Journal of the American Oriental Society,
   46
journals, 46–47

Kadi, Wadad, 41, 41n77, 106
Kadivar, Jamileh, 34n57
Kane, Ousmane, *Beyond Timbuktu*, 80,
   82–84, 88–89, 109
Karim, Jamillah, 21
Kassam, Tazim, 122
Katz, Marion, 52, 75n28
Keeler, Annabel, 39n70
Keersten, Carool, 25
Khadija bint Muhammad al-'Aqil, 88
Khan, Sayyid Ahmad. See *Sayyid
   Ahmad Khan* (Cambridge
   Companions series)
Khoja-Moolji, Shenila, 156–57
Kinberg, Leah, 39n70
Klein, Lauren, *Data Feminism*, 75
Koopman, Colin, 25
Krishnamurthy, Meena, 73, 93, 99

terrorism, 9, 139, 152
Texas, 138
textbooks, 146–52, 166, 191–93
theology, 3, 9, 50
Thompson, Jennifer, 11n20
Thonemann, Peter, 27
titles. *See* names and titles
tokenism, 180–81
Tourage, Mahdi, 24n22
trade books, 191–93
Trump, Donald, 6, 119
Truschke, Audrey, 118, 126
Truthout (news site), 138
Tucker, Judith, 76n29

universities. *See* academia
U.S. Supreme Court, 138

Vasmaghi, Sedigheh, 34n57
veiling, 63n4, 63n5, 67, 86, 139, 153,
   157–58, 161
violence, as topic of scholarship, 120.
   See also domestic violence

Wabash Center for Teaching and
   Learning, 144
wadud, amina, 54, 66n3, 66n4, 68,
   82n49, 91, 93, 99, 125–26; *Inside
   the Gender Jihad*, 99; *Qur'an and
   Woman*, 66, 68, 150
Wahhabism, 98
Waines, David, 147
Wakin, Jeanette, 41–42
Waldman, Marilyn, 20, 21n12
Ware, Rudolph, III, *The Walking
   Qur'an*, 80–83, 87–88, 108–9
Watt, W. Montgomery, 105
Weiss, Bernard, 35, 36
Welchman, Lynn, 72n19
Wheaton College, 118
Wheeler, Kayla, 154–55; "Black Islam
   Syllabus," 156
Whelan, Estelle, 41–42, 41n78
white feminism, 66, 127, 128, 138

whites and whiteness: and anti-choice
   movements, 138–39; assumed supe-
   riority of, 107–8, 131; attacks on
   non-whites and women by, 129;
   institutionalization of, 72; terrorism
   attributable to, 139. *See also* white
   women
white supremacy, 9, 31, 139. *See also*
   racism
white women: as converts to Islam, 4,
   4n11, 25; overrepresentation of, in
   Islamic studies contexts, 5, 25–26,
   39, 78–79, 84, 148; self-assessment
   of, 184–85. *See also* non-Muslim
   women
*Wiley Blackwell Concise Companion to
   the Hadith, The*, 168–69
Wilson, Jessica, 73, 93, 99
Winegar, Jessica, 7n14, 47
Winfrey, Oprah, 184
women: attacks on critiques made
   by, 1, 12–15, 62, 76n30, 116–17, 136;
   diminishment of, 99–109, 132n45,
   136; harassment and intimidation
   of, 116–19; main text mentions of,
   25, 68, 74, 77, 78, 82–94, 96, 100–109,
   151; marginalization of, in Islamic
   studies, 18–20, 27–28, 51–58, 61–66,
   68–69, 74, 76–109; and shariah, 89.
   See also critique; gender; gender
   bias; Muslim women; non-Muslim
   women; sexism and misogyny; white
   women; women's scholarship
Women, Ethics and Islamic Knowledge online summer school,
   51n106
#WomenAlsoKnowHistory initiative,
   167
women's scholarship: citations of, 21–23,
   26n29, 26n30, 74–109; engagement
   with/acknowledgment of (and
   failures thereof), 1, 10, 11, 17–26,
   40–42, 51–58, 61–64, 69–70, 72,
   74–109, 174–75, 182–87; feminist, 93,

A NOTE ON THE TYPE

This book has been composed in Arno, an Old-style serif typeface in the classic Venetian tradition, designed by Robert Slimbach at Adobe.